PROFESSIONAL SEXUAL ETHICS

PROFESSIONAL SEXUAL ETHICS

A HOLISTIC MINISTRY APPROACH

PATRICIA BEATTIE JUNG AND DARRYL W. STEPHENS, EDITORS

Fortress Press

Minneapolis

PROFESSIONAL SEXUAL ETHICS

A Holistic Ministry Approach

Scripture quotations are from the New Revised Standard Version Bible, copyright © 1989 by the Division of Christian Education of the National Council of the Churches of Christ in the USA. Used by permission. All rights reserved.

Chapter 10 is reprinted with kind permission from Springer Science+Business Media: *Pastoral Psychology*," Ministry with Adolescents: Tending Boundaries, Telling Truths," 62/5, 2013, 639-647, Robert C. Dykstra, © Springer Science+Business 2013. Chapter 18 is a revision of a talk Adam Hamilton shared at the Willow Creek Leadership Summit in August of 2010. See http://www.willowcreek.com/ProdInfo.asp?invtid=PR34836.

Cover design: Alisha Lofgren. Cover image: © Shutterstock/ Irina QQQ

Library of Congress Cataloging-in-Publication Data

Professional sexual ethics : a holistic ministry approach / [edited by] Darryl W. Stephens and Patricia Beattie Jung.

pages cm

Includes index.

ISBN 978-0-8006-9943-7 (pbk. : alk. paper) — ISBN 978-1-4514-3091-2 (ebook)

1. Clergy–Professional ethics. 2. Sexual ethics. I. Stephens, Darryl W., editor of compilation.

BV4011.5.P76 2013   174'.925–dc23   2013034860

The paper used in this publication meets the minimum requirements of American National Standard for Information Sciences—Permanence of Paper for Printed Library Materials, ANSI Z329.48-1984.

Manufactured in the U.S.A.

This book was produced using PressBooks.com, and PDF rendering was done by PrinceXML.

CONTENTS

Part III. Practices of Ministry

Part IV. Pastoral Leadership

Contributors

Steven Charleston is a Visiting Professor of Native American Ministries at Saint Paul School of Theology at Oklahoma City University.

Miguel A. De La Torre is a Professor of Social Ethics and Latino/a Studies at Iliff School of Theology.

Robert C. Dykstra is the Charlotte W. Newcombe Professor of Pastoral Theology at Princeton Theological Seminary.

Adam Hamilton is the Senior Pastor at the United Methodist Church of the Resurrection in Leawood, Kansas.

Youtha Hardman-Cromwell is the Assistant Dean for Mount Vernon Square and a Professor of Practice in Ministry and Mission at Wesley Theological Seminary.

Stanley Hauerwas is the Gilbert T. Rowe Professor of Theological Ethics at Duke University.

Jeanne Hoeft is an Associate Professor of Pastoral Theology and Pastoral Care at Saint Paul School of Theology.

John C. Holbert is the Lois Craddock Perkins Professor Emeritus of Homiletics at the Perkins School of Theology at Southern Methodist University.

Patricia B. Jung is a Professor of Christian Ethics and the Oubri A. Poppele Professor of Health and Welfare Ministries at Saint Paul School of Theology.

Boyung Lee is an Associate Professor of Educational Ministries at the Pacific School of Religion.

Joretta Marshall is the Executive Vice President, Dean, and a Professor of Pastoral Theology and Pastoral Care and Counseling at Brite Divinity School at Texas Christian University.

John S. McClure is the Charles G. Finney Professor of Preaching and Worship at Vanderbilt University.

Joyce Ann Mercer is a Professor of Practical Theology at Virginia Theological Seminary.

Bonnie J. Miller-McLemore is the E. Rhodes and Leona B. Carpenter Professor of Pastoral Theology at Vanderbilt University.

Kate M. Ott is an Assistant Professor of Christian Social Ethics at Drew University.

F. Douglas Powe is the James C. Logan Professor of Evangelism and Professor of Urban Ministry at Wesley Theological Seminary.

Rosemary Radford Ruether is a Visiting Professor of Feminist Theology at the Claremont School of Theology.

Susan A. Ross is a Professor of Theology and a Faculty Scholar at Loyola University–Chicago.

Don E. Saliers is the Wm. R. Cannon Distinguished Professor of Theology and Liturgy, Emeritus, at the Candler School of Theology at Emory University.

Darryl W. Stephens is the Assistant General Secretary for Advocacy and Sexual Ethics at the General Commission on the Status and Role of Women in The United Methodist Church.

Cristina L. H. Traina is a Professor of Religion at Northwestern University.

Acknowledgements

This book builds on the work of many dedicated individuals and institutions advocating for healthy interpersonal boundaries in ministry, improved sexual health of clergy, and increased attention to the ethics of ministerial leadership. References and citations throughout this volume witness to the scholars and pioneers preceding this work, for whom we are immensely grateful. We would like especially to thank M. Garlinda Burton, formerly General Secretary of the General Commission on the Status and Role of Women (GCSRW) in The United Methodist Church (UMC), for her tireless work on behalf of women survivors of clergy sexual abuse and her vision to improve theological education on this issue. Her encouragement and support for this book has been invaluable. A thank you, also, to Rev. Dr. HiRho Park of the General Board of Higher Education and Ministry of the UMC, for her suggestion to write an article on the fiduciary duty of clergy—the genesis of this volume.

We are indebted as well to Saint Paul School of Theology, which like many other seminaries, has long been committed to addressing these issues. Indeed, this volume was conceived at a workshop held there on these issues. Additionally, a word of gratitude for the collegiality and networking made possible through our membership and participation in the Society of Christian Ethics and the American Academy of Religion, without which this collaboration would hardly have been possible.

We offer a heartfelt thanks to the contributors to this volume—passionate, dedicated scholars and church leaders who believed sufficiently in the importance of this project to make it a priority in their busy schedules. Each has brought a vital and important perspective to the ongoing conversation we hope to engender with this book. We are grateful for their openness and receptivity to our requests, suggestions, edits, and questions. The task of editing was truly a collaborative effort. Patti's experience and wisdom guided our process from vision to contract and from invitations to contributions. While both of us read and responded to each contributor's essay, the bulk of the design, organization and detail work associated with editing this volume was shouldered by Darryl. As such, most of the credit for editing this volume belongs to him.

We are privileged to work with the capable team at Fortress Press. A big thank you goes to Ross H. Miller, former Senior Acquisitions Editor at Fortress Press, for his early support of this project. Thank you also to Will Bergkamp,

Publisher and Managing Director, who ably accompanied us through the development of the manuscript and to Lisa Gruenisen, Development Editor, for her close reading of our manuscript.

Introduction

Lay and ordained, paid and volunteer, part-time and full-time—ministerial leaders are called apart and authorized by communities of faith to proclaim and embody the scandalous good news of an incarnational God. We who are ministers represent this Christ-embodied church and, thereby, represent God. Yet sometimes we need to be reminded that ministers are people, too.

Parishioners tend to put us on a pedestal, expecting no sins or faults. At the same time, members of the faith community sometimes walk all over leaders as if we are doormats-for-Jesus, offering ourselves to the world 24/7. That we might have needs of our own and be bound by human finitude often goes unrecognized. To complicate matters, Christians have a long history of denying sexuality—in ourselves and our leaders. This does not contribute to healthy ministers or healthy ministry. Indeed, media reports of the unhealthy and abusive behavior of ministerial leaders have become all-too-frequent. In the years since 2002, when the Boston Globe first reported on a cover-up of child sexual abuse by priests, the Roman Catholic Church and many Protestant denominations have begun to grapple more openly with the problem of sexual abuse in church settings. Not just children but adults, too, have survived sexual exploitation by those entrusted to care for their spiritual needs. Ministers are all-too-human.

A HOLISTIC APPROACH TO MINISTRY

Many people who enter ministry are unprepared to handle issues of professional power, intimacy, and interpersonal boundaries, leading to preventable cases of sexual misconduct within the church. While better training can make the church a healthier, more credible witness to the gospel, no amount of education will eliminate sin from the church or its ministry. Sexual predators undoubtedly belong to our communities. Safe church protocols for the prevention of abuse, effective judicatory procedures in response to abuse, and the care and healing for all involved are critical in such circumstances. Nevertheless, this book is primarily written for those of us who are living in the murkier waters of daily life—ministerial leaders striving to be true to ourselves, our communities, and God. We are merely people—albeit called to sacred roles—who struggle, fail, learn, and grow in discipleship, even as we lead others to do the same. In order to flourish as ministerial leaders and followers of Christ, we need nurture and

1

guidance. We need practical guidelines and realistic expectations. We need a holistic approach to ministry and the place of sexuality in it.

PROFESSIONAL SEXUAL ETHICS

Bringing our whole, human selves into ministry allows us to be genuine and fully present as we fulfill our respective callings within the body of Christ. This includes our sexuality and its appropriately expressed and cared for needs and desires. Whether a teacher, chaplain, musician, prayer leader, preacher, or treasurer—each person in a ministerial role of leadership communicates profound messages about God's love. Authentically embodying God's unbounded, indiscriminate, infinite love, however, demands that we recognize and acknowledge our own limitations and boundaries. Upholding the sacred trust of ministry requires leaders who are attuned to the complicated dynamics of power, interpersonal boundaries, and consent within ministerial relationships. "Professional sexual ethics" refers to all of this—the integration of professional ethics, sexual ethics, and sexuality education for ministerial leaders.

Professional ethics in ministry pertains to the role of ministerial leader. When one's call to leadership is publicly affirmed, one is given authority within the community of faith. This authority (whatever the specific role) conveys certain responsibilities. Professional ethics is the intentional practice of reflecting on, deliberating about, and acting on the right use of this power and authority. Simply put, these special obligations stem from the role of ministerial leader. These are "professional" duties, even if the person in ministry is lay, part-time, or unpaid. When a ministerial leader abuses the power of her role by sexually exploiting a person in her care, this is a violation of *professional* sexual ethics. Marie Fortune, Founder and Senior Analyst of the FaithTrust Institute, offers this definition of sexual misconduct in ministry:

> When any person in a ministerial role of leadership or pastoral counseling (clergy, religious, or lay) engages in sexual contact or sexualized behavior with a congregant, client, employee, student or staff member (adult, teenager, or child) in a professional [ministerial] relationship.[1]

Fortune's pioneering work in healthy boundaries for ministry and the prevention of sexual abuse by ministerial leaders has had a profound impact on

---

1. Marie M. Fortune, *Responding to Clergy Misconduct: A Handbook* (Seattle: FaithTrust Institute, 2009), 30.

the work of many contributors to this volume. Awareness of professional sexual ethics for ministry has increased significantly in the past twenty-five years, coincident with greater awareness and enforcement of U.S. federal guidelines regarding sexual harassment in the workplace.

Holistic sexual ethics and sexuality education pertains to the ministerial leader as a sexual person—a rare topic in churches and in theological literature. Aside from discussions about vowed celibacy for priests and debates about ordaining partnered gay and lesbian persons, faith communities are reticent to acknowledge the minister as a sexual person. Much more has been written about clergy health generally (for example, healthy work/life balance) and about sexuality education for all Christians than about the sexual lives of clergy. When sexuality and ministry are discussed together, it is usually framed in terms of risk, danger, and prevention. Much more has been written about the abuses of sexuality by those in ministry than has been written about healthy sexuality for ministerial leaders.[2] Yet, awareness of professional sexual ethics and the need for resources is on the increase within denominational structures with the power to influence theological education.

In 2010, the Unitarian Universalist Association, according to its own press release, became "the first major religious denomination in the country to require that its candidates for ordination demonstrate the capability to address sexuality issues in ministry."[3] This action was heavily influenced by the Religious Institute, which offers the following characteristics of a sexually healthy religious professional:

- Knowledgeable about human sexuality.
- Familiar with their tradition's sacred text(s) on sexuality.
- Able to engage in theological reflection about how best to integrate sexuality and spirituality.
- Able to examine the impact of racism, sexism, heterosexism and homophobia on ministry.
- Trained in pastoral counseling approaches that facilitate resolution of interpersonal conflict, specifically when dealing with sexual matters, for individuals, families and groups.

---

2. Notable exceptions include Karen Lebacqz and Ronald G. Barton, *Sex in the Parish* (Louisville: Westminster John Knox, 1991); G. Lloyd Rediger, *Beyond the Scandals: A Guide to Healthy Sexuality for Clergy* (Minneapolis: Fortress Press, 2003); and Scott Edelstein, *Sex and the Spiritual Teacher: Why It Happens, When It's a Problem, and What We All Can Do* (Boston: Wisdom, 2011).

3. Unitarian Universalist Association, "Unitarian Universalist Seminarians to be Trained in Sexuality Issues and Ethics," news release, February 9, 2010, http://www.uua.org/news/pressroom/pressreleases/158197.shtml.

- Able to serve as role models, discussing sexual issues with ease and comfort.
- Knowledgeable about their denomination's policies on sexuality.
- Able to speak out for sexual justice within their denomination and in the larger community.
- Skillful in preaching about sexuality-related issues.
- Able to recognize their own personal limitations and boundaries when it comes to handling sexuality issues.
- Able to deal appropriately with sexual feelings that may arise for congregants, and vice-versa.[4]

This view recognizes that sexual health is an essential part of maintaining professional relationships in ministry.

In 2012, The United Methodist Church (UMC) approved a comprehensive set of guidelines for teaching professional sexual ethics in educational programs of ministerial preparation. United Methodist candidates for licensed and ordained ministry are now expected to reach the following goals and competencies in seminary (or alternate track of theological education).[5]

GOALS

FUTURE MINISTERIAL LEADERS ARE EXPECTED TO:

- Understand healthy interpersonal boundaries as integral to enabling the trust necessary for ministry.
- Recognize sexual ethics in ministry as an issue of appropriate use of power and avoidance of abuse rather than exclusively an issue of "sexual morality."
- Understand the importance of professional ethics, including one's own denominational policies and expectations.
- Learn the role of judicatories in prevention and response to clergy sexual misconduct.

---

4. Debra W. Haffner, *A Time to Build: Creating Sexually Healthy Faith Communities*, 2nd ed. (Westport, CT: Religious Institute, 2012), 13. Over the past decade the Religious Institute, a non-profit organization, has sought to develop models of sexual health for ministerial formation and congregational practice. For additional resources see http://www.religiousinstitute.org/resources.

5. United Methodist Church, "Sexual Ethics as Integral Part of Formation for Ministerial Leadership," in *The Book of Resolutions of The United Methodist Church 2012* (Nashville: United Methodist Publishing House, 2012), 146–52. For an earlier example of an articulation of desired outcomes for theological education to address and prevent clergy sexual misconduct, see Nils C. Friberg and Mark R. Laaser, *Before the Fall: Preventing Pastoral Sexual Abuse* (Collegeville, MN: Liturgical, 1998), 125–28.

- Become knowledgeable about human sexuality, one's own sexual self, and how to deal with sexual feelings that may arise for congregants, and vice versa.
- Appreciate how sexual integrity contributes to spiritual wholeness and how it is vital to ministerial formation and personal health.
- Become conversant with scriptural and theological resources for all of the above.

COMPETENCIES

MINISTERIAL CANDIDATES ARE FURTHER EXPECTED TO:

- Practice healthy life choices and work-life balance.
- Be sexually self-aware.
- Become comfortable talking about issues of sexuality.
- Develop skills to provide pastoral care and worship leadership on sexuality issues.
- Be committed to sexual justice in the congregation and in society at large.

Expressing its hope that implementation of these goals and competencies become integral to formation, the UMC asserts, "At its best, professional formation for ministerial leadership should not be confined to one subject, class, or academic discipline but should rather pervade the entire core curriculum, ethos and co-curricular experience of ministerial education."[6] This book embraces this hope, discussing concerns related to professional sexual ethics in relation to both traditional theological core disciplines and in connection with some of the common practices of ministry.

HOW TO USE THIS BOOK

This book is for you, the ministerial leader. It is appropriate for advanced leadership training for laity, seminary and other courses of study for ministerial formation, and continuing education for clergy. Furthermore, this book is about you, the ministerial leader. These chapters consistently focus on the person, role, and behavior of the ministerial leader. Read this book early in your leadership journey and review it often. Discuss it with others. Wrestle with and debate its conclusions.

---

6. United Methodist Church, "Sexual Ethics as Integral," 149. For a constructive approach to implementing these curricular guidelines, see Darryl W. Stephens, "Teaching Professional Sexual Ethics Across the Seminary Curriculum," *Religious Education* 108, no. 2 (March-April 2013), 193–209.

Contributors to this book represent the breadth of theological disciplines and bring a wide range of expertise in sexuality and professional ethics for ministry. In these chapters, established scholars (lay and clergy) and pastoral leaders offer a cross-curricular, inter-disciplinary, and ecumenical conversation about sexuality in the context of ethical ministerial leadership. Focusing on implications for the practice of ministry, chapters feature analyses of common ministry situations and practical guidelines. Each chapter includes discussion questions, designed for classroom or group study, and a trove of resources for further study.[7]

Part 1, "Ethical Landscape of Ministry," presents foundational issues in professional sexual ethics. These chapters could be assigned in preparation for a leadership training event, for a student orientation, in an introduction to ministry course, or as a common text for a first-year ministerial formation group. In chapter 1, Kate M. Ott makes a case for sexual health and wholeness as essential to faithful and effective ministry, focusing on integrity in one's sexual identity, personal attitudes, values, and history. In chapter 2, Darryl W. Stephens discusses safeguards and warning signs as guidelines for a professional ethics approach through vignettes depicting sexual exploitation, blurred boundaries, and dating. Stanley Hauerwas, in chapter 3, reframes the issue of professional sexual ethics by encouraging faith leaders to resist societal confusions and to speak truthfully and frankly about sex. Concluding Part 1, Cristina L. H. Traina, in chapter 4, establishes the virtue of attunement as essential to forming strong, trusting bonds in ministry, arguing for an embrace and appropriate restraint of the erotic in ministerial relationships.

Part 2, "Sources of Wisdom," draws upon four deep wells: inherited traditions of church teachings, interpretation of scripture, traditions of theological reasoning, and an ethic arising from experiences of the disenfranchised. In chapter 5, Rosemary Radford Ruether surveys the church's inheritance of Augustine's teachings on sexuality, suggesting ways in which that heritage needs to be reconstructed for sexual ethics today. In chapter 6, John C. Holbert interprets the story of David and Bathsheba as a warning regarding his own potential to abuse the power of the pastoral office—a risk that all ministerial leaders share. Susan A. Ross, in chapter 7, explores feminist developments of Protestant and Catholic theological traditions about love of self, suggesting appropriate practices of self-care for ministerial leaders. Concluding Part 2, Miguel A. De La Torre, in chapter 8, develops a constructive ethic of sexual pleasure, based on experiences of "those who reside

---

7. See also James S. Evinger, "Clergy Sexual Abuse Bibliography," 22nd ed., http://www.faithtrustinstitute.org/resources/bibliographies/clergy-sexual-abuse/?searchterm=evinger.

on the margins of power and privilege"—an ethic with the potential to overturn unjust social structures.

Part 3, "Practices of Ministry," explores professional sexual ethics from the perspective of a wide range of theological disciplines, focusing on the practicalities of ministry. In chapter 9, Joretta Marshall discusses pseudo-intimacy, vulnerability, clergy dating, collegiality, and intersections of oppressions as central issues facing ministers in the practice of pastoral care. In chapter 10, Robert C. Dykstra, through an engaging discussion of a character in a young adult novel, explores the risks and benefits youth ministers face when talking to teens about their sexual lives. In chapter 11, Boyung Lee examines sexuality education in congregations, increasing the pedagogical awareness of faith leaders and empowering us for more effective teaching throughout all ministries of the church. In chapter 12, F. Douglas Powe argues for prophetic resistance to individualistic distortions of the David narrative by pastors in African American churches, encouraging accountability and healing so that congregations may become more effective evangelistically. In chapter 13, Steven Charleston offers guidance for maintaining appropriate interpersonal boundaries and respecting cultural differences during missional encounters. John S. McClure, in chapter 14, interrogates the embodied sexuality of the preacher and the power of the pulpit, attending especially to differences in the ways women and men experience these aspects of ministerial leadership. Concluding Part 3, Don E. Saliers, in chapter 15, examines perceptions and intentions of liturgical leaders during the embodied, ritual acts of the gathered congregation, discussing embedded, contemporary cultural images and drawing upon ancient practices and virtues for truth-telling and resistance.

Part 4, "Pastoral Leadership," provides holistic guidance to the ministerial leader, applying themes of earlier chapters to common challenges in the church. In chapter 16, Jeanne Hoeft offers practical guidelines for monitoring power within the relational dynamics of ministry, with special attention to friendship and intimacy. In chapter 17, Joyce Ann Mercer discusses significant areas of concern regarding the use of technology in ministry, including virtual selves, digital privacy (or lack thereof), disinhibition in social networking, pornography use, and appropriate self-care for ministerial leaders. In chapter 18, Adam Hamilton offers leadership advice based on the experience of his congregation's response to sexual misconduct among two of its ministry staff. Youtha Hardman-Cromwell, in chapter 19, offers a frank discussion of an array of sexual topics in the lives of young people and in the Bible, urging openness to life-long learning by ministerial leaders and communal deliberation and discernment in congregations as new issues and insights emerge. The book concludes with chapter 20, by Bonnie J. Miller-McLemore, who writes elegantly about the need for ministerial leaders to attend to their own sex lives—outside of their professional context.

The end is the beginning of continued conversations and insights that go well beyond this book. You, the reader, will likely find much to disagree with—and agree with—in these pages. We hope that this book inspires you to examine your own ministry, your own sexuality, and your own professional ethics, with the aim of creating a healthier, more responsible, more effective, and more passionate witness for Christ.

Lent 2013

PART I

Ethical Landscape of Ministry

1

Sexuality, Health, and Integrity

Kate M. Ott

James, a recent seminary graduate, is serving as assistant pastor in a suburban congregation. In his last semester of seminary, he made a personal decision to be celibate after his fiancée cheated on him. As the assistant pastor, he hopes he will not be called upon to do any premarital counseling as the experience left him distrustful and damaged his self-esteem and body image. In his role supporting the youth minister, James is asked to lead the upcoming week's lesson on "Sexuality and Faith." James tries unsuccessfully to dodge the invitation. He hasn't yet figured out how he feels about dating or sexuality in general, and is hoping to avoid dealing with the issue for a while.

In a recent conversation with another local clergy friend, Maria complains about lack of free time adding to her stress and impeding her spiritual growth. At the same time, she avoids unstructured free time because she feels lonely. She admits that after her divorce, as a way of coping, she put all her energy into growing membership and programming in her small urban congregation. Her friend suggests she try online dating, but Maria is concerned about how her congregation would react. Many members of the congregation see her as a motherly figure who has devoted her life to the church. Furthermore, she dreads having to talk with the council members about guidelines for transparency and accountability if she were to become serious with someone.

Victor and his partner have been together for about ten years. Recently, they have been struggling to rekindle the "spark" in their relationship. They have taken a few extended vacations, which has given them time to re-connect, but little changes once they get home. They have also begun counseling. In their conversations, it has become clear that a lack of privacy is taking a toll on their relationship. They live in a parsonage on the church grounds and have always welcomed congregants to stop by at anytime. The house is located close to the church parking lot and gets a lot of traffic as folks come and go to meetings and programs. When asked to name what they enjoyed most about vacation, they talked about daily moments of holding hands, exchanging kisses, and even snuggling while watching a movie.

The stories of Victor, Maria, and James represent only a few aspects of sexual health and wholeness with which ministers struggle. The general perception about ministers is that either we are above the worldly distractions of sexuality, or that if we are in a sexual relationship, it is perfect. These perceptions are compounded by the mixed messages we all receive about sexuality and relationships. Stuck between a hyper-sexualized culture and a church setting generally silent about sex, most ministerial leaders do not receive adequate sexuality education in their youth, in seminary training, or through continuing education. Required training for clergy is usually limited to abuse and harassment prevention, which is extremely necessary but not completely sufficient.

Too often, Christians continue to think that sexuality education is about telling people "what not to do" or withholding information, lest it lead one down a path of sinfulness—a myth popularized by abstinence-only education. In most cases, we fail adequately to address the struggles associated with marital strife, infertility, eating disorders, coming-out, gender violence, sexual abuse, serial dating, sexual dysfunction, and so on. Silence and discrimination mitigate against sexual health. As religious leaders, we need to understand our own sexual histories, values, and identity—for our own health and well-being, in addition to responsibly serving congregants.

Defining Sexuality

In the classroom, as well as in trainings I have conducted, many individuals treat sexuality as synonymous with sexual behaviors (usually penile-vaginal intercourse) or sexual orientation (usually homosexuality). James makes this mistake in the case study above. He concludes that celibacy will be a way to avoid dealing with his sexuality, instead of seeing sexuality as part of his everyday life, regardless of relationship status or sexual behaviors. Sexuality is so intrinsic to our being that we cannot understand ourselves apart from it. Sexuality "compels our emotional, affective, sensual, and spiritual relationships. Sexuality does not determine all our feelings, thoughts and interactions, but it certainly permeates and affects them."[1] This is why it is difficult to describe

---

1. Kelly Brown Douglas, *Sexuality and the Black Church: A Womanist Perspective* (Maryknoll, NY: Orbis, 1999), 6.

sexuality: no single definition could be completely accurate in its comprehensiveness while still being truthful in its particularity.

Our sexuality is informed by our sexual behaviors but is not limited to them. Sexuality is comprised of a variety of aspects, including the biology and physiology of our bodies and the sexual and reproductive systems, as well as how we care for our bodies. Sensuality (how our bodies respond to pleasure primarily through our senses) and intimacy (the experience of reciprocated emotional closeness to another person or higher power) are also aspects of sexuality. In addition, our sexual identity refers to sexual orientation along with sex, gender identity, and gender roles. Sexuality includes these aspects and more; however, at any given time, they are not all experienced or expressed.[2]

Sexuality develops in relationships (both personal and systemic) shaped by social, biological, psychological, cultural and spiritual forces. In our relationships with self, others, and God, we come to know our sexuality. We do not have complete control over interpretations of our sexuality; some definitions and understandings are forced upon us. In the stories above, for example, Maria struggles with how her congregation perceives her, while Victor and his partner have stopped showing physical affection publicly based on their perception of others' (dis)comfort. Messages from our culture, religion, and history construct for us many different, conflicting, and at times unhealthy ways to interpret our sexuality.[3] Those messages change with age. They may differ based on our racial/ethnic background, gender identity, geographic location, or cultural and religious surroundings. In other words, our sexuality is shaped by the time and space in which we live. For example, we all have a body and thus an image of that body. How we relate to our bodies—the comfort or discomfort we feel—is shaped by what our culture values, by what friends and family say or look like, and by our faith. Unfortunately, the positive message that we are created in the image of God is often lost, an affirmation drowned in a sea of enhanced images of "perfect bodies" or comments that we are ugly, fat, too skinny, too hairy, too wimpy, the wrong color, and so on.

---

2. *Our Whole Lives* is a lifespan sexuality education program jointly published by the United Church of Christ and the Unitarian Universalist Association. The curriculum uses a pictorial definition of holistic sexuality that includes the four areas mentioned above—sexual orientation, sex, gender identity, and gender roles—as well as sexualization. The following paragraph describes sexualization more generally in the context of relational development. See United Church of Christ, *Our Whole Lives: Lifespan Sexuality Education Curriculum* (Cleveland: United Church Board for Homeland Ministries, 1999-2000).

3. Sylvia Thorson-Smith, "Becoming 'Possessed': Toward Sexual health and Well-Being," in *Body and Soul: Re-thinking Sexuality as Justice-Love*, ed. Marvin M. Ellison and Sylvia Thorson-Smith (Cleveland: Pilgrim, 2003), 239.

It is impossible to experience our sexuality free of an evaluative lens or ethical framework. Integrally important to sexuality education and faith development, then, is creating the space for individuals to discover and define their sexuality in a way that is most consistent with whom they know themselves to be as God's beloved. As ministers, we need to create opportunities for such education and faith development by exploring our understanding of sexuality and the roots of our sexual ethics. Many of us did not have these opportunities in our seminary education and have even less time for them in our current ministries, leaving us to define, reflect upon, and set healthy boundaries on the fly or, worse, in response to a personal or professional crisis.

SEXUALITY AND CHRISTIANITY

Sexual self-knowledge is crucial to understanding how sexual integrity contributes to spiritual wholeness. In light of this, what might be the most helpful theological framework to use when considering professional sexual ethics for ministry? How do scripture and tradition contribute to defining and reflecting on sexuality and sexual health?

CREATION

We cannot exist apart from our bodies. They are part of how God created us to know and love the world, ourselves, and God (Gen. 1:26). Our bodies are not only part of God's creation, but were made in God's likeness and affirmed as "very good" (Gen. 1:31). The central teachings that flow from our creation as human beings call for a virtue of self-care and thankfulness related to our bodies. As Christians, we are to respect and steward our bodies as we would any part of creation. Affirming our bodies as part of the "very good" creation requires that we:

- Learn about and prepare for bodily changes across the lifespan, as well as the ways in which sexual feelings and thoughts are part of our body's biological and psychological response.
- Take care of our reproductive and sexual health needs, including checkups and using protection to prevent STDs or unintended pregnancy.
- Be comfortable as we grow, using accurate and age-appropriate sexuality language to talk about our body parts and bodily responses.
- Not use our body (or those of others) as an object, and appreciate the diversity of beauty in God's creation.

We are embodied creatures and sexuality is an integral part of that created nature. In that respect, we are sexual beings from birth to death; even as our sexuality changes over time with physical, emotional, psychological, and relationship developments, we never cease being sexual. James's story suggests he is reducing sexuality to relationships or behaviors to avoid dealing with the personal struggle he has with body image. Individuals who choose celibacy are still sexual. How we live in our skin affects not only our romantic relationships, but the confidence we have in all aspects of our lives, including our professional presence.

INCARNATION

It is ironic that Christians have historically had a difficult time accepting and honoring the body when we are a people of an incarnate God (John 1:14). The incarnation—the life and death of Jesus as God in flesh, a central component of Christian teaching—"promotes the value and significance of the body, which is never to be disregarded or treated with contempt."[4] Jesus understood what it means to live in a body with all its limitations, as well as its beauty. He ate with his followers, washed with them, woke up with sleep in his eyes, and was dunked under water for his baptism. These are all things that require a body to be experienced. Jesus knew the pleasure of touch when his mother held him, when his friends greeted him, when Mary anointed him. He also experienced violence to his body when he was beaten and crucified.

We do not know definitively if Jesus was celibate or single, what sexual behaviors he engaged in, or romantic relationships he had. Some interpret this lack of facts to suggest Jesus was not sexual, thereby projecting internalized discomfort with sexuality onto Jesus. Maria feels a similar judgment from her congregation, even avoiding dating because it may mean the congregation would have to recognize her as a sexual person. The incarnation shows us that our bodies are wonderful and integral to how we experience and know the world and live in a variety of relationships.

Our sexuality is part of who we are as human bodies. It was the same for Jesus. We are relational and it is our bodies that open us not only to the potential for great harm, but also to life-enhancing connection. "Far from being a first line of defense against the world," our bodies "are in fact the very field upon which the self is called daily to meet the world."[5] With embodiment

4. M. Shawn Copeland, *Enfleshing Freedom: Body, Race, and Being* (Minneapolis: Fortress Press, 2010), 56. In Chapter Three, "Marking the Body of Jesus, the Body of Christ," Copeland argues that we purposefully ignore the body in service of empire, marking particular bodies as less than human without acknowledging the systems we use to do so with regard to race, ethnicity, sexuality, gender, and so on.

comes vulnerability experienced in and through relationship with self, others, and God.

LOVE COMMANDMENT

The great commandment gives us three very important guidelines for understanding sexuality as it relates to the formation of healthy relationships (Luke 10:27). First, it reinforces the creation message about love of self and positive affirmation of one's unique personhood. Second, Jesus reminds us that balancing our love for God, ourselves, and others is ultimately our Christian calling and that all other actions will flow from that. Third, loving our neighbor as ourselves calls us to support and care for our neighbor in promoting his or her sexual development and health.

Many of us know the grace of a basically positive, even if challenging, relationship with God and are able to affirm our sexuality as a good part of our humanity. In describing the spiritual dimension of our sexuality, Todd Salzman and Michael Lawler write:

> Far from being an impediment to authentic spirituality, truly human sexuality and sexual acts, embraced and used as gifts of the creator God, can enhance, deepen, and develop one's spirituality. Christian spirituality is a person's foundational relationship with the triune God. . . . This foundational relationship shapes all other relationships, including sexual relationships.[6]

That is to say, through our spirituality we deepen and grow in our experience and understanding of our sexuality.

When we have such a relationship in our lives, the great commandment calls us to make it possible for others. For example, rather than hiding their affection, Victor and his partner might consider how their example could open space for others to express and affirm their love. Loving our neighbors as ourselves is an act of social justice that includes affirming the uniqueness of whom God created them to be as well as an equal opportunity for them to share and find love in relationships they choose. This means we have a moral

5. Thomas E. Breidenthal, "Sanctifying Nearness," in *Our Selves, Our Souls and Our Bodies: Sexuality and the Household of God*, ed. Charles Hefling (Boston: Crowley Publications, 1996), 47.

6. Todd A. Salzman and Michael G. Lawler, *The Sexual Person: Toward a Renewed Catholic Anthropology* (Washington, DC: Georgetown University Press, 2008), 134; see 127–38 for a description of the five aspects of sexuality. See also Todd A. Salzman and Michael G. Lawler, *Sexual Ethics: A Theological Introduction* (Washington, DC: Georgetown University Press, 2012), 50–60.

obligation or commitment to create safe space for all individuals to be free from abuse, violence, and harm as they develop life-giving and life-enhancing relationships with God, themselves, and each other.

Jesus gives us the great love commandment to guide all our relationships. It has special significance to our sexual relationships, which require the following:

- Balance of commitments to God, self, and others, including friends, family, romantic partners, and those we are called to serve.
- Recognition that respecting and honoring self, neighbor, and God in sexual relationships means we can have sexual feelings without acting on them, and that we may never coerce someone into a sexual behavior they do not want.
- Understanding Jesus' call to create a world where each person has the ability and chance to live the love commandment by seeking life-giving relationships as an act of justice for herself and her neighbors.

Being embodied and relational creatures deeply impacts how Christians understand sexuality. Having a clearer sense of what we mean by sexuality and sexual health is thus an important part of professional sexual ethics.

Sexual Health and Wholeness

Sexual health and wholeness rest on an ethical evaluation of how we ought to be sexual beings in this world. Our bodies change; our relationships grow, end, and begin; our self-understanding is shaped and altered by new life circumstances; and so on. Sexuality is affected by and changes with these experiences. Health and wholeness are not a finish line we can cross; they are a state of being that must be constantly evaluated, pursued and sustained.

Christians must respect the theological and ethical claims made above in relation to creation, incarnation, and the love commandment. For Christians, as for secular humanitarians, sexual health minimally requires the acknowledgement of the anthropological claims associated with our embodiment and relationality. Consent and safety are key components of sexual health when it comes to expressing attraction and engaging in behaviors. Additionally, there is also a social dynamic to sexual health; my own access to and opportunity for sexual health are tied to yours. The World Health Organization defines sexual health as:

A state of physical, emotional, mental and social well-being in relation to sexuality, and not merely the absence of disease, dysfunction or infirmity. Sexual health requires a positive and respectful approach to sexuality and sexual relationships, as well as the possibility of having pleasurable and safe sexual experiences, free of coercion, discrimination and violence. For sexual health to be attained and maintained, the sexual rights of all people must be respected, protected and fulfilled.[7]

Like other aspects of our health, our sexuality requires care and attention. Disease and unhealthy sexual expression and relationships arise when we deny our sexuality or limit it to only one dimension, such as physical/biological functioning.

Consider how James and Victor are affected by the compartmentalization of their sexuality. Victor's relationship is strained and his personal satisfaction is diminished. It is common for couples to get so stuck on sexual intercourse as the primary sexual behavior, both theologically and practically, and they stop engaging in a variety of sexual behaviors common during courtship and early partnerships, such as making out, mutual masturbation, holding hands, massaging, and so on. James, on the other hand, evades dealing with the pain of broken trust by cutting off all relational opportunities, to the point of avoiding talking about sexuality. This stark dichotomy is fed by our cultural denial of the sensual and intimate needs of single people, older adults, and those with physical and mental disabilities through forced celibacy,[8] limited understandings of sexuality, and the perpetuation of the idea that sexual self-pleasure is sinful. In response, we need to open ourselves to "new visions of wholeness and holiness, health and healing" through practices that integrate and honor the various dimensions of our sexuality."[9]

Many may know well their tradition and its policies, and perhaps even advocate for sexual justice issues. However, as these vignettes make clear, many are uncomfortable discussing sexuality in the context of their faith community, and many church professionals struggle with sexual integrity. Maria has neglected self-care by consuming herself with work in order to avoid dealing with the personal (and social) loss that can accompany divorce. James is avoiding particular types of counseling and education in the congregational context because of his own sexuality experiences. Victor is struggling to set

---

7. World Health Organization, *Defining Sexual Health: Report of a Technical Consultation on Sexual Health, 28–31 January 2002, Geneva*" (Geneva, Switzerland: WHO Press, 2006), 5, http://www.who.int/reproductivehealth/publications/sexual_health/defining_sexual_health.pdf.

8. When celibacy is a choice, it can be life-enhancing and nurturing to various aspects of one's sexuality.

9. Thorson-Smith, "Becoming 'Possessed,'" 236.

personal limits that allow his relationship to flourish while offering a positive example to the faith community.

The combination of theological education, pastoral care training, and basic sexuality education can provide the means for most religious professionals to meet the goals and competencies outlined in the introduction to this volume. Yet, it is not simply a matter of knowledge or skill acquisition. Both self-evaluation and commitment toward one's sexual health are required. We know that "all forms of social health and well-being are intimately related to our personal experiences of sexual health and well-being."[10] Professional sexual ethics calls us to work on our own sexual health as well as that of our faith community and larger society.

SEXUAL INTEGRITY AS CORNERSTONE FOR MINISTRY

Sexual health and wholeness are a state of being that we reach toward, fall short of, and partially attain. Many of us have been taught that particular sexual behaviors and identities alone determine morality. Thus, how we evaluate a person's sexual fitness for ministry or any relationship often relies on hidden characteristics. As Mary Hunt defines it, "Integrity has a dynamic of its own, a sense of wholeness and certitude that is obvious, albeit only on careful examination. It has both an individual dimension—I feel whole—and a communal dimension—people tell me I seem whole."[11] Being whole requires us to be honest with ourselves about who we are and who God calls us to be.

Sexual integrity is not a "free pass" for any and all sexual behaviors or relationship configurations. Quite the contrary, sexual integrity calls us to honesty with and care for ourselves before God and in relationship with others. Christian values and norms follow from the virtue of sexual integrity as described by Marvin Ellison: "when we discern that a person is seeking to live with integrity, it is fair to assume that the person is invested in relationships based on honesty, fairness, commitment, mutual care, and respect—and, further, that he or she wants to contribute to the well-being of others and to the community at large."[12] These norms serve as a measuring stick—for example, to show that instances of an adult touching a minor, or forced intercourse on a date, or sexual innuendos made from a ministerial staff person to a congregant are violations of sexual integrity. These norms establish a higher standard for

10. Ibid., 244.

11. Mary E. Hunt, "Sexual Integrity," *WATERWheel* 7, no.3 (Fall 1994): 1–3.

12. Marvin M. Ellison, "Practicing Safer Spirituality," in *Out of the Shadows and Into the Light: Christianity and Homosexuality*, ed. Miguel A. De La Torre (St. Louis: Chalice, 2009), 9–10.

our relationships than past religious configurations which relied on gender, orientation, racial identity, or family construction to determine morality.

Sexual integrity as a cornerstone in one's professional ministry can positively affect the congregation. Because of lack of training and preparation, "responding to individuals who have sexual concerns is one of the most difficult circumstances that clergy face today. The intensity of feelings, including a pastor's own, can make it hard to provide the guidance about sexuality that is sought."[13] Education and training will help religious professionals be better prepared. But there is also a personal journey toward self-knowledge that is needed. We have a moral obligation to God, ourselves, and our neighbor to be informed, responsible, and celebratory of our sexuality, a "very good" part of our embodied, relational being created by God.

DISCUSSION QUESTIONS

1. What Christian values guide your ministry related to sexuality issues?

2. Review the framework for sexually healthy religious professionals (discussed in the introduction). In what sexuality-related areas might you need more training? How will you seek out resources?

3. Draw your sexuality timeline, naming physical and emotional changes, behaviors, and relationships from your birth until now. How have various aspects of your sexuality been over or under developed at different stages of your life?

4. The daily practice of ministry teaches about sexuality even when we do not explicitly address it. For example, what does the "Kiss of Peace" or "greetings" in your liturgical context communicate about boundaries and aspects of sexuality mentioned above (for example, embodiment, relationality, sensuality, intimacy, and so on)?

5. Rate how comfortable you are talking about the following sexuality issues with various congregants—from 1 (*very uncomfortable*) to 3 (*I could do it, but I'm not actively volunteering*) to 5 (*very comfortable*). Where are areas for growth and training?

_____ Sexual abuse prevention with Sunday school children and teachers together?

_____ Separately?

13. Andrew Weaver, John D. Preston, and Charlene Hosenfeld, *Counseling on Sexual Issues: A Handbook for Pastors and Other Helping Professionals* (Cleveland: Pilgrim, 2005), 5.

_____ Sexual-decision making with the youth group and their parents together?

_____ Separately?

_____ Sexual behaviors of a couple in pastoral care?

_____ Dating and/or cohabitation practices of the older adults in your congregation?

_____ Liturgical prayers for miscarriage, infertility and/or abortion?

RECOMMENDED READINGS

Ellison, Marvin M. *Making Love Just: Sexual Ethics in Perplexing Times.* Minneapolis: Fortress Press, 2012.

Haffner, Debra W. *A Time to Build: Creating Sexually Healthy Faith Communities.* 2nd ed. Westport, CT: Religious Institute, 2012.

Thorson-Smith, Sylvia. "Becoming 'Possessed': Toward Sexual health and Well-Being." In *Body and Soul: Re-thinking Sexuality as Justice-Love*, edited by Marvin M. Ellison and Sylvia Thorson-Smith, 232–50. Cleveland: Pilgrim, 2003.

United Church of Christ. *Our Whole Lives: Lifespan Sexuality Education Curriculum.* Cleveland: United Church Board for Homeland Ministries, 1999–2000.

———. *Sexuality and Our Faith: A Companion to Our Whole Lives.* Cleveland: United Church Board for Homeland Ministries, 1999–2000.

Weaver, Andrew, John D. Preston, and Charlene Hosenfeld. *Counseling on Sexual Issues: A Handbook for Pastors and Other Helping Professionals.* Cleveland: Pilgrim, 2005.

2

Fiduciary Duty and Sacred Trust

Darryl W. Stephens

Jerome, a single man in his late twenties, is in his third year as pastor of Grace Church, a growing congregation in a bustling suburb.[1] Marjorie, a single woman in her middle twenties, joined Grace Church two years ago after a difficult divorce. Recently, she has begun to pay more and more attention to her pastor. It is clear to others in the congregation that they have a mutual attraction to each other, and some members gossip about how they might encourage this budding romance. Eventually, Jerome asks Marjorie on a date so that the two of them can get to know each other in a more personal way. Soon, they are dating regularly. Jerome chooses to keep things quiet and not to involve the church leadership in his personal affairs.

Sandra is a vivacious and dynamic lay leader at First Church. She is thirty-four, married, and has two preschool-age children. This is her fourth year in ministry with the congregation's youth group, and Sandra has developed very close relationships with many of the youth. The parents at First Church are pleased that the youth group is growing under her leadership and they appreciate Sandra's willingness to be available to her youth group members any time of day or night via telephone, text, or email. Indeed, many youth do confide in Sandra and often call her at odd hours about their personal problems. Sandra is also very affectionate, especially with the boys, often greeting them with a full-body hug and a kiss whenever they meet—to make them feel loved, she explains. In the church youth lounge, she is often found sitting on the sofa

---

1. This chapter is a revision of an article first published in the online publication, *Living the Sacred Trust: Clergy Sexual Ethics* (Nashville, TN: General Board of Higher Education and Ministry of The United Methodist Church, 2010), section II, 3–17, http://www.gbhem.org/site/c.lsKSL3POLvF/ b.6426417/k.13A2/Living_the_Sacred_Trust_Clergy_Sexual_Ethics.htm. A version of this article also appears as, "The Sacred Trust of Ministry," in *When Pastors Prey: Overcoming Clergy Sexual Abuse of Women*, ed. Valli Boobal Batchelor (Geneva: WCC, 2013), 41–52.

next to one or more of the youth, holding hands or giving backrubs. The youth consider her a friend.

Donald is a dynamic and charismatic senior pastor of Church of the Magdalene, a large, urban congregation. During the past five years of his fifteen-year ministry at Magdalene, three laywomen in his congregation—Nancy, Carol, and Johanna—have gone to the bishop with accusations that Donald has acted inappropriately toward them. Each woman independently tells the bishop that Donald repeatedly groped, kissed, and fondled her in the church office. When confronted by the bishop, Donald defends himself, claiming that ladies in the church are often attracted to him, that this is not the first time he has been accused by jealous women unable to lure him from his wife, and that his award-winning record of evangelism for the past twenty-five years speaks for itself. The bishop feels that her hands are tied since Donald will neither confirm nor deny the allegations and none of the women is willing to sign an official complaint out of fear of reprisal. In fact, Donald *has* done the things the women accuse him of, but he thinks that he is entitled to sexual favors since he "sacrifices so much" for the church.

Each of the above case studies depicts a leader who violated the trust of ministry through sexual behavior with a congregant. Donald is a sexual predator. He feels entitled to sex from his female parishioners, and he evades responsibility for his actions when confronted by the bishop. It is easy to understand his behavior as unethical and to see the wrong in his actions. Jerome, on the other hand, is not a predator. In fact, some people—including contributors to this volume—have difficulty understanding his actions as misconduct at all. The case of Sandra depicts a ministerial leader whose lack of clearly defined interpersonal boundaries creates emotional confusion and puts her at risk of abusing the youth in her care. She may be a wanderer, a predator, or neither. In my opinion, each of these ministerial leaders has put the needs of self ahead of the needs of those whom they serve.

DEFINITIONS

The "sacred trust"[2] of ministry invokes the concepts of fiduciary duty, power, interpersonal boundaries, and consent. Sacred trust refers to a fundamental

2. The United Methodist Church has referred to ordination as "a sacred trust" since at least as far back as 1980. See *The Book of Discipline of The United Methodist Church 1980* (Nashville: United Methodist Publishing House, 1980), 230. This phrase was popularized by a curriculum for clergy boundaries training published by the Faith Trust Institute (formerly, the Center for the Prevention of Sexual and Domestic Violence), *A Sacred Trust: Boundary Issues for Clergy and Spiritual Teachers* (Seattle: CPSDV, 2003).

ethical obligation of the ministerial leader. All Christians are called, through baptism, to ministry. Some Christians are called by God and confirmed by the faith community as having the gifts and graces for ministry wherein they represent the church/congregation. These ministerial leaders, whether lay or ordained, serve in countless ways—preachers, choir directors, church school teachers, and adult volunteers with the youth group all occupy a ministerial role. These roles of leadership indicate the trust of a faith community and obligate the persons in those roles to uphold this trust. The sacred trust of ministry demands, at a minimum, that ministerial leaders will act in the best interests of those whom they serve. "Fiduciary duty" is the legal term describing this professional obligation not to exploit others. Doctors, lawyers, social workers, teachers, law-enforcement officers—each of these helping professions accepts a responsibility to promote the best interests of others rather than self. For those in such roles, sexual misconduct is never simply an "affair." It is a violation of the power and authority of the professional role.

The Bible and Christian liturgy are replete with messages about justice and faithful ministry. The predominant theme of justice in the Hebrew Bible is protection of the vulnerable, those without power. King David exemplifies the leader who misuses power for personal gratification. Ezekiel brings sharp condemnation on so-called shepherds who would prey on their own flock (Ezek. 34:4). In the New Testament, Jesus warns that "just as you did [not do] it to one of the least of these, you did [not do] it to me" (Matt. 25:40, 45). Paul counsels those in ministry: "Do not seek your own advantage, but that of the other" (1 Cor. 10:24). In the United Methodist liturgy of baptism, the community of faith pledges to "live according to the example of Christ" and to "surround these persons with a community of love and forgiveness, that they may grow in their trust of God."[3] Misconduct of a sexual nature is a violation of this love and trust.

Let us now examine the issues of abuse of power, inappropriate interpersonal boundaries, and absence of consent, as illustrated by the problematic behaviors of Donald, Sandra, and Jerome.

ABUSE OF POWER AND DONALD'S CASE

Power and its abuse are key factors in ministerial misconduct, but many clergy are genuinely confused when discussions of professional ethics focus on the concept of power. "I don't *feel* powerful" is a common response of a pastor striving to exemplify "servant leadership." However, the power of the

---

3. *The United Methodist Hymnal* (Nashville: UM Publishing House, 1989), 35.

ministerial role is a reality we can and must learn to recognize. While age, race/ethnicity, gender, wealth, education, citizenship status, and language all contribute to the power differential between persons, when a pastor interacts with a congregant, his status as clergy is a primary factor in determining the relative power between them. People bring their most intimate concerns to those in ministerial leadership, trusting that they have the training, expertise, and sensitivity to understand the human condition and to speak a word of divine grace, judgment, and forgiveness. In short, ministers are entrusted to care for people's deepest needs, hurts, desires, and hopes. This is a powerful position to occupy.

Donald exemplifies the dangerous pastor to whom Ezekiel speaks a word of judgment. Donald feels entitled to act in the way he does towards the women in his congregation, and he leverages his effectiveness as an evangelist and prowess as a preacher to deflect criticism. His power derives not only from his role as pastor but also from his political influence in the conference. In this instance, he exerts his power by pressuring Nancy, Carol, and Johanna not to file a signed complaint and by pressuring his bishop to let the matter drop. He is a dangerous manipulator who casts himself as the victim, claiming to be the "vulnerable" party.

The term "vulnerability" refers to a relative lack of power and resources.[4] As with power, vulnerability is not dependent on the way someone feels. Clergy may feel "vulnerable" when striving to model sensitivity, openness, or servant leadership, but this feeling does not indicate a lack of power. To the contrary, many clergy are empowered to display a great degree of emotional and spiritual openness with their congregation precisely because of their role and the institutional resources available to them. Having a lot to lose is an indication of power, not powerlessness. In Donald's case, he has a twenty-five-year career, a tall steeple church, and a public image at stake (in addition to his marriage and family life). To protect himself and his personal interests, he spuriously claims to be vulnerable while leveraging tremendous institutional resources to have his way.[5]

---

4. Marie M. Fortune, *Love Does No Harm: Sexual Ethics for the Rest of Us* (New York: Continuum, 1995), 42.

5. This is not to say that clergy can never be the victims of harassment and abuse. Young women clergy, in particular, can be vulnerable to harassment and abuse by male laypersons, especially those whose age, race, wealth, and other social factors provide them with a relatively more powerful position. Nevertheless, the person in the ministerial role is always responsible for maintaining appropriate professional boundaries.

Inappropriate Interpersonal Boundaries and Sandra's Case

Interpersonal boundaries appropriately delimit the ministerial relationship. When a clergyperson interacts with a person in her congregation, she represents more than herself. She represents the congregation, the institutional church, the profession of ministry, and even God. When she dons the "collar" (either literally or figuratively), she functions in a public role with public expectations. She does not act on her own behalf. This is true whether leading public worship or providing one-to-one spiritual guidance. This is also true of laity in ministerial roles of leadership. Observing and honoring interpersonal boundaries allow ministerial leaders to uphold the covenant of expectation placed upon that role. The sacred trust of ministry is built on the assurance of limits.

Professional relationships differ from personal relationships in their degree of reciprocity. Ministerial relationships are asymmetrical: the pastor is there to serve the needs of the parishioner (fiduciary duty), not the other way around. The pastor is expected to provide certain services, to have professional training and expertise, and to be institutionally accountable for carrying out her duties. The pastor is expected to satisfy her own needs outside of pastoral relationships. Personal relationships, on the other hand, are mutual and less well defined. The mutuality of friendship means reciprocal personal sharing back and forth and support of each other. Sexual intimacy, for example, should be characterized by mutuality and reciprocity. This is not true of the relationship between pastor and parishioner.

I offer the following guidelines as an early warning system for ministerial ethics. Five safeguards remind us of the fiduciary duty and sacred trust of the ministerial role. Additionally, five danger signs indicate when we may be entering an ethically grey area that could lead to misconduct.

SAFEGUARDS

Safeguards
1. Bullhorn test
2. Fiduciary duty
3. Legitimate function of ministry
4. Collegial accountability and supervision
5. Do no harm

First, the bullhorn test: How would my actions as a ministerial leader be perceived if they were made public? Second, fiduciary duty: Are my actions as a ministerial leader in the best interests of the congregant? Or am I attempting to have my own, personal needs met through this relationship? Third, legitimate function of ministry: What ministerial service am I providing? Providing emotional and spiritual support during difficult times is a genuine function of ministry. Sexual intimacy is not a service of the profession of ministry! Fourth, collegial accountability and supervision: Can I stand by my actions? How would my supervisor and colleagues respond to my behavior? (Note: If I am unwilling honestly and openly to share my behavior with them, I have failed the bullhorn test.) Fifth, do no harm: Is anyone put at risk by my actions? Who? Is that risk warranted?

DANGER SIGNS

Danger Signs
1. Misperception
2. Self-importance
3. Creating dependence
4. Unhealthy precedent
5. Self-deception

First, misperception: Might my actions be misperceived? This is the test of staying above reproach, avoiding even the appearance of impropriety. Second, self-importance: Do I feel indispensable? Am I motivated by a need to be needed? Not only does this put me at risk of boundary violations, it also indicates poor self-care. Third, creating dependence: Does the person with whom I am in ministry exhibit unhealthy signs of emotional dependence on me? This danger sign is a companion to the warning about self-importance. The feeling of being personally needed by others is a powerful form of co-dependency and can go in both directions. Fourth, unhealthy precedent: What kind of precedent am I setting? Am I normalizing questionable practices? If I contribute to a congregational culture that routinely accepts risky ministerial behavior, then I set an unhealthy precedent that enables a future predator easy access to vulnerable parishioners. Fifth, self-deception or self-delusion: Do I feel that this ministerial relationship is an exception to the usual rules and limits? If I think that this relationship is special in a way that allows me to justify crossing the usual boundaries, I am at risk of self-deception. If I am observing guideline four above, then my colleagues and supervisor should alert me to this danger.

These guidelines do not by themselves determine if I am at risk of misconduct. However, failure to follow any of these guidelines is a red flag warning of possible boundary violations.[6]

Sandra's case raises several red flags according to these safeguards and danger signs. Her availability 24/7 indicates a lack of boundaries and the danger of self-importance. Sandra's actions indicate that she perceives herself as indispensable to the youth she serves. Her physical affections with the youth raise the question of her intentions. We don't know how the male youth perceive her hugs and kisses, nor do we know how others in the congregation perceive her behavior. Sandra is behaving in ways that could be easily misperceived, if indeed her actions are innocent. Sandra is also acting in ways that indicate she may be trying to meet her own needs for intimacy, touch, and friendship through her ministerial relationships.

Sandra's behavior raises other questions about her professional conduct. Are kisses, backrubs, and handholding legitimate services of ministry? There are certainly contexts when these actions could be an appropriate part of ministerial support: comforting someone in a hospital, during grieving at a funeral, and so on. However, Sandra uses physical intimacy as an everyday tool of ministry. Sandra may also be causing harm to others if some of the teenagers develop unhealthy emotional and physical attachments to her. Finally, Sandra's behavior is creating an unhealthy precedent. The youth and other congregants are being trained to accept as normal some questionable ministerial practices that could lead to abuse by other ministerial leaders. Would the congregation be as accepting of a male youth minister behaving in the same way? These guidelines do not prove that Sandra is guilty of sexual misconduct. However, the multiple warning signs indicate a situation that could easily lead to misconduct if it has not occurred already. Sandra is clearly guilty of violating ministerial boundaries.

ABSENCE OF CONSENT AND JEROME'S CASE

Consent is a prerequisite to acceptable sexual intimacy, but a ministerial relationship is a context in which meaningful consent by the parishioner is often impossible. Consent involves not only the ability to say "yes," but also the ability to say "no." When it comes to sexual intimacy, there is no meaningful consent possible between the minister and the person seeking pastoral care.[7] This type

---

6. I draw inspiration from Rebekah L. Miles's tools for negotiating the ambiguities of the moral terrain of ministry in *The Pastor as Moral Guide* (Minneapolis: Fortress Press, 1999), 54–56.

of dual relationship is incompatible with ministry and is often indicative of poor habits of self-care.

Dual relationships are common in ministry. Unlike other professionals, such as psychiatrists, clergy cannot categorically avoid friendships with those they serve. Because pastors live and work within a community, they often have multiple relationships with the persons in their pews. The pastor might buy books at the store owned by a parishioner, the pastor's dentist might join the church and desire to be baptized, and the pastor's children might attend school taught by men and women who sing in the choir or serve as church trustees.

When pastors have many different kinds of relationships with the persons in their congregations, they often have to work harder than other professionals to establish and maintain appropriate boundaries. Entering into responsible dual relationships requires intentional and often explicit negotiation of appropriate boundaries, since the work of ministry is not typically confined to office hours by appointment in a designated place of ministry. When a doctor and her patient coincidentally find themselves at the same grocery store, the doctor is clearly off duty and would not appreciate a spontaneous request for a medical opinion. However, a pastor might find that grocery shopping is a good occasion to offer invitation, assurance, and spiritual support. There is a real sense in which a pastor is never "off duty." This is not just an emergency exception. No matter the time of day or occasion, the pastor cannot shed the professional role when around potential, current, or even past members of the congregation. Indeed, the challenge for clergy is how to take time off.

Self-care for clergy and other ministerial leaders is vital to a healthy work-life balance and appropriate boundaries in ministry.[8] How can clergy set aside time and opportunity to attend to their own needs? In order to be fully present for and attend to the best interests of those we serve, ministerial leaders must

7. The concept of "meaningful consent" is based on the ability of each party to say "no" without fear of reprisal. Consent is maximized in a relationship of equals. The ability of the more vulnerable party in a relationship to consent to sexual activity is diminished as the power differential increases. In a fiduciary relationship, the professional is trusted not to exploit the imbalance of power to her own advantage. On the lack of meaningful consent to sexual intimacy in ministerial relationships, see Marie M. Fortune, *Responding to Clergy Misconduct: A Handbook* (Seattle: FaithTrust Institute, 2009), 28, 49–50; Karen Lebacqz and Ronald G. Barton, *Sex in the Parish* (Louisville: Westminster John Knox, 1991), 113–131; Karen A. McClintock, *Preventing Sexual Abuse in Congregations: A Resource for Leaders* (Herndon, VA: Alban Institute, 2004), 78–82.

8. Work/life balance is one of thirteen key factors highly correlated with clergy health, according to a survey of United Methodist clergy. General Board of Higher Education and Ministry and General Board of Pensions and Health Benefits, *Church Systems Task Force Report, May 2011*, 13, http://www.gbophb.org/TheWell/Root/CFH/4225.pdf.

also have personal time and personal relationships that allow their own needs to be met. If clergy attempted to be in ministry all of the time with everyone who enters their lives, they would do themselves and others a great disservice. They would inevitably begin using their ministerial relationships to satisfy their personal needs. Self-care for clergy means, at the least, taking a day off every week, turning off phone and email at certain times of day, and cultivating friendships with persons completely removed from their ministerial setting. Regarding their own sexual needs, clergy must recognize that they cannot be a person's lover and pastor at the same time.[9]

Jerome's case illustrates some of the complexities of dating for clergy. He and Marjorie clearly have a ministerial relationship: she joined the church under his leadership, and he has served as her pastor for two years. The pastoral relationship precedes their dating relationship chronologically and takes priority for Jerome even after their romantic liaison commences. What may appear to be a consensual relationship involving sexual intimacy between two adults is most likely not a relationship to which Marjorie is free to consent.

The guidelines above offer several red flag warnings for Jerome. Jerome fails the bullhorn test. There is also no evidence that he is seeking collegial support and supervision. He thus fails the accountability test. Jerome is also operating as if his relationship were an exception to the dangers inherent in dating a parishioner, indicating the likelihood of self-deception. Jerome still maintains the façade of a pastoral relationship with Marjorie even as they begin dating. Clearly, he has prioritized his own needs over the fiduciary responsibility he owes to her. Furthermore, who is being put at risk in this situation? Examining this dual relationship closely reveals that Jerome is putting Marjorie at more risk than he is willing to assume himself. If this romance encounters rocky terrain, to whom can Marjorie turn for pastoral support? She would need to turn to someone other than Jerome. Jerome's primary role in her life has changed from pastor to lover. However, it is not at all clear from Jerome's behavior that he shares this priority. Otherwise, he would be more transparent about and accountable for his actions. Marjorie has already lost a pastor, and Jerome has not helped her find a new one. The congregation is also being put at risk. When a romance goes sour, people take sides. What would happen to this congregation if this couple had a messy breakup? In many actual cases, the congregation becomes divided and community is significantly ruptured.

---

9. See Fortune, *Love Does No Harm*, 83–84.

How could this dating scenario be improved so as to reduce the risks and increase accountability?[10] First, Jerome should acknowledge that he cannot be both pastor and lover to Marjorie. If they desire an amorous relationship, one or both of them will have to find a new church. Second, transparency requires that Jerome and Marjorie be open about this dating relationship. Jerome should contact his district superintendent for guidance, and he should alert the congregation's staff-parish relations committee. Third, these parties, along with some trusted colleagues, should hold him accountable to his professional duties and help him establish safeguards to reduce the possibility of doing harm to others. Fourth, he will have to work carefully to avoid normalizing this behavior in the life of the congregation. If the congregation comes to accept the situation of their pastor dating a parishioner as normal, Jerome will be setting a precedent that may prove destructive to healthy ministry. If single women joining this church thought that they were being viewed as potential dating partners for the pastor, this would detrimentally affect the ability of the pastor to minister to them.

One of the most disturbing aspects of this scenario, even if these safeguards were put into place, is the likelihood that Marjorie is not really free to consent to sexual intimacy with Jerome. She joined this congregation immediately after a difficult divorce. If she has worked through her grieving of the end of this marriage, it is likely that this church and its pastor, Jerome, played a significant part in providing spiritual support. This would have increased the power imbalance already inherent in the ministerial relationship. If, on the other hand, she has not worked through her grief, she is even more vulnerable on an emotional level. The ability genuinely to consent to a sexual relationship decreases in proportion to the depth of pastoral relationship.

CONCLUSION

At the heart of the ethical obligation of ministry is fiduciary duty—a commitment by all persons in ministerial roles of leadership to act in the best interests of those whom they serve. Failure to observe prudent safeguards and to avoid common dangers puts many people at risk. Faithfulness to ethical standards of ministry creates safer and healthier congregational communities, more fully enabling the Church to live out its call to be Christ for the world.

10. Karen Lebacqz and Ronald G. Barton caution that the burden of proof is on the pastor to demonstrate that the relationship is genuinely consensual and that the couple are meeting as equals, as well as to acknowledge that the cultural reality of sexism renders a relationship between a male pastor and a female congregant unlikely to be free of power and coercion. Lebacqz and Barton, *Sex in the Parish*, 130.

Discussion Questions

1. How does the "sacred trust" of the ministerial office enable the honesty and openness we find so essential to ministerial relationships? How would the absence of that trust affect our ability to give and receive spiritual care?

2. Reflect on a situation in your own life when you felt an imbalance of power between yourself and another person. How did this imbalance affect your ability to influence (or be influenced) by the other person?

3. As a ministerial leader, what is your plan for handling a sexual advance by a parishioner? What is your plan for appropriately responding to your own sexual attraction to a parishioner?

4. If a church does not have a policy against single clergy dating their own parishioners, how would this affect the ways in which single laypersons might interact with an unmarried clergyperson?

Recommended Readings

Fortune, Marie M. *Is Nothing Sacred? The Story of a Pastor, the Women He Sexually Abused, and the Congregation He Nearly Destroyed.* Eugene, OR: Wipf & Stock, 2008.

———. *Healthy Boundaries: 101–Fundamentals and 201–Beyond Basics.* Seattle: FaithTrust Institute, 2012.

Gula, Richard M. *Just Ministry: Professional Ethics for Pastoral Ministers.* New York: Paulist, 2010.

Lebacqz, Karen, and Ronald G. Barton. *Sex in the Parish.* Louisville: Westminster John Knox, 1991.

McClintock, Karen A. *Preventing Sexual Abuse in Congregations: A Resource for Leaders.* Herndon, VA: Alban Institute, 2004.

Peterson, Marilyn R. *At Personal Risk: Boundary Violations in Professional-Client Relationships.* New York: W.W. Norton, 1992.

3, 4, 5, 8, 14, 16, 17
18 + 20

Chapters

3

Sexing the Ministry

Stanley Hauerwas

I often observe that it is not the ordination of gays that threatens the ministry. Rather, at least for those in the Methodist ministry, the biggest problem is adultery. I then observe that I wish that adultery could be attributed to lust, but most people in the ministry do not have that much energy. Rather, I attribute many of the cases of adultery by those in the ministry to loneliness. For I take it that in the ministry—and this is true not only for people in the Methodist ministry—loneliness surrounds those who occupy the office of priest or minister.

I think it is important to ask why this is the case. I suspect it has to do with the lack of understanding by those the minister serves of what the ministry entails. Many operate under the presumption that those in the ministry do not work for a living, as they are only required to work one day a week. Beyond this single day of work, what is required of those in the ministry is that they be personable. At the very least, this means they are to be superficially friendly with everyone in the congregation. If the minister becomes a genuine friend with some members in the congregation, it may seem the minister is playing favorites and, therefore, cannot deliver pastoral services in a fair manner to everyone in the congregation.

Pastoral services, moreover, can be one of the sources that create the profound loneliness associated with the ministry. Ministers are often given permission to be present to people in some of the most agonizing events in life. Divorce, death, and destruction name some events in which ministers are asked to participate in order provide comfort. During the crisis, the family or other members of the church are glad the minister is there to pray for them. But too often, after the crisis has passed, those who have gone through it do not want anything to do with the minister because the minister has witnessed them in their most vulnerable moments. Having been naked with emotion, they fear those with such knowledge. The minister is, so-to-speak, stiff-armed. The intensity of the events into which they were invited cannot be shared, given the obligations of confidentiality associated with such privilege. This makes the minister even more isolated from those they serve.

All of this is complicated by the politics of ministerial placement. It is hard to be friends with other ministers in your own denomination because you may be in competition with them. In Methodism, that means you have a constituency of one—the district superintendent. Friendship is possible with other clergy, but they are usually in another denomination. Moreover, such friendships too often consist of sharing war stories about how bad the congregations you serve may be. But friendships based on such dismal data are not likely to last.

Moreover, given the view that those in the ministry only work one day a week, those in the congregation often assume they can place infinite demands on their minister. It does not take long, therefore, for those in the ministry to feel as if they have been nibbled to death by ducks. Some ministers try to escape through the route of Clinical Pastoral Education. Others retreat into their family lives because some parishioners recognize that ministers indeed have family duties. But this creates its own problems, in that no spouse is required to love another spouse that much. Spouses may be friends, but it is not a condition necessary to make a marriage a marriage.

I realize that this characterization of how the ministry can result in making ministers feel alone may be a far too dour a view, but I suspect most in the ministry will detect some truth to the picture I have painted. I think, moreover, that what I have described helps us understand how those in the ministry often find themselves in compromised sexual circumstances. Clergy are often desperate to be known by another human being. It is not accidental that sexual relations are often described in the Bible as a "knowing."

For example, one of the tasks that often fall on those in the ministry is to counsel people whose marriages are in trouble. Counseling itself can produce a form of (false) intimacy. It is easy to imagine, given the loneliness I have suggested is characteristic of the ministry, finding yourself attracted to the person you are counseling. Too often, the touch of the hand to comfort someone who has broken into tears can lead to touching that had not been planned. Before you know it, you have been pulled into a "spontaneous" relationship you had not anticipated. It is thought to be all the more significant exactly because it "just happened"—because the passion that fueled the sexual encounter was felt to be overwhelming.

Some may well think this is a far too innocent an account of sexual misconduct by those in the ministry. I am sure that sexual misconduct by those in the ministry has multiple sources. I am also sure that the ministry attracts out-and-out sexual predators. It is often said that such people, like rapists, are not really attracted to sex. They are really attracted to power over others. Given the powerlessness that those in the ministry often feel, one can see how the exercise of power through sex may be misconstrued as a form of compensation. But I have never been convinced it is merely a matter of power. It really is a matter of sex. That it really is a matter of sex, moreover, is a reminder that sex, whether between strangers or those who have been long married, can be and often is a very violent physical act.

I do not want to be misunderstood. I am not suggesting that ministerial misconduct in sexual matters is not an abuse of power. I have no doubt that just as a teacher is not to be sexually involved with a student, those in the ministry abuse the power they have been given if they become involved sexually with one of the members of their congregation. What I am objecting to, however, is the presumption that what is wrong with that kind of ministerial misconduct can be captured solely by the description "the abuse of power." That the abuse of power takes the form of sexual misconduct is not irrelevant for how we should think about these matters. I suspect the temptation to describe such misconduct as an abuse of power suggests part of the problem is that the church no longer knows what it wants to or needs to say about sex. As a result, those in the ministry, as well as those they serve, are left with little guidance about how we should conduct ourselves sexually.

We are unsure where even to begin to think morally about sex. What I am sure is the case, however, is that we will not have a sufficient ethic about the sexual behavior of those in the ministry by focusing on sex itself. Indeed I do not believe you can have a sexual ethic for anyone by focusing on sex alone. Rather, how you think about what is appropriate or inappropriate sexual behavior will, by necessity, draw on more determinative ways of life than sexuality. That I have diagnosed one of the reasons for sexual misconduct as a response to the loneliness of the lives of those in the ministry reflects my presumption that the sexual character of our lives must be surrounded by richer aspects of life than sex itself. For example, if the church is a community committed to speaking the truth to one another, this should make a difference for how we relate sexually. To engage in sex outside of marriage involves secrecy—and secrecy is the breeding ground of the lie. Accordingly, it becomes extremely important to see the connections between significant practices that must be interrelated if we are to live with integrity.

Indeed, I suspect the over-determination of the importance of sex in our U.S. society has everything to do with the loss of other significant forms of human relatedness. For example, ask yourself why people in significant friendships think it important *not* to be involved sexually with one another. Sex is a far too complicated aspect of life to be introduced into the relation between friends. When friends become sexually involved, you can be sure that something other than friendship has begun.

In truth, contrary to what we often tell the young, you do not need to know another person to have what you might consider "good sex." It is often forgotten that Christians for centuries assumed people who had not known one another until the day of the marriage would have sex after they have been declared married—not because they "loved" or even knew one another but because they were married. They might come to love one another by being married, and that love might involve their sexual behavior, but what made their sexual relations legitimate was the reality that they could be held responsible for any children that resulted from their sexual relation. In other words, marriage meant they were having sex "in public."

In the absence of significant relations that should surround how sex might contribute to how our lives can be lived with purpose, I fear that we now live in a society in which sex is used as entertainment or as a desperate way to overwhelm our loneliness. It is not only those in the ministry who live lives of loneliness. In truth, all our lives are gripped by a profound sense of loneliness. Crowds at sporting events are desperate attempts to overcome loneliness by identification with a team. Sex, like the crowd, too often becomes an ultimately unsatisfying way to connect with another human being, even if I have no other connections with them. Pornography is the ultimate attempt to make sex in itself self-fulfilling. The result, interestingly enough, is boredom.

I assume that Christians, including those in the ministry, are no less determined by the way sex is construed in our culture than those who are not Christian. Sex has become the last sacrament; that is, it is assumed that some meaning or reality will result from sexual behavior no matter what intentions you bring to the act. This assumption has become particularly destructive for young people who now engage in sexual relations with one another in a manner that makes sex a far too manipulative reality in their lives. Why, for example, do we not call it rape when the sixteen-year-old varsity football player manipulates the naïve, insecure thirteen-year-old to engage in intercourse?

To tell young people that sex is such a precious form of relating that they should save it for when they are "really in love," is a formula for disaster. The result is that kids who should not be in love—whatever it might mean to be in love—think they are in love because they are having sex. They are having sex, moreover, because sex turns out to be more interesting than anything else in their lives. It is the way they try to understand what adult relations may entail. The result is the development of a perspective on sex that makes it just another form of "relating." It is, of course, another form of relating, but it is one fraught with bodily implications that most people are ill-prepared to negotiate. Just to take off one's clothes—to become naked—in the presence of another creates an intimacy that is often unanticipated.

I mention these general attitudes and behaviors surrounding sex in the world because our inability to have a language to talk about sex in church is an indication of the loneliness I am suggesting shapes our lives. One of the difficulties ministers face, not only when it comes to sex in their lives but also in the lives of those they serve, is that we seem to have lost the ability to talk about sex in a manner that is not deceptive. One of the reasons for our inability to talk to one another about sex, as I suggest above, is the loss of any determinative behavior that gives purpose to our lives when it comes to sex. In other words, we cannot develop an adequate account of the role of sex in our lives by focusing on sexual acts or something called "our sexuality" that allegedly always needs to be expressed. Rather, we can only get a handle on sex by identifying those forms of life that give purpose to our sexual behavior. For that to take place, we must have an adequate way of talking to one another about our lives sexually that preserves the intimacy that rightly surrounds sexual expression by those committed to keeping faith with one another.

For that to happen, I think, the church will have to discover determinative practices—practices, as I suggest above, as basic as speaking the truth to one another—some of which may seem quite odd. For example, I think what must be said about sex by Christians is that sex is not all it is cracked up to be. You are not less a human being, and you are certainly not less a Christian, if you have never had a sexual relation with another human being. It is often forgotten that one of the most significant developments in the early church was the presumption that, if you were a Christian, you did not have to marry or to have children. I do not think this presumption was the result of Christian disdain for sexual activity, but rather, it was an expression of the Christian commitment to grow the church through witness and conversion instead of biology. Of course, Christians could marry, but those who married, interestingly, bore the burden of proof, given that they did not need to do so to be a Christian. For what the single gave up was not sex—though they were certainly expected to live exemplary lives—but heirs. Those called to marriage understood their calling might well entail the willingness to welcome new life. For if I am right that those called to marriage in the Christian community bear the burden of proof, one of the questions they must ask is whether they are willing to receive those who may come from—be born of—this marriage. Marriage is not the end in itself, but rather an institution of hope in a world of despair. I am not suggesting that every act of sexual intercourse must be open to procreation, but rather that marriage as a practice is unintelligible if the role of children is not constitutive of what marriage is about.

A community so determined must be one in which those who constitute it have the gift of friendship. For singleness cannot be sustained without friendship. (Neither, of course, can marriage or parenting.) But the friendship made possible by being Christian is the result of having good work to share. In other words, friendship is not an end in itself, but rather comes from the discovery that we need one another, given the task of being God's people in a world that knows not the God of Jesus Christ. When the ministry is threatened by sexual misconduct, we have an indication that the church has lost sight of the work we have been given to do, that is, of our purpose.

Friendship requires the ability of friends (whether married or single) to be able to talk to one another about what they fear. What most of us fear is that we cannot be loved. Sex often becomes a way to assure ourselves that we are capable of being loved. But that turns out to be a doubtful strategy for the long run because it results in manipulative behavior that is hard to recognize—exactly because the behavior is thought to be an expression of love. Ministers, as well as their congregants, discover they are being held captive to accounts of sex they often recognize as destructive, but from which they have no way to free themselves—precisely because they have lost the ability to speak honestly about our lives.

So, I think if we want to make a start to help those in the ministry have an adequate sexual ethic, we must begin by asking them to think twice about the language we use about sex. For example, it is not a bad place to start to call into question the very notions of "sexual ethics," "professional ethics," and "professional sexual ethics." Those phrases suggest that professional sexual ethics can be isolated from other aspects of our lives in such a way as only to enforce the problems we are confronting in the first place. To try to develop a sexual ethic divorced from the traditional Christian position that some are called to the life of singleness—a life that may entail vowed celibacy—while others are called to marriage, cannot avoid misconstruing the crucial theological moves entailed in serious discernment about these matters.

To try to develop a sexual ethic on the basis of what makes sex good will never work, because sex is a far too complex form of behavior to be "controlled" by isolating it. To try to address sexual ethics as an end in itself is about as silly as telling someone obsessed by sex to try not to think about sex. The very attempt not to think about sex means you cannot help but think about sex most of the time. The only way to help someone obsessed by sex is to give them some good work to do, that is, work that is so demanding that they discover new habits that shape their imaginations. Of course, it is not just their imaginations that are so shaped, but it is their bodies.

I suspect, for example, that one of the most important developments to free women from the male gaze has been the involvement of women in sports and in the professions. Women have been given good work to do that challenges the male presumption that women are primarily to be regarded in terms of their sexual attractiveness. I am not suggesting that athletic women are not attractive, but rather women athletes present an alternative image that contradicts the all-too-prevalent images of female seduction in our society.

The analysis I have given and the constructive alternative I have tried to provide may seem not to have addressed issues surrounding ministerial sexual misconduct. In my defense, I have tried to reframe how we should think about ministerial sexual ethics. By directing attention to our societal confusions about sex, as well as the reproduction of those confusions in the church itself, I have tried to suggest why we have failed to understand how and why sexual misconduct is such a threat to the ministry. The loneliness of the minister is only made more destructive by the inability of the church to have a language that makes possible communication between people about our sexual lives. We need to be able to talk frankly with one another about sex, but that requires trust.

The development of such trust surely depends on the acknowledgment that whatever sexual history we may bring to such discussions, it is not determinative for what we as Christians think we now need to say. What I suspect destroys many is not what they have done sexually but the justifications they have given for what they have done. Too often, those justifications turn out to be exercises in self-deception that mire us deeper in ways of life that force us into secrecy. As a result, we end up becoming strangers to ourselves and strangers to those with whom we worship.

There is no quick fix for the fix we find ourselves in when it comes to sex and, in particular, how the ministry has been sexed. I do not think this is necessarily bad news. But it does require Christians to resist the myths that surround sex in our society. Such resistance will require people who are determined to speak truthfully to one another about the confusions that constitute our lives when it comes to sex. Such people, I would hope, might be called "reverend" or "pastor." In short, they are people who lead lives that make it possible for them to tell us the truth. So understood, they are people who have good but difficult work to do. But what a blessing this is in a time when so many now think there is no good work to be done.

Discussion Questions

1. Have you ever considered a life of vowed celibacy as a Christian vocation? How might this choice, as an alternative to marriage, be perceived and supported within your faith community?
2. Respond to the author's description of loneliness in pastoral ministry by creating a word-collage of the supportive, personal friendships that enrich your own life and the false intimacies you have experienced as a ministerial leader. Then, discuss this with a trusted friend who is not part of your faith community.
3. What practices does your faith community engage in to offer a counter-narrative to "the way sex is construed in our culture?"
4. What prevents us from speaking truthfully to ourselves and each other about sex?

Recommended Readings

Birch, Bruce C. *To Love as We Are Loved: The Bible and Relationships.* Nashville: Abingdon, 1992.

Hauerwas, Stanley. "Resisting Capitalism: On Marriage and Homosexuality," *Quarterly Review* 20, no. 3 (2000): 314–15.

Stephens, Darryl W. "Moral Exemplar or Ethical Professional? Clergy and Sexual Sin in Methodist Church Law," *Methodist Review* 3 (2011): 55–99.

Wesley, John. *Thoughts on a Single Life.* London: 1784.

———. *Thoughts on Marriage and a Single Life.* Bristol: 1743.

4

Erotic Attunement

Rethinking Love across Pastoral Power Gradients

Cristina L.H. Traina

Boundaries are essential in ministry. But just as "do not strike your child" is an inadequate description of parental love, "do not close the door of your office when meeting with one person" is an inadequate description of pastoral love. Yet we rarely talk about this love and the exhilaration it gives us, let alone describe it carefully.

Most ministers love their congregants—or some of them! Most ministers draw energy from moments of emotional resonance, the excitement of shared projects, and the satisfaction of learning that they have connected meaningfully with others. Most ministers feel that these rewarding moments require cultivating an emotional intimacy that seems to melt away the power of their pastoral role. At the same time, most ministers have been taught that role preservation is essential for maintaining good boundaries. Most ministers, particularly those in the Protestant traditions, have been taught to strive for Christ-like *agape* (disinterested love) and *kenosis* (self-emptying love)—the opposite of the intimacy and satisfaction they find so sustaining.[1] And most ministers either don't stop to think about these contradictions or feel a bit ashamed when they do. After all, the very things they "know" they should avoid are what keep them going: intimate emotional connection with members of their congregations, forged through shared projects and experiences.

The message of this chapter is simple: to minister well, we must resist the impulse to repress these pleasures of deep connection as selfish or to dismiss them as by-products of "real" agapic ministry. Instead, we must embrace them.

---

1. The classic text is Anders Nygren, *Agape and Eros,* trans. Philip S. Watson (Philadelphia: Westminster Press, 1953).

They arise inevitably in all truly human relationships, including relationships between unequals. They are true, sustaining, and good if handled reflectively and justly. Ignoring the pleasures of ministry is the surest way to find oneself crossing boundaries of power, care, and sexuality.

AN ETHIC OF EROTIC LOVE

In our culture, desiring love—or *eros*—has become synonymous with sexual attraction. But erotic love is simply attraction to and desire for whatever is good. As Augustine tells us, it is the compass that sets our course toward smaller, more contingent goods and toward the ultimate good, God.[2] Eros is a "because of" love, appreciating the goodness in what it loves, unlike agape, which is frequently an "in spite of" love, ignoring the distasteful in what it loves. Agape is indispensable; often we are called to love people who not only seem to have few redeeming qualities but who also make our lives difficult. But whether or not God is infinite, we are certainly finite; we must refuel. Eros sustains us by connecting us to the good in and with others.

Why is it so important for ministerial leaders to reflect on these normal, intimate connections? Because power inequalities are at play, this good, desiring love can obscure issues of justice if we are not aware if its effects on us and on the people with whom we minister. We must avoid creating situations in which our generosity and apparent stability, added to our relative power, could exploit another person's vulnerability or enthusiasm. For our power is a gift, a sacred trust we hold specifically for the good of others. Their welfare must remain at the center of our love for them.

EROTIC ATTUNEMENT

The habit of acknowledging our desires—at least to ourselves—is essential to responsible ministerial leadership. Certainly, speaking to a parishioner about our enjoyment of our relationship with them might leave them feeling obligated, and expressing this affection physically would only intensify this potential burden. The pastor's feelings suddenly and unjustly take center stage. But attempting to banish such feelings often results in just locking them away, leaving them to be unleashed later in the form of even less premeditated, more unjust behavior. Instead, especially for anyone holding power in a relationship, the first response to an awareness of desire—whether aversion or attraction—must be attentive embrace of the feeling. This is a matter of

2. Wendy Farley, *The Wounding and Healing of Desire: Weaving Heaven and Earth* (Louisville: Westminster John Knox, 2005), 1–17.

unhurried reflection, another commodity that is rare but necessary for pastors. What is it, exactly, that I find fascinating or attractive in this person? What do I love in her, and why? And what might constitute appropriate desires and actions toward her?

If we stopped here, the virtue of temperance would be enough for us.[3] Temperance reminds us that food and drink are good—we can't live without them—but it calibrates our desires so that we want (and seek) neither more nor less of something than is appropriate for us. For example, temperance counsels us to cultivate the habit of desiring and consuming neither too much nor too little nor the wrong kind of food, but eating what is appropriate for our health. The balance temperance recommends is flexible, reasonable, and practical. If I weigh 120 pounds and spend most of my time at my desk, my needs are different from those of a 200-pound colleague in training for a marathon. One size does not fit all. Likewise, relationships are essential to ministry, but pastors' needs for friendship and for the stimulation supplied by others' enthusiasm are very different. The same goes for touch: some of us thrive on a steady diet of hugs, and others are more reserved. A reflective person could learn what sorts of relationships sustain her and calibrate them with care.

However, virtuous relationships cannot be schooled adequately by temperance alone. Food and drink are inanimate objects that we consume, but people are subjects with their own wants and needs, ends in themselves. When they touch us, literally or emotionally, they are touched as well. So, although temperance may be analogously helpful, what we really need is a virtue that describes how we use power to sustain loving interpersonal relationships in a way that honors others' subjectivity.

Attunement, a term often used to describe mothers' ability to notice and respond to subtle signals from their infants, is a closer fit to the kind of erotic virtue we require.[4] Attunement is perceptive attention and adjustment to feelings, needs, and desires—both one's own and others'. In egalitarian relationships, responsibility for attunement is shared. But in relations between unequals, the more powerful person bears the greater burden. And pastoral relationships, like most relationships, are unequal.

An example of attunement from parenting may help. As anyone with children knows, first-time parents faced with a helpless, unfamiliar infant often

---

3. See Diana Fritz Cates, "The Virtue of Temperance (IIa IIae, qq. 141-170)," in *The Ethics of Aquinas,* ed. Stephen J. Pope (Washington, DC: Georgetown University Press, 2002), 321–39; and Jean Porter, "Chastity as a Virtue," *Scottish Journal of Theology* 58 no. 3 (2005): 285–301.

4. Cristina L. H. Traina, *Erotic Attunement: Parenthood and the Ethics of Sensuality between Unequals* (Chicago: University of Chicago Press, 2011), esp. 241–249.

feel powerless before the challenge of meeting their child's needs. But in most cases they are able to overcome this anxiety by cultivating their perception, realizing that their feelings of ineptitude are masking their *real* capacity—and responsibility—to learn how to care for the child they love. In the process, they acknowledge their nervousness explicitly and yet respond to the child as she is, with her weaknesses and limitations, engaging in the complex dance of discovering and meeting her needs as she grows, gradually weaning her from dependence on them.

Still, parenting is such a wearing and extended task that it is hard to imagine surviving, much less enjoying, the vocation without its exquisite pleasures: the comfort of cuddling a sleepy infant or the wonder of attending a high-schooler's artistic or athletic performance. These moments are so rewarding that parents mourn parenting when it ends. But as pleasant as parenting can be, the measure of successful parenting is the child's strength and maturity, not the parents' pleasure. Justice requires that the child's genuine good be always at the center of the parenting effort. When parents are not attuned to their own needs and desires—when their own unacknowledged needs for security and fulfillment sneak to the center of their relations with their children—they also lose sight of their children's true needs and desires. They misuse their parental power, and abuse and exploitation result. As in ministry, the violation occasionally takes a sexual form, but typically the root problem is not sexual perversion. It is the parents' practice of unknowingly letting their own interests and anxieties obscure their vision of their child's needs, letting their enjoyment rather than the child's flourishing be their goal.[5] It is precisely because the two are not completely separable—because a child's genuine success also breeds unmeasured joy in a truly loving parent—that it is so necessary to work hard at the distinction.

Likewise, although all adults should cultivate attunement, pastors—who hold power both with their congregants and over them—are ultimately responsible for monitoring their own desires and needs. They must be alert to them, ensuring they are met in appropriate ways, to prevent them from sliding unnoticed into the center of even the most pleasant relationships with their congregants, obscuring their realistic vision of the people entrusted to them.

---

5. Making others' good the norm does not entail always putting others' demands ahead of one's own good. Genuine flourishing for both, the less powerful and the more powerful, often involves creating boundaries. For example, a pastor who asks not to be called after 9:30 p.m. sets a boundary that not only preserves her sleep but also helps her congregants to distinguish between important matters that can wait and real emergencies.

This cultivation hints at attunement's final quality: it is not a single act but a virtue, cultivated and practiced over time.

EROTIC RESTRAINT

U.S. culture attaches erotic love to pursuit: people in the throes of desiring love go on elaborate quests to gain the objects of their affections. This implies falsely that desiring love is both irrational and overwhelming. In fact, such excess depends upon a false reading of the beloved: that she is perfect or that he will make us perfectly happy, qualities that, Augustine reminds us, belong to God alone. Genuine erotic love desires the person not as we fantasize her to be but *as she is*—incomplete and quirky, bumps, warts, and all. It enjoys and celebrates her gifts and strengths but is also concerned for her holistic welfare. Nor does genuine erotic love overestimate itself. Rather than attempting to be the source of everything good for the beloved, it often stands back to let that person receive what she needs to grow in other ways. Parenting involves teaching, befriending, and coaching, but parents know that, for their children to grow well, much of their education, friendship, and encouragement must come from others. Parents must often restrain themselves, standing aside when they least feel like doing so, precisely for the sake of desiring love. Likewise, pastors must exercise erotic restraint, for the good of their congregants, their congregations, and themselves. What does this look like in practice?

CASES

The following cases of Margie White and Antoine Powell show that body boundaries are only a starting point: attuned relationships are the core of pastoral power used lovingly. A third case illustrates the need for judicatory leaders to model attunement for the pastors they supervise.

CASE OF MARGIE WHITE

Recently retired, Margie White is a minister of care who has known Jaime and Adelita Hernandez since working with them at a rummage sale at her suburban Catholic parish three years ago. For the last four months she has been bringing communion to Jaime and his widowed father weekly. The elder Hernandez has been struggling with leukemia, and Jaime has taken a leave from work to care for him. Because Margie's father is also suffering from late-stage cancer, she and the outgoing Jaime have formed an extra bond, comparing notes on care and sharing worries and victories. Margie knows Adelita much less well because she not only is working overtime to cover Jaime's lost salary, but is also very shy and does not feel confident speaking English.

Three days ago, Jaime's father died, and yesterday, Margie's father started palliative hospice care. Today, preparing to greet Jaime and Adelita at Jaime's father's wake, Margie's emotions surge almost uncontrollably, but she remembers her role and tries to keep them in check. As she and her husband, Bob, approach, Jaime steps forward with arms open and enfolds her in a long hug. Margie's eyes fill with tears as she turns toward Adelita. Adelita stands a bit awkwardly, and Margie reaches out to grasp Adelita's hands gently. Adelita remains stationary and nods, and Margie steps back. Bob then grasps first Jaime's hands and then Adelita's.

In the car on the way home Margie asks Bob for help dissecting the awkward moment. "I just feel strange," Margie says. "Maybe Dad's illness is affecting me more than I realize. I was trying to put that out of my mind and just be responsive to both Jaime and Adelita. They've been through so much." Bob asks, "Is it that you don't trust your instincts? Or do you think Adelita worries that you and Jaime are a little too close?"

CASE OF ANTOINE POWELL

The week has been long and gloomy, punctuated by an unexpected funeral and family pressures. At the bottom of the pecking order at her new job, Pastor Antoine's wife, Shirley, has been saddled with a complicated assignment and has been working distractedly every night after the kids are in bed and through much of the weekend. As Tuesday's church council meeting approaches, Antoine feels tired, insecure, and increasingly anxious. How will the council react to the food pantry proposal he and Justine, the council's social outreach chair, have put together?

Antoine has been at Good Shepherd only nine months but knows how strongly the Women's Board has reacted in the past to encroachments on the space they control in the old, undersized building. The conversation leans in this direction until Adele, the vice-chair of the Women's Board, speaks in support. Opposition dissolves, the proposal passes, and Justine and Antoine exchange a discreet glance of satisfaction. Good old Justine! She had walked Adele over to a Community House meeting earlier in the week, where clients and staff were worrying over the recent closure of two pantries.

After the meeting, outside at their cars, Justine and Antoine excitedly begin naming tasks to be done before the pantry can open. They make a coffee date for the next day to brainstorm a comprehensive list. Both are excited to be working together, confident in their partnership, and eager to move forward.

But the next morning Antoine and Shirley's three-year-old daughter, Kiara, wakes up with the flu. No daycare today. Shirley is due in a meeting at nine o'clock. Antoine protests briefly, but there is nothing for it; he will have to stay home. As he picks up the phone to call Justine, he is more disappointed than he had expected to be.

DISCUSSION OF MARGIE'S AND ANTOINE'S CASES

Both Antoine's and Margie's behaviors are outwardly faultless. Their relationships are public, ministry-centered, and appropriate. But this is only the first question. Are they also attuned? Vignettes are inadequate bases for judgment, because attunement is an ongoing practice. Yet, we can fill out the picture with some hypotheses.

As she arrives at the wake, Margie is aware of her own emotional vulnerability. She is also responsive to Jaime, whose characteristic gesture communicates shared suffering. She restrains a desire to hug Adelita out of respect for her typical reserve. She not only is aware of the moment's awkwardness, unsure whether her different responses to Jaime and Adelita have honored their marriage, but immediately asks Bob for his reading of the moment. His perceptive questions suggest that she consults him frequently and honestly. If Margie is as practiced in attunement as she seems, she will reach out to Adelita in the near future. She will discuss the moment in her parish's monthly ministry leadership meeting, contemplating whether she might have preempted Jaime's hug with a handshake or hugged Adelita. And she will call a close friend for a conversation about her own father's impeding death. This last item is especially important, as Margie may not have realized how much her exchanges with Jaime, while genuinely focused on empathy for him and his father, have relieved her own emotional anguish, or how much she may be tempted to lean inappropriately on him now that the reason for pastoral visits has ended.

Antoine, apparently a young pastor, may not be as far along the path of attunement as Margie. In the "honeymoon year" with a new congregation, he is experiencing the exhilaration and stress of forming new relationships and starting fresh projects. His family is also in a challenging stage, juggling young children and two careers. The deck is stacked against self-awareness. Thus, at the first glimmer of disappointment, he should put the phone down for a moment and reflect. What is this feeling telling him? In the midst of a bleak week, he is hungry to make progress on the new project and, frankly, craves Justine's collaborative, creative energy. He could invite Justine to the parsonage for coffee; for insurance, he could call George, the church secretary, to tell him of the plan. This would fulfill his desires to move the project forward on schedule. But Justine, recently divorced, is good at friendly banter. Inviting her over would raise his spirits but possibly also her unconscious expectations and others' eyebrows. Here is a moment for restraint. Out of love for the project, Justine, his family, and himself, Antoine will need to postpone the meeting, invite Adele to attend as well, and consult colleagues during the social time at the weekly pastor's bible study. Just as important, he should plan a date with Shirley this weekend.

CASE OF JANET GUNDERSON

Janet Gunderson had been frustrated that her mostly rural conference had been ignoring the denomination's mandate for sexual abuse and boundary education for clergy. Her first project as bishop was to plan a training day. To her happy surprise, 65 percent of the pastors in the conference had turned out.

Toward the end of the day, Janet summed up the speakers' messages: "Maintaining safe boundaries is crucial for you, for your families, and for your congregations. We encourage you to talk with one another or with conference staff if anything occurs that makes you uncomfortable, or if you need help deciding how to proceed in a relationship with a parishioner that has become awkward for you. We also remind you of mandatory reporting rules. If you observe or hear of any behavior that you suspect may run afoul of the law, either in your congregation or in another, you must report it to the police. If you see behavior that, while not illegal, may signal an issue, we encourage you to take it up with the colleague in question. If you are unsure whether to do so, we are here to consult with and counsel you. We want this conference to be a safe place for women and children. We are all in this together."

Janet's summary points to the progress the church has made articulating healthy sexual and emotional boundaries in ministry, as well as how far it still has to go. Everything she communicated was true and well-intentioned: It is imperative to report abuse. It is good to discuss anxieties about colleagues' behavior with them. The conference staff-persons are important resources to pastors and should be ready to help them deal with their foggiest, most vexing challenges. Solidarity is essential. Openness and "daylight" are the best guarantors of healthy pastoral relationships. Finally, sexual abuse and harassment are unacceptable everywhere, but especially in the church, which is supposed to be a zone of safety and trust.

That said, Janet's words alone would be unlikely to encourage frank conversations among clergy. The stick—reporting—is much larger than the carrot—which is merely that "nothing terrible happens." The guarantees of safety and the rewards of openness need to be more palpable, because the risk of raising questions about a colleague or about oneself—especially in a denomination with a clergy glut and in which bishops are heavily involved in placement—is enormous. Janet does not address understandable anxiety about consequences and about future power relations. If I am in line to become district superintendent, will my request for pastoral assistance from my bishop derail that ambition? What if I raise a question about a current or potential future bishop—will there be retribution against me? Janet does not describe the most benign version of erotic susceptibility, affection for others born of devotion to and intensive work on a common project, nor does she emphasize that all pastors worth their salt (including the bishop and her colleagues who put the day together) experience it regularly. She does not discuss the strategies she and other successful pastors use to stay aware of their desires and their own current emotional and spiritual weaknesses. She does not tell any stories about herself, stories that might help her colleagues connect more personally with the strategies and circumstances she describes. Consequently, she fails to use her power to model the change she recommends.

Little is likely to change; attuned pastors will continue their good practices, and distracted pastors will continue to think the advice applies to others. That is, little is likely to change unless such teaching moments are calibrated carefully to respond to Janet's situation-specific knowledge that her colleagues need a crisp, hard-line message at this moment; unless her own bearing and behavior have modeled attunement in the past and will in the future; and unless she shares her own stories on other occasions.

Conclusion

Power differences between bishops and clergy and between pastors and laypeople are not evils to be eradicated but inevitable facts of collegial ministry. The challenge is using them to empower and assist. Erotic, desiring love helps us to use the unavoidable power differentials of pastoral ministry to preserve safe boundaries. To employ erotic love justly, ministerial leaders must:

- Consciously embrace erotic desires, prayerfully delighting in and fostering the good in projects and people.
- Become attuned to self and to others, aware of our own attractions and needs as well as theirs, and of the power relations in ministerial relationships and in the wider community.
- Practice erotic restraint, gauging our behavior toward others by what they and the community really need from us in our pastoral roles.

- Cultivate safe conversations in which we can regularly assess our desire, attunement, and restraint and discuss appropriate ways of expressing them in ministry.
- Take good care of our own spiritual, emotional, physical, and sexual needs.

Erotic attunement—responsive, caring love that values and nurtures particular gifts and answers genuine needs, both ours and others'—is a means of forming strong, trusting bonds across pastoral power differentials. It is a virtue, a practice modeled intentionally and lovingly over a lifetime.

DISCUSSION QUESTIONS

1. Rewrite Bishop Gunderson's closing words, accounting for power relations between clergy and congregants, among clergy, and between the clergy and the bishop's office. Think creatively about structures, examples, or services that might promote the ends she seeks. What other qualities of her ministry as bishop might reinforce or stymie her message?

2. What are the deterrents to attunement to ourselves and others? Why do pastors often feel that they can manage emotionally challenging or intense pastoral relationships without support from peers or confidants?

3. What are the deterrents to discussing attunement with colleagues? How can pastors balance the obligation to preserve confidentiality in relations with congregants and colleagues with the obligation to confer about these relations?

4. When you have the power to structure an ethos—whether it is for three days at confirmation camp or for a decade in a large staff ministry—how might you create safe places for such discussions? How might you model attunement?

RECOMMENDED READINGS

Cooper-White, Pamela. *Shared Wisdom: The Use of the Self in Pastoral Care and Counseling.* Minneapolis: Fortress Press, 2004.

Farley, Wendy. *The Wounding and Healing of Desire: Weaving Heaven and Earth.* Louisville: Westminster John Knox, 2005.

Fortune, Marie M. *Sexual Violence: The Sin Revisited.* Cleveland: Pilgrim, 2005.

Holler, Linda. *Erotic Morality: The Role of Touch in Moral Agency.* New Brunswick, NJ: Rutgers University Press, 2002.

Oxenhandler, Noelle. *The Eros of Parenthood: Explorations in Light and Dark.* New York: St. Martin's, 2001.

Traina, Cristina L. H. *Erotic Attunement: Parenthood and the Ethics of Sensuality between Unequals.* Chicago: University of Chicago Press, 2011.

Vacek, Edward Collins, S.J. *Love, Human and Divine: The Heart of Christian Ethics.* Washington, DC: Georgetown University Press, 1994.

PART II

Sources of Wisdom

5

Sexual Ethics in Church History

Rosemary Radford Ruether

In this chapter, I survey some key issues of sexual ethics in Western church history, focusing on the thought of St. Augustine, which has deeply shaped the Western Christian tradition on sexual ethics. I begin with key themes in the New Testament that were reshaped by Augustine. After giving a somewhat detailed view of how Augustine's teaching on sexuality was shaped by his life journey, I then discuss how his heritage was reshaped by Thomas Aquinas in the thirteenth century and again by Martin Luther and John Calvin during the Reformation in the sixteenth century. I then touch on the revival of a rigid Augustinian view of sexual ethics in the 1968 papal encyclical, *Humanae vitae*, which sought to repress the call for a reform of Catholic teachings on sexuality and contraception. I conclude with some suggestions for how the Augustinian heritage on sexual ethics needs to be reconstructed today.

NEW TESTAMENT

The New Testament does not have a systematic teaching on sexual ethics. The early church was deeply shaped by an anti-family perspective, a fact largely overlooked by modern Christianity with its pro-family assumptions. The Jesus movement consisted largely of a gathering of marginal men and women called out of their families and occupations into a counter-cultural community. Their priority was following Jesus at the expense of the family in the belief that the eschatological transformation of history was imminent. This was expressed in shocking demands, such as that recorded in Luke 14:26, "Whoever comes to me and does not hate father and mother, wife and children, brothers and sisters, yes, and even life itself, cannot be my disciple."[1]

---

1. All scriptural quotations are from the New Revised Standard Version.

Jesus is depicted as an itinerant with "nowhere to lay his head" (Luke 9:58). Yet, a variety of households assist Jesus and his followers in their travels, many led by women. His disciples did not give up all property and family relations. Peter has a house in Capernaum, and Jesus heals Peter's mother-in-law, which suggests a wife somewhere in the background. Jesus' relation to his own family, his mother and siblings, seems to have been tense. When his mother, brothers, and sisters come and ask to speak to him, he repudiates them, claiming his followers as his true family (Mark 3:31-35). Yet his mother and brothers are described as members of the Jerusalem community of Pentecost (Acts 1:14).

This complex perspective came to be interpreted as a choice of celibacy in the light of the imminent coming of the kingdom of God, where marriage will be transcended. Jesus is portrayed as teaching that only those men and women who "neither marry nor are given in marriage" will be worthy of a place in that age (Luke 20:34-35).

It is Paul, writing decades later for the Christian movement he led, who sought to affirm some place for marriage and marital sexuality within the larger vision of the superiority of celibacy in the light of the coming kingdom of God. Paul affirms celibacy as best for himself, but he is dubious of the ability of some of the other Christian men to maintain the same practice of sexual abstinence. For such men, it is better to marry and not to deprive themselves of sexual relations. They may set aside times for prayer when they and their wives abstain from sex, but "then [they should] come together again, so that Satan may not tempt [them] because of [their] lack of self-control" (1 Cor.7:5).

He goes on to argue that the unmarried and the widows should remain as they are, but if they are not practicing self-control, they should marry: "For it is better to marry than to be aflame with [sexual] passion" (1 Cor. 7:9). The married should not separate from each other, and believers should not separate from spouses who are non-believers. But if the non-believers leave the marriage, it is just as well. Everyone should lead the life that God has assigned to them—married or unmarried, circumcised or uncircumcised, slave or free. This is all in the light of the reality that the "appointed time has grown short; from now on, let even those who have wives be as though they had none" (1 Cor. 7:29). This last phrase reinforces that, for Paul, sexual abstinence is always the highest option. He wishes "that all were as I myself am" (celibate) but teaches that married sex is better than fornication (1 Cor. 7:7). Paul never mentions children as a purpose of sexual relations in marriage. Marital sex is discussed only in the context of the satisfaction of (male) sexual desires, in order to prevent the worse sin of fornication.

AUGUSTINE

These New Testament themes were rethought by Augustine three centuries later. Augustine's views were deeply shaped by his struggles with his own sexuality. The way he interpreted that struggle in relation to his aspiration for union with God would define his sexual ethics. Augustine was born in 354 in the provincial town of Tagaste in North Africa, as the Christian church was becoming the established religion of the Roman Empire. The son of a pious Catholic mother and a pagan father of middle-class means, Augustine sought to rise through education from his hometown to the provincial capital of Carthage and on to the imperial cities of Rome and Milan, culminating in an alliance with the imperial ruling class and in a marriage into a Roman noble family.

This career trajectory meant Augustine could not marry as a youth to a local woman but had to delay his marriage until he had reached this projected goal. But he experienced insistent sexual desires and so, as an eighteen year old, took a concubine of lower class status with whom he could satisfy his sexual needs but would not marry, a solution conventional for his society. In the first year of their relationship, Augustine's concubine gave birth to a son whom they named Adeodatus (Gift of God). Although Adeodatus became much beloved, Augustine was determined to have no more children through this relationship. At this time, he also joined the Manichaean sect, which believed in a strict dualism of spirit and matter as good and evil and sought to escape from matter into spirit by, among other things, avoiding procreation. Although allowing marriage and sexuality for their ordinary members, as distinct from their elite who practiced celibacy, the Manichaeans recommended practices of contraception to prevent birth. Augustine and his concubine continued to live together and enjoy sexual relations for the next twelve years, but had no more children, a fact which makes it very likely that he practiced some form of contraception, a practice he would later decry as sinful.

By 385, Augustine was beginning to achieve his career goals. He departed for Rome in 383 and went on to Milan, where his skills as a rhetorician, as well as his heterodoxy, were both appreciated by the Roman elite. He took his concubine and son with him to Italy, but evaded his mother, who strongly condemned his Manichaeanism. Because she was then a widow and expected him to take her into his household, she followed him to Rome and Milan. By 385, Augustine had contracted to marry a young girl of elite family, but she was not yet of the marriageable age of twelve, so he had to wait two years before consummating the marriage.

His mother, seeing the presence of a concubine in his household as an offense to his coming marriage, forced her to leave. She returned to North

Africa, vowing never to marry but to remain faithful to Augustine. He describes this event touchingly, revealing his deep affection for this companion of his youth and, perhaps, a little pride at her vow of fidelity.[2]

> The woman with whom I habitually slept was torn away from my side because she was a hindrance to my marriage. My heart which was deeply attached was cut and wounded, and left a trail of blood. She had returned to Africa vowing that she would never go with another man. She left with me the natural son I had by her.[3]

Augustine, however, feeling unable to live without sexual relations, took another concubine while he waited for his bride to be old enough to marry. He described his state during this interlude:

> But I was unhappy, incapable of following a woman's example, and impatient of delay. I was to get the girl I proposed to only at the end of two years. As I was not a lover of marriage but a slave of lust, I procured another woman, not of course as a wife. By this liaison the disease of my soul would be sustained and kept active. . . . But my wound, inflicted by the earlier parting, was not healed. After inflammation and sharp pain, it festered.[4]

What is striking is Augustine's lack of inner relation to these latter two women, his second concubine and his child bride, in contrast to his deep feeling for his first concubine. He depicts these later relationships as simply vehicles of his lust. As a sophisticated intellectual of thirty, the relation with his impending bride was also that of a tool, now of social class attainment.

However, Augustine was now struggling to repudiate this whole career trajectory, which he saw as fueled by his pride and sullied by his lust. Under the influence of the brilliant teachings of Ambrose, bishop of Milan, he sought to commit himself to the Catholic faith and be baptized, a decision which he identified with acceptance of celibacy—the repudiation of his concubine and his future bride—as well as his imperial appointment. He experienced this conversion as a struggle between two female forces: the force of lust that

2. See Margaret R. Miles, "Not Nameless but Unnamed: The Woman Torn from Augustine's Side," in *Feminist Interpretations of Augustine*, ed. Judith Chelius Stark (University Park, PA: The Pennsylvania State University Press, 2007), 167–188.

3. Saint Augustine, *Confessions*, trans. Henry Chadwick (Oxford: Oxford University Press, 2008), 6.15.25.

4. Ibid. This quote is cited and discussed in Miles, "Not Nameless but Unnamed," 167–188.

"tugged at the garment of my flesh and whispered: 'Are you getting rid of us?'" and the beautiful, virginal Continence, spouse of Christ, who held out her arms to embrace him.[5]

Once converted and baptized, Augustine retired with likeminded friends, as well as his son and mother, to a country estate where they could discourse on the meaning of the Christian life. His first writings, much under the influence of Neoplatonism—such as *Solioquies, On the Happy Life, On the Immortality of the Soul,* and *On Free Will*—were written during this period. At this time, Augustine saw the decision of conversion to God as an expression of his true self acting in freedom of the will. But this view would be reshaped by his reflection on his bondage to sin, manifest in his pride and sexual needs. He would come to see the fallen self as in bondage, transformed only by acts of divine grace that transcended the fallen self.

After this period of retirement, Augustine decided to return to his home town of Tagaste, where he intended to create a small monastic community. But the leaders of the local church were not about to allow such as brilliant thinker and rhetorician simply to disappear into monasticism. He was called into the priesthood and then became a bishop. The second half of his life, from 391 to his death in 430, would see Augustine as ruler of the church, reshaping his thought and teaching in controversies with adversaries, such as the Manichaeans, the Donatists, and the Pelagians. How sex and marriage were to fit into a proper understanding of Christian life was to be a major theme of later writings, such as *Marriage and Concupiscence, The Good of Marriage, The Good of Widowhood,* and *Holy Virginity.*

To understand the relation of human nature to gender, sex and sin, Augustine repeatedly returned to the key biblical passages of Genesis 1–3. He came to reject the Eastern Church's Platonic view of an original, spiritual, non-gendered creation, in favor of a belief that Adam and Eve were created with real physical and sexually differentiated bodies. In the original creation, Adam and Eve would not have died, since their bodies would have been united with their souls in union with God. Yet, they would have had sexual intercourse and produced offspring. But, unlike fallen humanity, this sexual intercourse would have been free from any sexual desire, or "concupiscence." Like a farmer sowing his seed in a field, the act would have been purely rational.

Eve would have remained virginal in intercourse and childbirth. Yet, even in Paradise, Eve would have been subordinate to Adam. Although Eve was created in the image of God and had a redeemable soul, as female, she

---

5. Augustine, *Confessions*, 8.11.26–27.

represented the lower self, created to serve the male as wife and child-bearer. In the original creation, this would have been freely accepted, rather than coerced.

But this lust-free and virginal intercourse never actually happened, because immediately after the creation of Eve, she enticed Adam into disobedience to God, and humanity fell into sin. The fall into sin deeply changed this original humanity. Humans lost their original union with God and hence the immortality of their bodies. They also lost the freedom of the will and its control over their bodies. This loss of control is manifest in the involuntary erection of the male penis; the male is unable to control the power of sexual desire over his body. Sexual intercourse is now accompanied by a rush of sexual pleasure, which Augustine saw as corrupting the act into sin and the means by which sin is transmitted to the next generation. In Augustine's understanding of "original sin," all humans are born into sin and alienation from God by the very act by which they were begotten in sexual desire. Yet God has, from all eternity, chosen a limited number of the elect, without any basis of their moral merits—since all humans are fallen and deserve hell—to receive the transforming grace of redemptive life.

This view of all sexual acts of fallen humanity as intrinsically sinful and transmitting sin to their offspring shaped Augustine's sexual ethics. Marriage was given to humans by God as the means to reproduce themselves, leading finally to the birth of Christ, our redeemer. But now that Christ has come, marriage and sexual reproduction are no longer necessary. Humans are now living in the last age of human history, awaiting the advent of eternal life. Chastity or renunciation of sexual relation is the appropriate ethic for humans in view of eternal life.

For those unable to contain their sexual desires, marriage is allowed. But since every sexual act, even in marriage, is sinful by its nature, married people should engage in sexual acts very abstemiously and only for the purpose of procreation. Producing children is still a good, so marital sex is allowable for this purpose. Sex is also allowable in old age or at other times of infertility, as a way of affirming the covenant of the relationship. But to engage in sex only for pleasure, preventing procreation, makes sex even in marriage sinful. Thus, for Augustine, any use of contraception, even in marriage, is sinful. This view would be passed down in the church's teaching, shaping sexual ethics up to the present day.

AUGUSTINIANISM IN MEDIEVAL SCHOLASTICISM: THOMAS AQUINAS

Although Thomas Aquinas follows the main lines of Augustine on sexual ethics, he shifts the emphasis slightly under the influence of Aristotle, who is more positive toward the body and its desires. Aquinas defines the soul as the "form" of the body. Although the soul can exist apart from the body, it is complete only when joined to the body and depends on the body for sense data. As originally created, humans were in a state of "original justice," in which the body was subject to the soul, sensuality to reason, and the whole in union with God. Although good, this was not a perfect state, which comes about only through grace and transforms the human into a state of beatitude when the resurrected body will be in communion with God. But here, too, the body is an integral part of the redeemed human.

The goal of the human journey for Aquinas is happiness, or complete fulfillment. This journey takes place on an overlapping hierarchy of natural and supernatural fulfillment. Natural fulfillment is good on its own level. This includes the natural desires of the body for food and sex. These desires are necessary for the body to sustain and reproduce itself. These desires have been distorted by sin, but unlike Augustine's view, this distortion of desire is not seen as more intense pleasure but less pleasure, caused by excesses. In paradise, sexual pleasure would have been complete with the unity of soul and body. But even in the distortion of sin, sexual pleasure is a necessary good. Yet the human is destined for the higher happiness brought by grace, transforming the body into supernatural beatitude in heaven, when the appetites of sex and food will be left behind as no longer necessary.

Aquinas follows Augustine in believing that original sin was passed down through the sexual act, but he changes the emphasis. The male seed doesn't transmit sin through its excesses of pleasure, but rather is unable to transmit original justice since it no longer possesses it. So the male seed generates a human being, which lacks this original harmony. Yet, the human being retains its basic orientation to virtue, which can be restored and perfected by redeeming grace.

Like Augustine, Aquinas thinks of woman as possessing an asexual soul in the image of God, and so she is equally able to enjoy eternal life in communion with God. But as female, woman was created as the subordinate helpmeet of the male in the work of procreation (not as a friend or companion of the male, which Aquinas, like Augustine, believes is better served by another male). But Aquinas worsens this view by adopting Aristotle's definition of woman as a "misbegotten male" who is defective in her physical strength, volitional self-control, and intellect, and cannot exercise sovereignty over herself or others but is by nature under male domination.

This definition of woman is based on Aristotle's belief that it is the male seed alone that provides the formative power of procreation. The female womb provides only the material substance that is shaped by the male seed. Normatively, every male seed would reproduce another male. But the defectiveness of the female means that, on a regular basis, the female matter fails to be fully formed by the male seed, and an inferior human being—woman—is created who is defective in mind, will, and body. Thus, the social hierarchy in which the male rules and the female is ruled is biologically necessary. This view of woman affects not only Aquinas's view of secular society, in which women can exercise no sovereignty, but also his Christology and ecclesiology. Christ had to be a male, and only a male can represent Christ in the priesthood, since the female does not represent the full human being.

AUGUSTINIANISM WITHIN REFORMED THOUGHT

Augustinian teaching on sexual ethics was passed down through the Middle Ages. Luther and Calvin would reject asceticism and the celibacy of the priesthood as unrealistic ideals for most but would carry on Augustine's view of humanity as fallen, alienated from God, without free will, and in need of transcendent grace for redemption. Since most men and women are incapable of the lifelong renunciation of sex, all should marry. Marriage was not just a remedy for lust, but it was also a natural good given by God for the reproduction of the species and companionship. Although marriage is not seen as a sacrament by most Protestants, they cultivated a more positive view of sex and marriage. Still, these early Protestants retained the view that sex is primarily for reproduction, and so birth control is wrong.

DEBATE OVER BIRTH CONTROL

In the late-nineteenth and early-twentieth centuries, campaigns for birth control began to be waged in Europe and the United States. In 1930, the Lambeth Conference of the worldwide Anglican Communion, although still recommending abstinence from sex as the primary method of birth control, conceded the morality of contraception within marriage. This opened the floodgates for dramatic change in Anglican and Protestant teaching on this issue. The Vatican reacted swiftly, reiterating its condemnation of birth control. By the early 1950s, the Catholic Church would allow the use of period abstinence or the "rhythm method," known today as natural family planning (NFP), to regulate birth. Through the 1940s and 1950s, the prohibition of contraception came to be seen as intrinsic to the faithful practice of Catholicism.

But this view began to be challenged among some Catholic thinkers by the 1960s. With the calling of the Second Vatican Council in 1962, many hoped that this issue could be discussed and reformed. Pope John XXIII decided to form a commission to study the issue of birth control. In its final report, by a vote of fifty-two to four, the Pontifical Commission on Birth Control voted to allow contraception in marriage, within a context of a general commitment to procreation. The four bishops who voted against this decision complained that such a reform would deeply undermine church authority. Pope Paul VI agreed and, in 1968, released the encyclical *Humanae vitae*, which reaffirmed Augustine's strict view that sex is allowed only in marriage and that any sexual act that impeded procreation is deeply immoral. There was a vehement worldwide response to this encyclical, which many saw as a betrayal of the results of the commission's careful attention to marital experience and modern science.

CONCLUSION

Western Christianity is in a state of conflict over its teaching on sexuality. The framework of Augustine's theological worldview still deeply shapes Protestant as well as Roman Catholic thought. The basic framework of Augustine's anthropology—that humans were created in sexually differentiated bodies for procreation; that the creation of children is a great good; and that women are ultimately equal to men in redemption—remain as positive affirmations for Western Christians. But much in the details of these views is problematic for modern Western Christians. What needs to be questioned and rethought most centrally is Augustine's belief that the rush of sexual pleasure in the sexual act is fundamentally sinful and is the means by which original sin is transmitted to the next generation. It is this view of sexual pleasure that shaped the heart of his view of sex and marriage. This view was questioned even in his own day by those who believed that sexual pleasure was necessary for coitus to be fertile.

Today, sexual pleasure is highly valued. Men and women cultivate techniques to assure the best of this experience. But sexual pleasure that is mutual needs to be differentiated from "lust," in the sense of a sexual pleasure that exploits and harms the other person. What would it mean for Christian sexual ethics if the Church fully embraced a view of egalitarian sexual pleasure as a natural good in itself, which God has created for our well-being and delight and not simply as a dubious adjunct to reproduction? This would not only overcome the lingering hostility to sexual pleasure that dogs Christianity but also encourage a sexuality whose pleasure lies most fully in a partnership relation.

Discussion Questions

1. Does your ecclesiological tradition take seriously a vocation to celibacy? How is this informed or motivated by the New Testament? By Augustine? Aquinas?

2. Assumptions about sexuality have changed dramatically since Augustine's time. How must today's church's leaders and members think about sexuality differently than Augustine did or could? For example, do you believe that "egalitarian sexual pleasure" can be viewed "as a natural good in itself"?

3. What sources of wisdom might be used to challenge Augustine's beliefs about the sinful nature of sexual pleasure? How can we reconstruct Augustinian thought in light of this?

4. How has Augustine's view about the transmission of original sin shaped your theological understanding of sexual intercourse? How have you questioned and rethought Augustine's viewpoint?

5. Is the use of birth control a pragmatic or a theological question in your church tradition? What theological understanding of sexuality underlies this practice?

Recommended Readings

Barnes, Corry. "Thomas Aquinas on the Body and Bodily Passions." In *The Embrace of Eros: Bodies, Desires and Sexuality in Christianity*, edited by Margaret D. Kamitsuka, 83–98. Minneapolis: Fortress Press, 2010.

Miles, Margaret R. "Not Nameless but Unnamed: The Woman Torn from Augustine's Side." In *Feminist Interpretations of Augustine*, edited by Judith Chelius Stark, 167–88. University Park, PA: The Pennsylvania State University Press, 2007.

Ruether, Rosemary Radford. "Augustine: Sexuality, Gender, and Women." In *Feminist Interpretations of Augustine*, edited by Judith Chelius Stark, 47–68. University Park, PA: The Pennsylvania State University Press, 2007.

———. *Christianity and the Making of the Modern Family*. Boston: Beacon, 2000.

———. *Women and Redemption: A Theological History*, 2nd ed. Minneapolis: Fortress Press, 2010.

6

David and Women and Power and I

John C. Holbert

It was a Friday night, nearly two decades ago. I had recently returned from a year living in the north of England on a sabbatical leave from my teaching post. All in all, it had been a very satisfying year, five thousand miles from home and all of its usual problems and issues and questions. One does not hear much of Dallas, Texas, in the north of England. And then the phone rang.

It was the United Methodist bishop of my annual conference. I was a teacher, no longer a local church pastor, and was housed and paid by my university. Though my bishop appointed me each year to teach school, I was, in the lingo of my denomination, "under special appointment," nomenclature that often means "out of sight, out of mind." Late Friday-night episcopal phone calls seldom come for clergy people like me.

He first asked how I was and then asked if I was sitting down. This was decidedly ominous. He then calmly asked me if I would consider becoming the interim senior minister of the largest church in our annual conference. I was stunned. My pastoral experience had consisted of a two-year stint as an associate pastor in another annual conference, eighteen years before. I was a tenured professor at my school, very happily doing what my graduate training had helped me do, namely, teach students with an eye toward the work of church ministry. Of course, I did preach and teach quite often in churches but had not pastored in a very long time. Silently, I questioned the Bishop's sanity, but audibly I said, "Why?" with the clear implication, "Why me?"

A deeply troubling reason had forced him to relieve the senior pastor of his pulpit. That pastor had been accused, multiple times, of sexual misconduct, and an investigation was under way. Hence, one Sunday, he was preaching, and the next, he was gone. And because litigation was involved, very little could be revealed of the reasons for his sudden absence. The bishop went on to say that he had considered several persons to perform this special task; however, he had settled on me. Because I was a member of the conference, I was relatively close to the church, and he knew I could preach reasonably well. That is what he wanted: someone to preach and hold things together while the investigation proceeded.

I thought and prayed overnight, called him back, and agreed to accept the job. And then my trouble began. No, I do not mean the great trouble this assignment turned out to hold for me, although God knows there was trouble enough for several assignments. I mean the trouble that arose in my own spirit as I tried to get my head around the supposed power I had been handed. I was now senior minister of an enormous church with thousands of members, with a very large staff, a huge, multi-million dollar budget, and a magnificent physical facility in the very heart of a vibrant city. There was a weekly television broadcast that beamed the worship service to millions, as well as a superb mission outreach that touched thousands of homeless and working poor people every week. This was a great downtown church with a long and rich history of significance for the annual conference, but also for many well beyond the confines of United Methodism. And I—I emphasize the "I"—was now the senior minister—I emphasize the "senior."

My head swelled to a size that could no longer easily accommodate my hats. As I headed off in the early-Sunday darkness for my first preaching day, I was so puffed up with myself that the great double doors of the sanctuary could barely open wide enough to allow my now gigantic person to enter. As I donned my robe and strode toward the throne-like preacher chair, the echoes of the organ sounding in my kingly ears, I sat triumphantly and gazed languidly out at the congregation that had assembled to hear my brilliant words. As I hiked up my robe to make myself more comfortable—though I was feeling decidedly very comfortable in my lofty perch—I looked at my socks, now exposed by my elevated trouser legs. To my horror, I saw that they did not match! I, the great senior minister of the huge church, chosen for power and grandeur, was about to preach the word of God to the hungry crowd, standing before them in mismatched hosiery.

After my initial shock at this sartorial travesty, I thought: "This is God's word to me. My puffed-up self needed this reminder of my frail humanity." And Paul's famous words floated into my mind (they actually did!), "God chose what is foolish in the world to shame the wise" (1 Cor. 1:27a). How I needed that foolishness, the recognition of my foolishness! My predecessor had plainly abused power in very destructive ways, but I saw myself that September morning as a fellow power abuser, and without the reminder of my own foolishness, I was well on the way to abusing power in ways I could hardly predict.

King David needed such a reminder, too, but unfortunately never received it until it was too late. One of the great ironies of my four-month stint as senior pastor was that over a year before, even before my time in England, this same church had asked me to come and offer a series of lectures on King David. I did those lectures during my interim ministry there, but little did I know what resonance they would have in the charged circumstances in which the lectures were delivered. The story of the second king of Israel was exactly the one the church needed to hear, and the one I needed to hear. David's use and abuse of women and his use and abuse of power are signal examples of the dangers any leader can fall into as we move among the corridors of leadership. That ancient story may again help us to rediscover warnings concerning the ever-present dangers of the abuse of power. Though David's abuses of power were primarily at the expense of women, as were those of my pastoral predecessor, it is power that drove the ego in these two men, rather than some sexual needs. My own burgeoning needs for power did not result in sexual abuse but did raise the ugly possibility of abuses of others and self.

In order to examine the biblical abuse of power more directly, I will focus my analysis on three sections of a long and immensely rich story. Anyone who breaks at least four of the Ten Commandments in one grim chapter (2 Samuel 11) is someone to be reckoned with! But I wish to begin with 1 Samuel 25 and the story of Abigail to introduce David the charismatic one. In this chapter, the character of David is revealed to us both as promise and warning.

Samuel, the prophet of Israel, finally died, but before his death, Saul, the first king of Israel, was publically humiliated and deposed by the old prophet, leading to immense confusion in the land. Is Saul still king or is the fast-rising son of Jesse, David, in fact the real king? He, after all, is the slayer of the giant, Goliath, and is also the sweet singer who alone can soothe the rages of the mighty Saul. Yet, the two leaders now hate one another for reasons that remain unclear to Israel. Now that Samuel has died, David sees the power vacuum created as a time when he can begin to assert his own power in the land. He begins that assertion with the land and wife of a churlish fellow named Nabal, who lives on a large ranch in the rich agricultural area of Carmel in the fertile northwest of Israel.

Nabal in Hebrew means "fool," so we can expect little from such a nasty man. Still, the storyteller does not give us a simple story of the "good" David and the "bad" Nabal. Simple stories rarely exist in the Bible, and we will not find one here. The narrator makes it clear that Nabal is a thoroughly unpleasant fellow—"surly and mean" (1 Sam. 25:3).[1] His wife, Abigail, is on the other hand both "clever and beautiful." David, surviving hand to mouth in the wilderness, hears that the wealthy Nabal is shearing his enormous flock of sheep. He instructs some of his men to speak carefully to Nabal, to offer him "shalom" and then to tell him that since David and his rough army have been attending to the flocks and herds of Nabal, he has found none missing. And because his flocks have remained safe and intact, David now expects some sort of payment. His men are to word the request as follows: "Please give whatever you have at hand to your servants and to your son David" (1 Sam. 25:8b).

What else is this request but a protection racket? David was not hired by Nabal; he has merely stood near in the wilderness, supposedly protecting Nabal's flocks, and now demanding to be rewarded for these unrequested actions. The implications are all too clear: no gift, no safety. Nabal responds crudely and forcefully: "Who is David? Who is the son of Jesse? . . . *Should I take my bread, water, and meat intended for my workers and give it to men who have come from someplace I do not know*" (1 Sam. 25:10-11)? Nabal calls David's bluff; he did not hire him and intends to offer him precisely what he deserves—nothing.

David is told and immediately commands, "*Everyone* strap on his sword" (1 Sam. 25: 13a)! He fully intends to slaughter the impudent Nabal, because not only has David been called out as the potential criminal that he is, but his vast pride has also been pricked. Wholesale slaughter is the only thing his mind can contemplate as he and four hundred of his men ride hard toward Nabal's ranch.

Fortunately for David, the clever Abigail is told by one of her men what has happened. She swings into action, gathering a huge cache of food and gifts for David's men in the wilderness, and rides out herself to meet the furious warrior. In a speech beautifully designed both to calm and flatter David, she stops the proposed bloodbath and offers herself to the handsome fighter. The foolish David was intent on killing Nabal and confiscating his goods, an act that would have had difficult consequences for an aspiring king; after all, murdering one's own subjects, no matter how unpleasant they may be, is no way to begin a successful monarchy. Without the winsome Abigail, David would have incurred a huge load of bloodguilt, a reality he would have had to live with for a very long time.

Conveniently, Nabal dies of an apparent stroke, and David proceeds to woo Abigail for a wife. She agrees in an obsequious speech: "Your servant is a slave to wash the feet of the servants of my lord" (1 Sam. 25:41). For her heroic and risky actions, what does Abigail gain? Freedom from the odious Nabal, along with marriage to the next great man in the land. Abigail has played

---

1. Bible quotations are from the New Revised Standard Version, but italicized words within Bible quotations are my own translations or paraphrases.

her part in the rise of David, but she now disappears from the story, another apparent female protagonist who gains little from the man she risked life and reputation to save.

David is thus revealed as a self-possessed, egocentric man with a violent temper. He can be most vindictive when he is thwarted by anyone who would deny him his desires. Ultimately, those several traits will lead to adultery and murder.

Among those women who served the needs of David's ascent to the throne was Saul's younger daughter, Michal, who had the misfortune of falling hard for the man. Then, she risked her life for him against her own father, and the terrible consequences of that risk are made clear in 2 Samuel 6.

Saul has died, and one of the results of his death is that David no longer needs Michal as a connection to the house of Saul. After all, Abner, Saul's general, has handed Saul's army over to David, with which David has taken the citadel of Jerusalem from the Jebusites. He has only now to consolidate his power over the whole land by bringing the sacred ark of the covenant up to the city. He does this by arranging a massive and triumphant parade with himself as grand marshall, dressed rather scantily and provocatively in a "linen ephod," a priestly garment perhaps best described as a glorified G-string. The virile king leaps and dances before the ark, as it wends its way up toward the new city of David.

But Michal, witnessing the joyous procession, with her powerful husband dancing with abandon, demonstrating his full masculinity for all to see, "*despises* him in her heart" (2 Sam. 6:16). After David has entered the city, sacrificed to YHWH, and fed his people with bread and raisin cakes, he goes home to bless his household. But the furious Michal rushes out to meet him, and verbally and publically assaults her husband for what she has seen as a disgusting display before even the "*maids of the servants*" (2 Sam. 6:20), just like the most vulgar and common man in the kingdom. And David responds precisely as we would expect any ego-based man to respond to such a challenge: "It was before *YHWH*, who chose me in place of your father and all his household, to appoint me as prince over Israel, the people of *YHWH*, that I have danced before *YHWH*" (2 Sam. 6:21). Rather than confine his retort to a religious one, he cannot resist hurling the reality of his ascension to power and Saul's defeat and death into the teeth of his wife, the dead king's own daughter. And the result? "Michal the daughter of Saul had no child to the day of her death" (2 Sam. 6:23). This fact has far less to do with the anger of YHWH than with David's refusal to sleep with Michal again.

And that leads us to the most infamous story of this king, 2 Samuel 11. David is now the secure king of an expanding realm. His army and general Joab are about to subdue the last enemy in the orbit of Israel, the Ammonites. Though it is the spring, "when kings *go forth* to battle" (2 Sam. 11:1), David this time does not go but stays in Jerusalem. He spies a beautiful woman, and even after being told that she is the wife of one of his own generals, Uriah, he demands that Bathsheba be brought to him. They sleep together, and Bathsheba becomes pregnant.

David may now act in several ways. He could confess to the deed; after all, he is king and can do what he pleases. Or he could act as if nothing has happened and allow Bathsheba to have the child, disavowing his paternity. He might even confess and beg Uriah's forgiveness, but such men rarely do that. What he does is despicable. He has Uriah murdered in a ruse of battle, engineered by the ruthless Joab, after David tries twice to get the faithful Uriah into his house with his wife to make it appear that the coming child is his. When David is told that Uriah is dead, he announces without remorse or concern, "*War is hell; these things happen in battle. Tell Joab, nice job*" (2 Sam. 11:25). David is little better than a mafia don in this sordid tale.

And where does such mad behavior lead? One of David's sons rapes his sister, another son murders the rapist, that son tosses his own father out of Jerusalem, taking over the kingdom for himself, and a third son claims the throne while the aging king is dying.

Lord Acton's familiar line, "Power corrupts, and absolute power corrupts absolutely," comes easily to mind. Yet, there is danger in quoting the line, tut-tutting about the massive sins of David, and then convincing ourselves that we would never do such obviously evil things. Well, I may have thought once or twice about murdering those who do not agree with my considered and obviously correct judgments, but I surely would never actually do it. I may have considered that my next-door neighbor's lovely new white Mercedes would look far better in my driveway than hers, but I would never plot the way to make the criminal transfer. And I, on occasion, may have cast my lusty eye on a nubile young woman or two, but I love my wife and would never imagine myself with any other woman. And, finally, I could be pastor of a huge congregation and never allow the sense of privilege and power to turn my head—or could I?

Power is given to those in positions of leadership. I went to my senior pastor post in the full flower of my naiveté. I fancied that I really did not have any real power; I was just old John, everyone's friend, immune to the siren song that power always sings. I quickly learned just how wrong I was. But I was fortunate to receive an early wake-up call from God due to my poor choice of socks. I listened intently to conversations from many of the women who had been abused and learned from them the wiles of power run amok. Their relationships with the previous pastor often began quite innocently. There was a problem—a death in the family, a difficult time in a marriage, a sense of lack of worth. They had come to the man of God who would listen and care. This is a man who could be trusted; he was the interpreter of the word of God, and as that interpreter, he wielded the power of God for the people. His power, in effect, derived from that very ability to interpret God's word. But, unfortunately, this man of God had deep troubles of his own, troubles he had masked through a long ministry. Thus, his power was a troubled power, and like David before him, he found using people easy and profitable for his own self enhancement.

Finally, it began to become clear to me that I was a man of power, too—real power, dangerous power. People saw me as a man of God, charged with the care of countless lives, given the responsibility of preaching and teaching the truths by which they hoped to lead their lives. That is awesome power indeed! I began to read material on this problem. I was first led to Marie Fortune and her Faith Trust Institute. I borrowed her extraordinary film, "Not in My Church" (1991), and showed it to the staff. That film, in a quite uncanny way, was a near mirror of the situation that our church faced.

Then I turned to James Poling's work on power, work that comes up in several articles in this book.[2] I then found Donald Capps' *The Depleted Self*, which gave me insight about the possible causes of power abuses—both my predecessor's and potentially my own.[3] All of us have very deep needs, says Capps, and we will choose various ways to fulfill them. Some of those ways are life-giving and some are death-dealing.

At the end of David's life, the mighty king was reduced to a husk of his former self, freezing in his bed, unable to stay warm despite the presence of a young and comely Abishag. One after another, Bathsheba and then Nathan appear in the king's bedroom and coerce him into making their favorite, Solomon, the king. He does so, and with that act releases a torrent of horror on the kingdom as Solomon consolidates his own power in blood and death. And at the last day of David's life, he calls this same Solomon to his bedside to confirm his wisdom on his son and heir. He first offers to Solomon fine advice, telling him to be strong and courageous, to walk in the ways of YHWH, and to keep YHWH's statutes and commandments and ordinances (1 Kgs. 2:1-5).

2. James Newton Poling, *The Abuse of Power: A Theological Problem* (Nashville: Abingdon, 1991).

3. Donald Capps, *The Depleted Self: Sin in a Narcissistic Age* (Minneapolis: Fortress Press, 1993).

But, alas, he does not stop there. He ends his advice with a demand that the new king get even with two old enemies. First, Joab must die, the general who had been David's henchman for over fifty years but whom the king had never forgiven for his murder of Abner (2 Samuel 3). Second, Shemei must die, because when Absalom had forced his father to vacate Jerusalem, Shemei had cursed David, tossing pebbles at him and calling him a man of blood (2 Sam. 16:5-14). After David's eventual defeat of Absalom, Shemei came to the king and begged forgiveness. David had said on that day that he would not kill the old man, but now, as he is dying, he charges Solomon to do the deed.

And the story ends with these chilling words: "Then David slept with his ancestors, and was buried in the city of David" (1 Kgs. 2:10). The final words out of the mouth of the sweet singer of Israel were contracts on two old enemies. Power has indeed corrupted the old king absolutely.

But what of me and you? We church leaders are David's heirs, and we have real power. Its abuse is ever near. Remember what YHWH says to the world's first killer, Cain. "If you do well, will you not be accepted? *But* if you do not do well, sin is *crouching* at the door; *and though its desire is for you, you must master it*" (Gen. 4:7). And with that warning ringing in his ears, Cain goes into a field and murders his brother. We must know our power, must face it squarely, and then master it, before it masters us. But how? Paul is our guide. In great words from his letter to the Romans he says, "So I find it to be a law that when I want to do what is good, evil lies close at hand. . . . Wretched *one* that I am! Who will *deliver* me from this body of death? Thanks be to God through Jesus Christ our Lord!" (Rom. 7:21, 24-25).

Discussion Questions

1. David appears to be the very model of a power abuser. Are there other biblical characters who demonstrate such an abuse of power? How might these other characters add to the portrait of power abuse?

2. The wisdom and deeply felt honesty of Paul in his letter to the Romans is a possible antidote to the abuse of power. Can you name other possible ways to address this significant problem, using the resources of the Bible?

3. In what ways do you feel "depleted" in your ministry, and how have you attempted to fill up that depletion? Recreation? Prayer? Relationships? Which of these, or others you can name, have proven helpful to you?

4. Look honestly at your life: where have you abused the power that your position affords you? Can you name a time when that power has been recognized and used for good rather than for your own desires?

Recommended Readings

Alter, Robert. *The David Story: A Translation with Commentary of 1 and 2 Samuel*. New York: W.W. Norton, 1999.

Capps, Donald. *The Depleted Self: Sin in a Narcissistic Age*. Minneapolis: Fortress Press, 1993.

Not in My Church. Directed by Maria Gargiulo. Seattle: FaithTrust Institute, 1991. DVD, 45 min.

Fortune, Marie M. *A Sacred Trust: Boundary Issues for Clergy and Spiritual Teachers*. Seattle: Faith Trust Institute, 2008.

Gunn, David M. *The Story of King David: Genre and Interpretation*. Sheffield: University of Sheffield Press, 1978.

Heath, Elaine A. *We Were the Least of These: Reading the Bible with Survivors of Sexual Abuse*. Grand Rapids: Brazos, 2011.

Poling, James Newton. *The Abuse of Power: A Theological Problem*. Nashville: Abingdon, 1991.

7

Self-Love and Ministerial Practice

Susan A. Ross

What does it mean to be a sexually healthy Christian in the twenty-first-century postmodern world? Such a question would have sounded somewhat strange just fifty years ago. For Catholics, it was assumed that the only good sex was between a married man and a married woman for the procreation of children. "Sexual health" would have meant, at its best, something like regular sexual intercourse between the couple that was mutually pleasurable, within the fairly strict confines that Catholicism set for married couples. For Protestants, what it meant to be a sexually healthy minister was a question that was rarely if ever asked, but we can assume that the norm was not unlike that for Catholics, with the difference that contraception was permitted. But much has happened in the last fifty years: movements for sexual freedom, for women's rights, and for gay rights have all changed the sexual landscape. Situations that were seen as scandalous then, such as movie stars having children "out of wedlock," are commonplace in the present, and situations that were commonplace then, such as a Protestant pastor marrying a parishioner, are considered scandalous today. In the second decade of the twenty-first century, issues surrounding sexuality are in the forefront of religious and political turmoil, and those in ministry face daunting challenges in both living and promoting a sexuality that is authentically Christian, fulfilling, and just. In this chapter, I hope to sketch out an understanding of sexuality that is faithful to the Christian theological tradition and at the same time can offer wisdom to ministers for their own and their congregations' sexual health.

Consider the situation of Rev. Emily C., a thirty-two-year-old Episcopal priest. For the first few years after seminary and ordination, she served at a large urban church alongside a rector who was a helpful mentor to her. He and his wife met her for dinner frequently, and she felt that her life was relatively well balanced, while still busy. The congregation was diverse, and she enjoyed a fulfilling pastoral work schedule, as well as a social life with some of her seminary colleagues who lived nearby. Although she had been in a few romantic relationships in college and seminary, none of them led to the marriage for which she still hopes. Now she is in her first solo pastorate in a suburban area far from where she went to school. While she feels basically supported by the congregation, she is finding it difficult to make friends. She is the congregation's first woman rector, and some members find this a difficult adjustment. In addition, her church took on an ambitious project of helping to resettle refugees, and she has found herself working nearly to exhaustion trying to maintain the church's full liturgical schedule, give pastoral care, as well as tend to the social justice projects to which she feels committed.

One evening, she is in the church's office filling out school forms for the refugee family's children alongside one of the members of her church, a dedicated and successful lawyer with a wife and three children. He has been very helpful in the process, donating his legal skills and expertise. They talk, and he comments that she looks like she needs a massage. She laughs and agrees, and before she knows it, he is massaging her neck and shoulders, a massage that soon becomes more erotic than therapeutic. Emily realizes how lonely she has become in her position and how attractive and kind her parishioner is, and they begin to kiss.

What happens next? That is up to the reader's imagination. But anyone who has ever worked to exhaustion in a pastoral setting will understand how pastoral leaders can be at risk when they do not care for themselves adequately, especially when they neglect their sexual, as well as their physical and emotional, health. Emily had always thought herself to be a good Christian. Herself the daughter of a priest, she had watched her father lead congregations successfully; but he was also supported by her mother, who considered her role as the pastor's wife almost as important as raising her children. Emily had no real role model for herself as a single woman priest with a demanding job but also with sexual desires and longings. Where can she, and we, turn to find wisdom in the Christian tradition?

CHRISTIAN THEOLOGICAL TRADITION AND SEXUALITY

Most pastoral leaders would acknowledge that Christian theological tradition in relation to sexuality is mixed. Jesus was, as far as we know, never married, and the bible attests to his mother's virginity. Although the earliest followers of Jesus, such as Peter, were married, sexual continence came to be seen as desirable for a number of complex reasons, including disdain for the body and its "lower functions." For women, celibacy offered the opportunity to live a life not wholly defined by husband and children. In addition, one cannot ignore the misogyny frequently expressed by some of the early Christian fathers, who, citing the bible, blamed women for the ills of the world and, hence, recommended that men avoid them. But certainly the most influential figure of Christianity's first millennium was Augustine, whose influence is still powerful more than 1,500 years after his death.

Augustine's preference for continence and his mistrust of sexual desires are familiar aspects of his intellectual legacy; the long shadow of his influence is still very much felt in the sense that sex and sin always seem somehow to be connected. And while a thousand years after Augustine, Martin Luther made the significant move to claim for marriage a vocation as holy as that of monasticism, the sexuality of the minister or priest was hardly a frequent topic of seminary formation. Perhaps only in the last twenty years, when revelations of clergy sex abuse have taken over the headlines, have those responsible for ministerial formation begun to take seriously the need to address the sexuality and sexual health of those aspiring to and practicing ministry.

Two strands in the tradition—rooted in both the Protestant and Catholic traditions—have helped to shape attitudes about clergy, sexuality, and sexual health. The Protestant tradition, as first exemplified by Luther, has a strong sense of human sinfulness and is suspicious of the ways that human beings try to deceive themselves about their own supposed virtue. Thus, self-sacrifice and self-abnegation are often seen as the virtues that Christians should practice above all. The self-sacrificial love of Jesus, as it reads in John 15:13—"No one has greater love than this, to lay down one's life for one's friends"—is often identified as the prototype of ideal Christian love. Jesus is the model par excellence of self-sacrificial love, and ministers are trained to see themselves as modeling the kind of love for their communities that Jesus showed for the world. In 1930, Anders Nygren, a Swedish Lutheran theologian, published his classic study *Agape and Eros*, in which he argued that the central message of Christianity is love—in particular, the ideal of agapic self-sacrificial love. Nygren described the other form of love often mentioned by philosophers, eros, as a love that seeks after self-fulfillment and, thus, is contrary to the love that Jesus evidenced in his self-sacrificial life and death. Nygren was highly critical of Augustine's attempt to join agape and eros in *caritas* (charity).

This suspicion of one's desires also emerges in other Protestant thinkers, such as Reinhold Niebuhr, who emphasized pride as the root of human sinfulness. Because of their sin, human beings tend to build themselves up and to think too well of themselves; thus, the best way to overcome this tendency is to put others first, as Jesus did. I will describe below the feminist critique of this understanding of universal human sin. But for the moment, this tendency to be suspicious of one's own desires as inevitably leading one to sin can serve as one, but not the only, strand of the tradition. Translated into the emotional and sexual life of the minister, this strand means that he or she must be the model of self-sacrifice, always thinking of others first.

The Catholic tradition is, historically, a bit more optimistic regarding the human condition and, thus, can benefit from the Protestant tradition's serious attention to sin. But it has its own problematic tendencies as well. Because of its tradition of clerical celibacy, a life of sexual activity, even with one's spouse, has long been seen as inferior to a life of sexual abstinence, although Vatican II's affirmation of the common priesthood of the faithful helped to allay this. To develop a healthy sexuality while remaining continent is a challenge, although not an impossible one. For those who are married, sexual intercourse must always be open to the procreation of children, and for those who are single, a chaste life of abstinence is required. Thus, sexual expression is always to be very carefully practiced, within strict boundaries, and with a strong suspicion of sexual pleasure for its own sake. Same-sex relationships are seen in Catholicism as contrary to nature, and while same-sex orientation has come to be seen as a "disordered" condition rather than a choice, acting on desires for someone of the same sex is considered "intrinsically disordered" and "contrary to the natural law."[1]

In recent decades, Pope John Paul II's "Theology of the Body" has become widely publicized, at least within Catholicism.[2] "Theology of the Body" stresses the fundamental goodness of the body and sexuality as created by God, as well as the complete self-gift of each opposite-sex partner to the other. Women in particular are created to be mothers, and so biologically and spiritually receptive to both divine and male leadership. Neither husband nor wife must ever "hold back" any part of oneself, including one's physicality, which would mean sinfully, and selfishly, thinking of oneself first. Sexuality is first and foremost relational, so any form of self-pleasure is also contrary to God's intent. While containing a welcome appreciation for the joys of mutual sexual pleasure, "Theology of the Body" maintains that this pleasure can never be separated from openness to children.

This very brief look at the Christian tradition on sexuality shows: (1) one should always think of others first, and this applies especially to those who serve in ministerial capacities—potentially even more so for women; and (2) sexual desires are suspect, probably connected with one's own (selfish) desires

---

1. *Catechism of the Catholic Church*, 2nd ed. (New York: Doubleday, 1995), sec. 2357.

2. John Paul II, *The Theology of the Body: Human Love in the Divine Plan* (Boston: Pauline Books & Media, 1997).

for pleasure, and both prohibited and dangerous outside of the institution of marriage. While the body and sexuality are created by God as good, this goodness is extremely fragile and needs to be kept within very careful boundaries. Going back to our example of Rev. Emily, these themes do not seem to leave her with much of an avenue to a healthy sense of herself as a sexual person. They can also leave her at risk and needy, with the potential for inappropriately crossing boundaries, placing her and those to whom she ministers in precarious situations.

Contemporary Theologies of Love, Justice, and Sexuality

Over fifty years ago, a graduate student in theology questioned Niebuhr's emphasis on pride and self-assertion as the main ways that original sin manifests itself. In her classic article, "The Human Situation: A Feminine View," Valerie Saiving asked whether women are primarily guilty of over-estimating their own worth. Her conclusion was that women often fail to see themselves as worthy of attention as those for whom they care, and that a failure to develop one's self and a tendency to devalue one's contributions were characteristically women's "sins."

While it took another ten years and more for Saiving's insights to be developed by the newly emerging field of feminist theology, her questioning of the universality of theologies of sinfulness has proven to be a central insight. In the years since, theologians—both feminist and those sympathetic to feminist issues—have addressed how human beings are to understand themselves as sexual, as loving, and as responsible. In this short chapter, it is impossible to do justice to all these works. But I can identify some of their insights that can assist in developing a healthy sexuality and appropriate care for self and others that may be of assistance in the formation of the minister.

The first important insight is that recent theological treatments of sexuality have placed it in a much wider context than previous understandings. Sexuality has been a subject of immense scholarly study in the last two decades. In sexual ethics and in Catholic moral theology, sexuality was often viewed from an "act-centered" moral perspective—that is, some sexual acts are licit (for example, heterosexual marital intercourse) and some are not (for example, masturbation and adultery). These acts were studied and evaluated apart from their contexts and their history. An increased recognition of the fact that our sexuality has a history, is always lived in a social and cultural context, and is more diverse and fluid than implied by a rigid male-female dichotomy has changed the direction of sexual ethics. Those studying for and practicing ministry have a responsibility to be as informed as possible about sexuality and its history, and to give thoughtful reflection to their own development as sexual persons. This is not only so that they can adequately minister to others but also that they themselves can live healthy and fulfilling lives as sexual persons, whether they are actively in sexual relationships with others or not.

Putting sexuality in a context does not mean dismissing the most valuable points made by theologians about sexuality over the centuries. Some of these would include respect for human dignity and autonomy, the importance of justice in relationships, openness to life in its many dimensions, and an appreciation for the beauty and joy of God's creation, as expressed in human sexuality. But some points may need to be jettisoned, such as the idea that all sexual pleasure is out of accord with virtue, that sex should always be oriented toward procreation, and that women's sexual desires are dangerous and, thus, women need to be controlled.

The suspicion of sexuality that we have inherited from our long history and tradition needs to be faced honestly and critically. The unqualified condemnation of self-pleasure is one example of a prohibition that needs careful reexamination. The Catholic tradition holds that masturbation is "an intrinsically and gravely disordered action"; whether practiced within or outside of marriage, it is a use of sexuality "contrary to its purpose."[3] Although the Catechism notes that psychological and social factors need to be taken into account in determining the moral gravity of masturbation in any particular situation, it is still seen as an intrinsically evil act. Margaret Farley acknowledges this history and suggests that Christian ethicists consider masturbation "morally neutral," to be considered in the light of the person's life direction and particular situation.[4] In addition, she proposes that just sexual relationships need to balance autonomy and relationality. Farley is concerned that sexuality be attentive to the "*shared concrete reality of human persons*"—that is, aware of the personal and social dimensions of our lives in all their complexity.[5] Farley is especially concerned that the social and cultural dimensions of human sexuality be noted, including gendered dimensions, since sexuality has different meanings across cultures. But her main point is that *justice* needs to be the criterion for sexuality (thus, the title of her book). In this understanding, justice applies not only to others but also to one's self.

This leads to a second insight: the importance of self-love and self-care. Barbara Hilkert Andolsen has developed the critiques made by Saiving and

3. *Catechism of the Catholic Church,* sec. 2352.

4. Margaret A. Farley, *Just Love: A Framework for Christian Sexual Ethics* (New York: Continuum, 2006), 236.

5. Ibid., 210.

others in her work. In particular, she argues that self-sacrifice "is not an appropriate virtue for women who are prone to excessive selflessness."[6] Andolsen notes how self-sacrificial love has been seen as the ideal for love in the private sphere, whereas justice is the ideal in the public sphere, because in this latter context, self-sacrificial love was determined to be unrealistic. Andolsen, however, rejects this separation. Her insights suggest that the field of pastoral ministry needs to be attentive to the role of self-sacrifice in its practices.

I would take Andolsen's point further and propose that the clergy as a whole are, in a sense, feminized and that they are also encouraged to be models of self-sacrificial behavior. While the thesis of the "feminization of religion" was first developed to understand American religion in the nineteenth century, the role of the clergyperson in subsequent centuries has come to be seen as one of the "helping" professions, where the minister cares for his or her flock. People in these professions—men and women—spend their lives caring for others and run the risk of neglecting to care for themselves. Such self-care should involve caring for one's whole person, including sexuality.

When Jesus was asked what one ought to do to gain eternal life, he responded simply: "Love God with all your heart, and love your neighbor as yourself" (see Mark 12:30-31). What does it mean to love oneself? Too often, self-love is identified with selfishness, but they are not the same. To love oneself properly is to realize that one is a beloved child of God. We are all aware that the child who is not loved will probably grow up to be an unhappy and unhealthy adult. To love oneself means to accept oneself *as one is* and not with regret that one is not another.

This can be difficult for women and for those in the "helping" professions, such as ministry. Those who care for others come to be acutely aware of the needs of the sick, the vulnerable, and the poor, and can find themselves overwhelmed with a sense of inadequacy in meeting the needs of others. With a regular focus on the demands of the Christian life, ministers know all too well how difficult it is to live up to them. Self-care follows from self-love. We make sure that those whom we love are adequately cared for, and this goes for ourselves as well. Tending to one's whole being, especially those dimensions that touch most closely on our sexuality, is important for everyone.

6. Barbara Hilkert Andolsen, "Agape in Feminist Ethics," in *Feminist Theological Ethics: A Reader*, ed. Lois K. Daly (Louisville: Westminster John Knox, 1994), 151.

Some "Best Practices"

Let us return to Rev. Emily. Emily needs to understand how the history we inherit affects how we see ourselves as worthy of love and care and that her sexuality is a gift from God and is, therefore, good. She needs to develop practices of self-love. She yearns for touch, which is why she is so at risk to the advances of her parishioner. She yearns for intimacy and friendship. These are all necessary for a healthy and fulfilling life. As a single woman, what options does she have? First, Emily's pattern of overwork has left her isolated. She needs to have supportive friends, with whom she can share her feelings honestly and without fear of judgment. As a priest, she should have a spiritual director, someone with whom she could talk about her situation. It is important for her to be as honest as she can be with her friends and her spiritual director. Most often, situations where boundaries get crossed inappropriately arise when a person is out of balance in relation to work and personal life. Emily needs to restore an appropriate balance to her life.

Second, Emily needs to take time for herself and to reflect on her sensual-sexual needs. She might consider finding a massage therapist, who can offer touch in a safe situation and restore a sense of physical comfort. She might consider getting a companion animal, who could offer the opportunity to receive and return love. Having a canine or feline companion means having responsibility for an "other." And even though it is not a human other, studies show that relationships with companion animals are, in general, good for physical and emotional health. She might consider taking up yoga, which helps to increase awareness of one's body and how one's emotional and spiritual energies play out in bodily ways. At the least, she should be sure that she cares for her body in ways that nourish her on as many levels as possible. These suggestions are geared towards an increased focus on bodily and sensual awareness.

Third, attending to one's relational and physical dimensions is essential to a healthy sense of oneself. It is important to note that healthy relationships come out of a strong and stable sense of self and that, while openness in a relationship is important, allowing oneself to be open to potential hurts as well as blessings is—or ought to be—a choice and not a "default" position. Emily's fatigue, loneliness, and overwork have left her with few resources to face temptation. Had she been more attentive to her own needs, she would have been less likely to respond positively and more likely to rebuff her parishioner's attention. And since she wants to develop a serious long-term relationship, she will be in a much better position to establish one that is healthy and just if she cares for herself as much as she cares for those to whom she ministers.

Fourth, Emily needs to reflect carefully on her time commitments to ensure that she has adequate time for peer relationships and to take care of her physical-sexual well-being. It is tempting for ministers to think that they are irreplaceable, but illness or unforeseen accidents bring home the reality that parish life will go on, whether they are there or not. Emily has solid theological grounds for insisting on a work life that has balance, time for prayer and contemplation, exercise, and companionship. And it is crucial to note that Emily's sexuality is not something that exists apart from these other dimensions of her life: it is an essential dimension of her being, intertwined with her intellectual, emotional, and spiritual dimensions.

Conclusion

These theological reflections will not find a partner for Emily nor will they tell her exactly what she needs to do to care more appropriately for herself. But they might help her reflect more deliberately on the assumptions that she carries about herself, her needs, and her work. Emily's vocation is central to her life, but it cannot be lived out well under her present circumstances. Considering the proper roles of love for self, others, and God will be a healthy exercise in Emily's development as a woman and as a minister.

Discussion Questions

1. Have you ever found yourself in a situation similar to Emily's? How did you deal with the situation and what did you learn about yourself from it?
2. The single minister who seeks a long-term relationship is in a delicate situation, both with regard to the faith community that the minister serves and with regard to church polity. What resources might be available to single ministers in Emily's situation from the church and the local community?
3. What kinds of Gospel messages about love of self do you find to be the most important for you? How do ministers deal with the contemporary "culture of narcissism"?

Recommended Readings

Andolsen, Barbara Hilkert. "Agape in Feminist Ethics." *Journal of Religious Ethics* 9, no. 1 (Spring 1981): 69–83; reprinted in *Feminist Theological Ethics:*

A Reader, edited by Lois K. Daly, 146-59. Louisville: Westminster John Knox, 1994.

Farley, Margaret A. *Just Love: A Framework for Christian Sexual Ethics.* New York: Continuum, 2006.

Ross, Susan A. "The Bridegroom and the Bride: The Theological Anthropology of John Paul II and its Relation to the Bible and Homosexuality." In *Sexual Diversity and Catholicism: Toward the Development of Moral Theology*, edited by Patricia Beattie Jung, 39–59. Collegeville, MN: Liturgical, 2001.

Saiving, Valerie. "The Human Situation: A Feminine View." *Journal of Religion* 40, no. 2 (April 1960), 100–112; reprinted in *Womanspirit Rising: A Feminist Reader in Religion*, edited by Carol P. Christ and Judith Plaskow, 25–42. New York: Harper, 1979.

Salzman, Todd A. and Michael G. Lawler. *Sexual Ethics: A Theological Introduction.* Washington, DC: Georgetown University Press, 2012.

Weaver, Darlene Fozard. *Self-Love and Christian Ethics.* New York: Cambridge University Press, 2002.

8

Orthoeros: A Biblically-Based Sexual Ethic

Miguel A. De La Torre

Toe-curling, earth-shaking, climax-reaching sex is great! God may have declared all of creation to be good (Gen. 1:31), but when it comes to human physical intimacy, sex is beyond simply good. Sex is great because it can be a basis for healthy and just communities. Not surprisingly, the very first instruction given by the Creator to humans, before forbidding eating from the tree of the knowledge of good and evil, was to "be fruitful and multiply" (Gen. 1:28),[1] a goal that can only be achieved through copulation. This is not to establish that reproduction is sex's ultimate or even necessary purpose. Yes, sex is how future generations are brought into the world; but, it can also be a source of communion and extreme pleasure (valuable for its own sake). And yet, while engaging in a conjugal relationship was recognized as a calling from God, historically Christianity developed a predominantly ascetic tradition that idealized sexual abstinence and often associated it alone with godliness, purity, and holiness. The concept of sexual sacredness leads many Christians to recoil. Many have come to conflate all sex outside of a monogamous, heterosexual marriage with promiscuity, holding those in such lifestyles responsible for the moral degradation of our culture. Sex, for such Christians, is constructed as a powerful and dangerous desire whose lack of restraint and control has led to skyrocketing divorce rates and broken families.

Neither conservatives' sexual legalism nor liberals' permissiveness provides satisfactory approaches toward sexual ethics. A crusade against so-called "sexual immorality" is waged by conservatives who reduce sex to an act involving nothing more than the genitals, with emphasis placed on whom one engages in sex. A fear-driven discourse is created when the consequences of sex—for

---

1. All biblical quotes were translated by the author from the original Hebrew or Greek.

example, pregnancy, contracting a sexually transmitted disease, or condemnation for being lascivious—are used to define such activity as something dirty and unholy. Sex, as the epitome of sin, fosters control of bodies through guilt. Because of desire, sex is labeled as something good but too powerful, thus needing to be contained. Fear and coercion are used to ensure compliance with the sexual mores of the culture. In the minds of many past (and some contemporary) Christian leaders and believers, good Christians avoid sex, and if they participate, avoid pleasure. So to be a lesbian, gay, bisexual, or transgender person, to engage in pre-marital sexual relationships, or to become pregnant while unmarried becomes, in the eyes of many conservatives presently framing the Christian conversation on sexual morality, a blatant flaunting of hedonism. The job of the clergy is to rein in the sexual perversions of others, either through homilies within the church or legislation within the secular culture. The godly response to sex becomes celibacy when single, heterosexual coitus when married. Advocating public policies and legislative initiatives that socially reinforce these standards becomes the responsibility of the clergy and, indeed, all the faithful who see themselves as safeguarding society from the destructive nature of unchecked sexuality.

For more liberal-minded individuals (including some Christians), sex is reduced to a biological function, a private act between two consenting adults, resulting from a dopamine-elevated state. What occurs between two or more consenting adults is no one else's business. Because of the liberal's presupposed dichotomy between the public and private sphere, sex clearly falls under the category of the private. Sex, for the liberal, becomes depoliticized—reduced to a personal choice that has no impact on the overall society. For more liberal-minded individuals, sex is simply another bodily appetite, like eating or sleeping. It is simply what human mammals do—no more, no less. Therefore, as long as no one is being hurt by the sexual encounter, two or more consenting adults can participate in whatever sexual interaction they wish. When dealing with matters of sexuality, individual reason and experiences guide a utilitarian-type approach.

Neither the conservative nor the liberal view is adequate. Both sides overly emphasize sexual acts, debating and seeking answers to what is or is not sexually permitted. Both approaches are indicative of a dominant, Eurocentric, hyper-individualist culture, and as such, both share common problematic assumptions and presuppositions about sexuality. For example, they share a tendency to reduce the Christian faith to a personal piety that dictates which acts should be or should not be permissible. As such, sex is understood as something private rather than communal. Sex may indeed be a personal act (for example, masturbation) or an interpersonal act, but it is not private. It does have public, social, and cultural ramifications. What is required is a new way of approaching Christian sexuality. But how does one construct a sexual ethic within a conservative religious atmosphere that usually equates sex with sin or within a liberal secularized society in which sexual images run rampant on film and television, on our advertising billboards, and on the Internet? If the message of the New Testament is the fulfillment of the law with the commandment of love, then any sexual ethics constructed should concentrate on what it means to love my neighbor—more specifically, my sexually oppressed neighbor. The ethical act of unconditional love for the other—the neighbor—is what makes transformative relationships possible.

This chapter will attempt to construct biblically-based, ethical principles for enjoying sex (in spite of the Bible's patriarchal tendencies). Additionally, it can serve to present those engaged in the practices of ministry with a more holistic approach to providing guidance on how a sexual ethics should be implemented. Aware of how sexism, heterosexism, and even racism and classism have influenced past and current conversations on sexual ethics, this chapter will avoid predominant "conservative" or "liberal" approaches to sexual ethics. Instead, looking toward a "liberative" methodology that seriously considers liberation theology, this chapter will attempt to develop a sexual ethics influenced by those who reside on the margins of power and privilege.[2]

Orthodoxy, Orthopraxis, and Orthoeros

To implement a liberative methodology means that sexual ethics must: (1) listen to testimonies usually ignored, specifically the voices of those abused by the prevailing sexual norms; (2) pay close attention as to who benefits, either through power or privilege, from the present sexual norms of society; and (3) challenge sexual norms that prevent individuals from living the abundant life promised to them by Christ (John 10:10). I argue that social injustices pervert human relationships and distort any definition or concept of love. Because justice-making (the fostering of non-oppressive structures) is an act done in obedience to unconditional love, any sexual ethics that ignores the communal ramification of sexual relationships will fall short of offering an alternative to either some stringent conservative purity code or some hyper-liberal view of "anything goes." For sex to be liberating, sexuality must be understood as

2. This chapter is based on my earlier book, *A Lily Among the Thorns: Imagining a New Christian Sexuality* (San Francisco: Jossey-Bass, 2007).

relational and, hence, a justice issue. Great love-making is needed for justice-making to take place, and vice-versa.

Those who ground their religious commitment on the insights provided by liberation theology participate in a liberative ethical framework that considers both "orthodoxy" (correct doctrine) and "orthopraxis" (correct action). Historically, Eurocentric, Christian theological thought has predominately emphasized only orthodoxy. What one believes in one's heart and professes through one's mouth becomes fundamental in defining whether one is truly Christian. Doctrine matters. And while believers may no doubt feel compelled to act upon their beliefs, in the final analysis, belief trumps action. In this view, it is more important to have correct doctrine than correct action.

In contrast, for historically disenfranchised Christian groups subsisting on the underside of the U.S. dominant culture, the emphasis is usually on orthopraxis, correct action. Orthopraxis is the cornerstone of living out liberation theology. The actions committed, specifically actions leading toward social justice, are what define one's Christian commitment. What then becomes the correct action of liberative sexual ethics? I suggest "orthoeros" (correct erotic sex).

The orthoeros that I'm calling for focuses its critical eye on the sexual prejudices of those in power. Those whom society empowers usually impose restrictions upon the powerless, so as to enhance and secure their privileged spaces. In an attempt to construct a proper "orthodoxy," a proper doctrine, many quickly move from saying sex is good (only in a monogamous, heterosexual marriage) to developing a list of "dos" and "don'ts." But such lists have more often than not led to sexual repression and oppression. Those privileged by the prevailing sexual patterns remain complicit with oppressive structures, specifically structures which lead to the domination of wives, partners, and/or their supposedly economic or racial "inferiors." From the underside of today's normative sexual patterns lie the seeds for producing a justice-based sexual ethics, but only if we are willing to listen to the stories and testimonies of the disenfranchised, learning from their experiences, resisting the temptation of paternalistically fixing the problem, and standing in solidarity with those abused by the present social structures.

The goal of this chapter is, therefore, not to limit what makes sex great but to enhance sexual pleasure and spiritual intimacy through the process of unmasking those oppressive structures put in place to control the "flesh" so that the "spirit" could supposedly flourish. And here lies the paradox that prevents so many from experiencing great sex: total surrender, each to the other, can never be achieved as long as one of the two parties is holding on to power over his or her partner. If we can construct this liberative orthoeros, we might bring to fruition the words of the psalmist: "Steadfast love and faithfulness will embrace, justice and peace will kiss" (Ps. 85:10).

BASIS OF MUTUAL GIVING AND VULNERABILITY

To love and be loved is part of what defines our humanity. Correct erotic sex, orthoeros, occurs within a familial relationship that is based on love and commitment while remaining vigilant against the suffering of others due to that relationship. When I refer to familial relationships, I realize that this does not necessarily signify a marriage. Although church or civil weddings are rituals publicly proclaiming the existence of a familial relationship, these events do not create family—people do. A church wedding simply blesses the relationship. A familial relationship may occur absent a religious ritual; likewise, a legally married couple where both spouses lack appropriate vulnerability or have not given freely of themselves would be "living in sin." There may be a marriage because a ritual occurred in a church building, but if a sexual relationship fails to meet the deepest physical, emotional, spiritual, and intellectual needs of both partners, there is no family. Orthoeros promotes a familial relationship based on mutual giving and vulnerability.

MUTUAL GIVING.

A scriptural guiding principle for all human relationships is the placing of others first. Paul, in his letter to the Ephesians, wrote: "Be subject to one another in the fear of the Lord" (5:21). Within an intimate familial relationship, putting the needs of one's partner before one's own needs become a biblical norm. Yes, this view is contested by many feminists—and for good reasons. No doubt, most Christian men have historically insisted that it be the women who must put male needs first. But this is a misreading, for patriarchy is the antithesis to mutual giving. Participating in mutual giving can never mean forfeiting personal autonomy. One can only give of oneself if one has authority over one's own personhood. Mutual giving (rather than taking) presupposes autonomy. Mutual giving means that the participants seek the best, each for the other. Sex must, therefore, occur in a safe environment, where the fear of abuse, abandonment, or domination can be eliminated. Giving of oneself to the drunkenness of love can only occur if it is mutual, and mutual giving can only be possible when both parties become totally vulnerable.

VULNERABILITY.

Mutual giving is marked by vulnerability. I suggest that the ideal paradigm for a vulnerable relationship can be found in the Genesis creation story. We are told that "the man and woman were both naked, yet felt no shame" (Gen. 2:25). This supposedly was the pristine relationship which existed prior to the "fall," prior to the establishment of patriarchy. To the ancient Hebrew mind, "nakedness" was a metaphor for vulnerability. Picture this, if you will: both the man and woman were standing stark naked before each other, totally vulnerable, yet they were not ashamed of their bodies, of their personhood.

Only when two individuals are totally vulnerable with each other and are able to stand naked—warts and all—are they truly free to become one flesh, fully sharing themselves with each other in body, spirit, and soul. When I am with my beloved in the privacy of our home, I can stand before her, totally naked, and feel no shame whatsoever. Even though I am unable to hide my sagging excess weight, stretch marks, wrinkles, and grayness, I can stand totally vulnerable and exposed to her gaze without fear of ridicule or abandonment. I stand before her not just physically naked but also emotionally, intellectually, and psychologically naked. And here is the good news: she can do likewise. We are able to stand fully before each other because for years, during good times and bad, we have created a familial relationship based on mutual giving and vulnerability.

FIVE PRINCIPLES

This orthoeros ethics for which I call, based on mutual giving and vulnerability, focuses upon strengthening, securing, and supporting familial relationship. Familial relationship is not so much a set of rules to be followed as a way of being. The focus is therefore not on the type of sex acts that occur between individuals. Rather, I argue, for orthoeros to blossom, sex must be safe, consensual, faithful, mutually pleasing, and intimate.

SAFE.

For a relationship to be vulnerable, it must be safe—safe from harm, danger, and abuse. The apostle Paul reminds us: "Nothing to me is forbidden, but not all things do good. All things to me are lawful, but not all things build up. Let no one seek their own advantage, but each that of the other" (1 Cor. 10:23-24). Sex is not forbidden, but not all sexual encounters are good or safe. No one should seek, through the use and abuse of others, mere gratification of his or her sexual desires. Instead, each should seek the sexual good of the other. Sex which brings no harm to self or others, but rather builds the other up, becomes safe.

CONSENSUAL.

For sex to be mutually giving, it presupposes that both partners are mature and equal in power. By definition, it eliminates adults in full capacity of their faculties from engaging in sex with the mentally impaired, children, subordinates, or anyone for whom they have a role based on fiduciary responsibility (like clergy in relation to members of their congregation). Even when apparent consent is given, an uneven relationship between the parties denies the existence of true consent. A mentally impaired person may agree to sex with a person having "full" mental capacities, while not realizing all that is entailed in the encounter. A child may agree to have sex with an adult family member as a perverse understanding of love. A student or employee may agree to engage in sex with his teacher or employer in hopes of a better grade, job security, attraction to the power the holder has over her, transference, or simply out of a fear of the consequences the power holder might inflict if the subordinate does not acquiesce.

FAITHFUL.

Another important point to recognize is that nowhere within the biblical text is monogamy established as the standard for all forms of Christian marriages, except perhaps as found in Titus 1:6, which requires elders to be the husbands of one wife. Still, if our hope is for sex to be great, then both mutual giving and vulnerability must be present. Trust and safety from rejection or abandonment fosters the ability of both partners to feel vulnerable enough to mutually and fully give of each other, which in turn leads to a bonding that enhances the physical sexual experience. For this reason, any violation of this bond shatters fidelity.

MUTUALLY PLEASING.

To touch, to feel, to nibble, to fondle, to penetrate or be penetrated is more than simply sultry pleasure. It is trust—trust in a partner who will neither hurt you nor deny you pleasure. Improper sex occurs when conducted solely in search of self-serving pleasure, when love is absent from love making. When the other is denied a share in its pleasures; when the other is reduced to a commodity to be used and abused for self-gratification; or when the other, due to an uneven power relationship, is forced to participate in sexual acts against her or his will, then orthoeros is absent.

INTIMATE.

For some, the act of sex with the same partner can become somewhat routine and predicable, if not repetitive. But what makes sex great is not the act of obtaining physical gratification with and through another body, but the intimacy which comes with vulnerability. Through the process of revealing our inner self to our beloved, an intimacy capable of bringing healing to our dysfunctionality is created, reassuring our deepest fears and satisfying our most intense yearnings. Even when sexual pleasure is unattainable due to illness, old age, or forced separation (for example, war or imprisonment), sex can still remain great so long as it enhances intimacy.

CONCLUSION

Now that we know what constitutes orthoeros, we are left to consider an important question: can relationships that are love-making prove to be justice-making? Consider the obverse. If our interpersonal, intimate relationships function in accordance with a hierarchical structure based on an active-passive oppressive model, why then are we surprised that this model is echoed within public sphere? Social structures mirror the patriarchal hierarchy existing within many households. The writer of 1 Peter clearly testifies to these connections. Believers are to be subject to the political structures of imperial Rome, even to the point of honoring the emperor (2:13-17), and they are to be subject to the economic structures imposed by their masters, even when masters are unfair (2:18-25). Similarly, women are to be subject to their "lords"—their husbands—even if their husbands are not believers (3:1-6). The same logic used to reinforce the obedience of women within the household is extended to the political sphere and the marketplace.

The basis for most unjust social structures is the denial of body rights—the right to clothe, feed, and shelter the body—through economic oppression. Denying the right of (any)body to participate in the fruits of society because of her gender, skin coloration, or sexual orientation is oppressive. Our society's obsession with the white, heterosexual, male, idealized body leads to injustices that are usually manifested in the form of classism, sexism, racism, and heterosexism. The idealized bodies born of these systems are privileged and are often granted power and control over against poorer, darker, and/or female bodies. This power and control often finds expression in male-centered, female-passive patriarchal sex, while eroticizing domination. Pleasure is found perversely both in domination and in being dominated. Christianity has come to be interpreted so as to justify spiritually white, heterosexual, male supremacy both in the home and in the broader society. Consequently, sexual justice cannot be understood and/or achieved apart from seeking class, gender, and racial justice.

Orthoeros, by providing an ethical pattern for our most intimate human relationships, attempts to remedy these public injustices. To seek justice deepens love for the other. Training one's heart to love others more deeply impacts one's love for one's beloved. Reaching deeper levels of love can only enhance one's sexual encounters. Now, if the major goal for justice-seeking is an equitable sharing of resources and power, then dismantling power structures designed to privilege one group at the expense of another becomes the major task for those seeking a justice-based social order. Because oppressive patriarchal structures exist in the bedchamber, then seeking justice "between the sheets" becomes an ethical issue. In this intimate space, power-sharing becomes the paragon upon which other social relationships are based.

Pope Benedict XVI hints at this in his 2006 encyclical *Deus Caritas Est,* where he argues that a mature form of sex is unselfishly concerned with others, creating a type of love that leads to justice. He wrote: "Love looks to the eternal. Love is indeed 'ecstasy', not in the sense of a moment of intoxication, but rather as a journey, an ongoing exodus out of the closed inward-looking self towards its liberation through self-giving, and thus towards authentic self-discovery and indeed the discovery of God."[3]

What we do with our flesh in the privacy of our bedroom with our beloved can be a means of learning how to love selflessly in the public sphere. It can become a model for the generous extension of compassion for others. Sex can humanize its participants, providing a self-giving paragon by which to relate to others. Sexuality ceases to be a private matter as it moves to the public sphere as a moral imperative. Even though sex may occur in private, it has social ramifications. It can school us to attend with love to the needs of others. Sex provides the opportunity to move beyond the self toward the other. To desire sex is, foremost, a plea for communion, where the psychological and physiological needs of lovers are met. Sexual fulfillment within a vulnerable and mutually giving relationship validates our humanity, because to be human is to be in relationship with our beloved, with our God, and with our neighbor.

---

3. Benedict XVI, *Deus caritas est* [*God is Love*], Encyclical letter on Christian love, Vatican Website, 2005, http://www.vatican.va/holy_father/benedict_xvi/encyclicals/documents/hf_ben-xvi_enc_20051225_deus-caritas-est_en.html, sec. I.6.

Although physical sex may be limited to the beloved, still, the principles of putting the needs of others first become the foundation for creating justice-based relationships.

Sex can be a pleasurable experience, both physically and spiritually, designed to achieve wholeness with completeness—*shalom* with *shlemut*. But let's be clear: seeking a sexual liberationist ethics does not provide a pseudo-religious permission wherein "anything goes." To fully engage in a liberative sexual ethics is to rely fully on the power of God's grace while affirming *shalom* with *shlemut* for the self as well as for the beloved. From the get-go, liberative sexual ethics dismisses any sexual relationship which prohibits *shalom* with *shlemut* from being established. Sexual abuse and exploitation are unequivocally defined as wrong and therefore evil. Will mistakes and errors occur in our quest for great sex? Of course, for after all, we are humans. But if we recognize that failures and mistakes are themselves powerful learning devices that lead to personal growth, and if we understand grace as God's healing from wrong choices and painful experiences, then we can boldly move forward in our quest for great sex without fear or incrimination.

Nevertheless, fear of and incrimination from sex runs rampant in many of our churches. For conservatives, such a liberative approach to sexual ethics is considered anti-family. Family values becomes the battle cry for reasserting, according to Christian ethicist Marvin Ellison, "white, affluent, male hegemony as the necessary social mechanism for preserving both the family (read 'male-dominated, affluent families') and the capitalist social order."[4] To establish orthoeros, the task is not to define the type of relationship (male-centered, patriarchal, heterosexual marriage) through which sex can occur but to establish biblically-based principles of justice within all relationships, sexual and nonsexual, so as to dismantle societal injustices.

DISCUSSION QUESTIONS

1. Think of a sexual experience which made you feel bad or "dirty." Why did you have these feelings? Were these feeling imposed due to societal mores? Was the sexual experience mutually giving and did it foster vulnerability?

2. How can sexual or sensual acts be deemed holy? Does the concept of orthoeros suggest ways that you can manifest this holiness in your own life?

4. Marvin M. Ellison, *Erotic Justice: A Liberating Ethic of Sexuality* (Louisville: Westminster John Knox, 1996), 12.

3. Five underlining principles are suggested for orthoeros. Are any of these principles problematic? If so, why? What other principles should be considered?

4. Do you agree that the way we construct our intimate relations influences societal relationships? Why or why not? If you agree, how then should your present intimate relationship(s) change to foster a more justice based society?

Recommended Readings

Althaus-Reid, Marcella. *Indecent Theology: Theological Perversions in Sex, Gender and Politics*. London: Routledge, 2000.

De La Torre, Miguel A. *A Lily Among the Thorns: Imagining a New Christian Sexuality*. San Francisco: Jossey-Bass, 2007.

Douglas, Kelly Brown. *Sexuality and the Black Church: A Womanist Perspective*. Maryknoll, NY: Orbis, 2003.

Ellison, Marvin. *Erotic Justice: A Liberating Ethic of Sexuality*. Louisville: Westminster John Knox, 1996.

———. *Making Love Just: Sexual Ethics for Perplexing Times*. Minneapolis: Fortress Press, 2012.

Schüssler Fiorenza, Elisabeth. *But She Said: Feminist Practices of Biblical Interpretation*. Boston: Beacon, 1992.

PART III

Practices of Ministry

9

Pastoral Care and Sexual Ethics

Joretta Marshall

A common challenge in training sessions on clergy sexual ethics emerges in this remark: "Are you telling me I can no longer care about my parishioners? These rules make it impossible to show I care." The beginning assumption of this chapter is this: the purpose of conversations about clergy sexual ethics is to create a holier and healthier community of faith that embodies its care in ways that are trustworthy. Because the church represents something beyond itself, congregations become places where hope is encouraged, comfort is experienced, and commitments to justice are embodied. For these reasons, communities of faith can become participants in healing processes and can also be experienced as damaging to individuals, families, and communities. Clarity about clergy sexual ethics contributes to the relational health and wholeness of a congregation; trespassing against the souls of others by violating norms of spiritual, physical, emotional, or sexual behavior can cause irreparable harm—a kind of damage that ought not to occur in a context where people turn to find solace and wisdom.

Pastoral care intersects with issues of clergy sexual ethics in at least three ways. First, the practice of pastoral care sets in place dynamics that contribute to the potential for healing *and* for damage. The crossing of emotional, physical, or sexual lines can often begin in the context of pastoral care. The cases that follow in this chapter offer insights into how the dynamics that lead to healing can also lead to potential harm, while also suggesting some strategies for pastoral care that respect healthy sexual ethics. Second, pastoral care requires a willingness to wrestle with the nuances of sexual ethics, relying less on "rules" and more on a thoughtful response to the messy boundaries inevitably involved. Good pastoral care enhances the flourishing of individuals, families, and communities by creating patterns of behavior attentive to dynamics of power and vulnerability. Decision-making about how best to care for others requires that we draw upon the wisdom of many voices, including those who have experienced a betrayal of trust in the context of pastoral care. They teach pastoral leaders the importance of walking with exceptional care when assisting others in moments of discernment about life's complexities.

Third, pastoral care intersects with sexual ethics once an alleged offense has been named. At that point, congregational care requires holding whole communities in steadfast concern, including offering care to various constituencies: congregational members who may be less sanguine about any allegations against a clergyperson; the one who named the offense and any family members connected to that person; the pastoral caregiver who allegedly crossed boundaries alongside any family members identified with that individual; and the larger community, judicatory, and denomination that surrounds the local congregation. The layers of pastoral care at these moments require integrated and complicated strategies. This chapter will not deal directly with responding to such situations, recognizing that others continue to work on developing appropriate strategies.[1] However, in what follows, connections emerge between the development of healthy relationships in the context of congregational life or specialized ministry and the aftercare that is needed once a violation has been reported.

Before looking at the intersection of pastoral care and sexual ethics, two caveats need to be named. First, it is important to differentiate between caregivers who find themselves in a precarious place because of situational stressors or other dynamics and the more habitual or chronic offenders who are adept at boundary-crossing over time and with multiple victims. Habitual abusers of power or those whom we might identify as interested only in satisfying their own needs (such as persons who are narcissistic) often use pastoral care as an entrance into their systematic abuse, as they prey on the most vulnerable. This chapter does not address those situations.[2]

A second caveat is to note that, while much of the language of this chapter refers to clergy, the potential to cross emotional, spiritual, physical, or sexual

---

1. See, for example, Marie M. Fortune, *Responding to Clergy Misconduct: A Handbook* (Seattle: FaithTrust Institute, 2009); Beth Ann Gaede, ed., *When a Congregation Is Betrayed: Responding to Clergy Misconduct* (Herndon, VA: Alban Institute, 2006); Nancy Myer Hopkins and Mark R. Laaser, eds., *Restoring the Soul of a Church: Healing Congregations Wounded by Clergy Sexual Misconduct* (Collegeville, MN: Liturgical, 1995); John Thoburn and Rob Baker, eds., with Maria Dal Maso, *Clergy Sexual Misconduct: A Systems Approach to Prevention, Intervention, and Oversight* (Carefree, AZ: Gentle Path, 2011).

2. Fortune draws a distinction between predators and wanderers. Educational materials may help wanderers avoid risky behavior but are unlikely to change the behavior of predators. Fortune, *Responding to Clergy Misconduct*, 23.

boundaries is present for anyone who is in a position of caregiver in any context. Every caregiver is at risk of causing damage by crossing a boundary. Certainly, lay leaders, spiritual care advisors, "Stephen" ministers, chaplains, or others who are designated care representatives of a congregation or faith community should be included in what follows.

PASTORAL CARE, PSEUDO-INTIMACY, AND VULNERABILITY

In the midst of caring for a husband who is incapacitated due to an illness that will eventually take his life, Sondra expresses deep appreciation for the care and attention of her pastor, Rev. Johnston. As the pastor continues to visit with her, he finds himself connected to her spiritual strength and compassion. Because he knows how to invite meaningful conversation, they often find themselves in intimate discussions about fear, loneliness, suffering, and the need for deep and abiding friendships. In an attempt to let Sondra know that she is not alone, Rev. Johnston shares frustrations about his ministry and life, offering opportunities for Sondra to move away from some of the intensity of her experience. Sondra and Rev. Johnston often end their time in prayer, holding hands as they pray, and then offering a hug to one another, as is the norm in their congregation. One day, as they are departing, both of them acknowledge the special connection they feel with one another because of the journey they share.

In many ways, the narrative above represents what we hope for in the ministry of care. Sondra, in the midst of an intense period of suffering and grief, experiences Rev. Johnston as a spiritual companion. Rev. Johnston offers care in ways that are normative for his congregation: sharing one another's burdens through physical presence, praying together, and symbolically offering a hug in moments that are beyond words. On the surface, there is nothing "bad" about Rev. Johnston's behavior. In fact, the pastoral care that he offers bears the possibility to embody comfort and healing—and therein lies part of the struggle. While pastoral care has the potential to offer solace at moments of our deepest pain, it also carries with it the potential to leave equally deep injuries and wounded people in its wake. But how does one tell the difference between good pastoral care and the inappropriate crossing of emotional, physical, spiritual, or sexual boundaries? Let me suggest four avenues for conversation that can assist caregivers in these moments.

First, how does Rev. Johnston both recognize the vulnerability of Sondra and cautiously walk with her in ways that embody the care of a church and, ultimately, of God? Sondra receives a great deal from Rev. Johnston's visits, which nurture and sustain her sense of community, reminding her that she is not alone and giving space for her pain. In the midst of an intensely personal, spiritual journey, Sondra receives care from a pastoral leader who makes her feel comforted and cherished as a child of God. A deep spiritual and emotional presence is confirmed by the holding of hands and the offering of a sign of peace (in this instance, a hug). There is no one else that knows as much about her feelings on this journey, and from her perspective, feelings of intimacy are nurtured in response to the genuine care. This sense of intimacy on the part of Sondra is precisely why Rev. Johnston needs to pay deep attention to how he walks this journey.

Second, Rev. Johnston needs to ask himself what intimacy needs of his own are being met in this relationship. Most pastoral leaders enter caring ministries because they know that a pastoral presence can make a difference in someone's life. Such a desire to care is an asset for those in ministry, but it does represent one of the burdens pastoral leaders carry into moments of intense relatedness. Our need to care about others sometimes makes it difficult for us to recognize when we are moving into risky territory emotionally, spiritually, or physically. While Sondra experiences this moment as "intimate" for reasons that are natural and good, Rev. Johnston is wise to recognize this as a moment of *pseudo-intimacy*. In other words, he is not sharing at the same level of vulnerability as Sondra, nor is this a mutual intimacy. Good pastoral presence heightens our sensitivities to others and, in return, caregivers feel honored and affirmed. Lest we be drawn in by the potency of the moment, pastoral caregivers need to embody additional humility in these moments. A pastor who knows himself and his weaknesses, recognizes his own intimacy needs, and finds ways to appropriately meet those needs is, ultimately, a gift to parishioners and communities.[3]

Third, Rev. Johnston and the congregation need to discuss the meaning and power of touch. Many congregations hold hands while praying or hug one another at the offering of the peace of Christ, and this, in and of itself, is not wrong. It is important, however, to talk about the meaning of such encounters in the context of the church. It is a disservice to congregations to let them assume that all people like to be hugged or that everyone appreciates the same kind of physical touch. Nor is it helpful to imagine that a hug is an adequate substitute for the verbal reminder that "God's love enfolds you at this moment."

---

3. There are multiple resources that discuss the dynamics of care, including a large literature on the classic definitions of transference. See, for example, Andrea Celenza, *Sexual Boundary Violations: Therapeutic, Supervisory, and Academic Contexts* (Lanham, MD: Jason Aronson, 2007); Karen A. McClintock, *Preventing Sexual Abuse in Congregations: A Resource for Leaders* (Herndon, VA: Alban Institute, 2004).

Congregations deserve pastoral leaders who can help them find language to communicate, even when some feelings exist beyond words.

Fourth, the congregation should consider who else needs to be part of Sondra's care. Pastoral caregivers sometimes fall into the illusion that the ministry of care belongs only to them, not recognizing that the ministry of care belongs to the church as a whole. Hence, pastoral caregivers often work in isolation, becoming a greater risk to themselves and to others in the process. Finding ways to share intense situations with a trusted colleague, mentor, judicatory leader, pastoral counselor, or other professional can assist caregivers to reflect on what is happening in their spiritual, emotional, and physical life. In addition, recognizing that the congregation is called to share in the ministry of caregiving broadens an otherwise narrow focus on the pastoral relationship.

SEXUAL ETHICS AND COLLEGIALITY

Rev. Carolyne asks to speak confidentially with Rev. Manuel about a pastoral care matter. The two colleagues meet for coffee, as is their custom, and as the conversation unfolds, Rev. Carolyne discloses that she and Bill, one of her parishioners, have begun dating. They are both single and see nothing wrong with exploring their relationship at this point since they are not engaging in any "sexual activity." When Rev. Manuel asks how their relationship began, he discovers that the parishioner came to the pastor to talk about matters of vocational discernment. The relationship developed as they discovered mutual interests and commitments, and their feelings blossomed into romance. Rev. Carolyne asks Rev. Manuel to keep this information confidential out of respect for their collegiality and friendship.

With this conversation, Rev. Manuel and Rev. Carolyne have opened up questions of honesty and accountability with one another, their respective churches and parishioners, and their denominations. This case represents the quagmires that surround us in our everyday pastoral care. Many judicatories and sexual ethics policies for clergy prohibit all romantic relationships between pastor and parishioner outright, naming them inherently abusive. Yet, many clergy continue to enter into and condone such relationships, especially if a pastoral care relationship had not yet been established. Still others draw the line elsewhere. Many consider themselves the exception to the rule in one way or other. Whether this relationship eventually becomes a genuine, mutual, caring, intimate relationship or not, it carries within it the potential for spiritual and emotional harm to a parishioner, a church, a pastoral leader, and the larger community of faith, and therefore, it deserves the utmost care in response.[4]

How might Rev. Manuel, Rev. Carolyne, Bill, and others connected to this community move forward?

First, a relationship between a pastoral leader and a parishioner is, by its very nature, one of unequal power and imbalance. Rev. Carolyne carries more power in this relationship by virtue of her pastoral role and the fact that she is being financially compensated to care for the members of the congregation. In this case, Bill approached Rev. Carolyne with a genuine concern about his vocational life, and as a result, Bill is the more vulnerable party. As they moved from a pastoral to a romantic relationship, they opened up complex and competing roles with one another. For example, Rev. Carolyne can no longer fulfill her obligations as Bill's pastor, and he is left without a pastoral caregiver, perhaps causing him to seek another community in which to worship. Now that they are exploring a romantic relationship, they will need assistance in reimagining and renegotiating these power dynamics. They will need to be absolutely and concretely clear in disclosing and discussing these imbalances of power with the larger community, lest they harm not only Bill but also the congregation, judicatory, and many others who might be affected.

Second, creating a special relationship with a parishioner can be detrimental to the care that is offered not only to this parishioner but also to the whole of the congregation. Tending preferentially to one parishioner sets up dynamics within the congregation that can hinder pastoral and prophetic leadership in larger ways. Bill is no longer simply a member of the congregation but has become a special person in Rev. Carolyne's personal life. While some in the congregation may celebrate the budding romance, there are others who will feel slighted or who will experience less attention and energy from the pastoral leader. In addition, if Bill is involved in important committees of the congregation, his intimate relationship with the pastor will affect how people

4. The contextual factors related to this case also contribute to how one analyzes the appropriateness or damage of the potential relationship. For example, the question of whether this pastor serves a congregation that is 150 members in which she is the only pastor, or a large congregation of 1,000 members in which she is one of several pastors, might make a difference in how one begins to assess the ethics of the behavior. A more extensive analysis is beyond the scope of this chapter. For more conversation on this matter see Karen Lebacqz and Ronald G. Barton, *Sex in the Parish* (Louisville: Westminster John Knox, 1991), as well as the classic argument between Carter Heyward, *When Boundaries Betray Us* (Cleveland: United Church Press, 2000) and Marie M. Fortune, *Is Nothing Sacred? The Story of a Pastor, the Women He Sexually Abused, and the Congregation He Nearly Destroyed* (Eugene, OR: Wipf & Stock, 2008), presented together in Katherine Hancock Ragsdale, ed., *Boundary Wars: Intimacy and Distance in Healing Relationships* (Cleveland: Pilgrim, 1996). See also Cristina L. H. Traina's analysis of and commentary on this debate in *Erotic Attunement: Parenthood and the Ethics of Sensuality between Unequals* (Chicago: University of Chicago Press, 2011), 217–40.

experience and interpret his leadership, causing them to wonder if he is acting on behalf of Rev. Carolyne or on his own behalf. Again, these complexities do not necessarily suggest that it is impossible for Rev. Carolyne and Bill to explore their personal relationship, but it does require that they recognize that their romantic intimacy has an impact on many more people than just themselves. They will have to choose between attempted secrecy and a more open disclosure about Bill's changing role in the life of Rev. Carolyne and the congregation.

Third, this case raises questions and concerns about the larger covenantal framework in which Rev. Manuel and Rev. Carolyne reside. What happens in her relationship is not hers alone but has implications for the local church as well as the judicatory or denomination, particularly if something changes in the relationship or if charges of sexual harassment or misconduct emerge. Confiding in Rev. Manuel also means that both of them must now make decisions as stewards of the information, discerning how to interact with their judicatories and other clergy colleagues. Pastoral leaders need to discuss what it means to retain confidences with one another in much the same way that we differentiate a secret from a confidence in other aspects of pastoral care. Caregivers never agree to carry secrets about damaging relationships between children and adults, potential suicide, or homicide. In a similar manner, pastoral colleagues must be completely honest about the need to disclose to judicatory officials or others the potential harm that may result from an inappropriate sexual relationship between a clergy person and a parishioner. When secrets and fear rule our responses to sexual ethics, lives are often damaged. At a minimum, there are others who need to know about the development of this relationship because of the harm or potential for harm that rests within it. Strategizing about how to invite judicatory leaders, as well as the congregation, into the conversation is an essential element in response to this situation.[5]

As I have noted in this section, dating parishioners presents significant difficulty because of the increased potential for harm to someone who has been entrusted to a pastor's care, thus requiring extra diligence in response. It is imperative that Rev. Carolyne take extra steps to ensure that the pastoral care needs of Bill and her congregation are being met. Open and forthright communication with the congregation, including its leadership, can help to prevent rumors about secret relationships. Some may still judge Rev. Carolyne's

5. See Barbara J. Blodgett, *Lives Entrusted: An Ethic of Trust for Ministry* (Minneapolis: Fortress Press, 2008), for a good conversation on issues of trust, confidentiality and gossip. Also, Kibbie Simmons Ruth and Karen A. McClintock, *Healthy Disclosure: Solving Communication Quandaries in Congregations* (Herndon, VA: Alban Institute, 2007).

involvement with Bill as an instance of pastoral abuse, but at the very least, Rev. Carolyne should think creatively with colleagues and judicatory leaders about how to provide for Bill's pastoral care needs. For these reasons, it is rarely a good idea for pastors to develop intimate romantic or sexual relationships with parishioners. And, it is never helpful for those relationships to operate or function in secret, as is evidenced in the next case.

THE INTERSECTION OF OPPRESSIONS AND CARE

Rev. Beverly is the pastor of a 200-member church that is moderate in its theology and warm and inviting in its hospitality. She is one of the few women pastors in the region. In addition, Rev. Beverly lives quietly as a self-identified, and single, lesbian. Many in the church assume this about her and are open to her leadership, believing that the "don't ask, don't tell" model works best for this congregation. As Rev. Beverly begins to develop friends outside of the church, she gains a reputation as someone who can address the spiritual issues of coming out. Juanita, a woman from the community who is also lesbian and who is in a public position that requires her to keep her orientation quiet, begins to attend Sunday services. It does not take long for Rev. Beverly and Juanita to name a mutual attraction.

This case builds on the conversation above, yet it also highlights the intersection of oppressions in the context of care and sexual ethics and the difficulty of seeking justice on behalf of sexualized minorities. In a church and culture where homophobia and heterosexism exist, there is increased pressure on the pastoral leader who is same-gender-loving not only to remain in the closet but also to create relationships that are bound by secrecy. Intimate relationships created in this context are often fraught with additional burdens because of the lack of outside support, friendships, and other social structures that couples normally use to help sustain their relationships over time. Juanita and Rev. Beverly, for example, are encouraged not to be open and honest in their community of faith about their sexual orientation, making it even more difficult to be open and honest about their sexual needs. Because of the intensity of living in the closet or trying to live quietly on the edges of multiple communities, both of them are caught in a powerful moment of experiencing closets within the closets of their spiritual, emotional, and relational lives. This, in turn, increases the sense of intimacy and boundedness for each woman.

Second, this case raises a question about what sexual justice and spiritual wholeness looks like, particularly for those who live closeted lives or who find themselves increasingly marginalized because of their gender identity or sexual orientation. Coming out is often taken lightly in congregations that assume there are few spiritual elements to the process. In reality, living in the closet and discerning how to be authentic in the congregation are important dynamics for both Rev. Beverly and Juanita. Both of them are looking for a sacred place to share the fullness of their spiritual lives, yet they find themselves in a community of faith that encourages them to keep silent.[6]

Third, there are countless untold stories of parishioners who have experienced clergy sexual misconduct and not reported it because of the personal risk of outing themselves. Reporting the abusive pastoral leader requires parishioners not only to talk about something that is taboo (clergy sexual misconduct), but also to disclose their own sexual orientation at the same time. Hence, the reporting of misconduct is complicated by an extra pressure on the parishioner to disclose not only something about the pastor but also something about herself.

For those pastoral caregivers who live at the intersection of cultural boundaries, it is imperative that they have an adequate support system beyond the church. The practice of living in closets becomes dangerous for parishioners and pastoral caregivers alike, but until we have more open and affirming churches and denominations, the closets within closets will continue and harm will occur in the lives of many others.

Conclusion

It is helpful to remember three directives for pastoral caregivers, congregations, judicatories, and denominations. First, we must continue to nurture open and honest conversation about sexual ethics, not simply at the judicatory or denominational level but also within local congregations. Parishioners, who deserve pastoral care that is trustworthy and that nurtures their spiritual lives, are the ones most vulnerable and least often included in direct conversations about pastoral sexual ethics. This has to change if we are to work toward the building up of a holier and healthier community of faith.

Second, pastoral caregivers are always at risk of inappropriately crossing emotional, physical, or sexual boundaries in the context of pastoral care. The moment that any caregiver thinks she is not susceptible to such behavior, parishioners are already in danger. Caregivers must be vigilant about the power they carry into ministry, as well as proactive about caring for their own needs

---

6. There is significant and growing literature on spiritual issues and coming out. See Kathleen Ritter and Craig O'Neill, *Coming Out Within: Stages of Spiritual Awakening for Lesbians and Gay Men* (San Francisco: HarperCollins, 1992) and Leanne M. Tigert, *Coming Out Through Fire: Surviving the Trauma of Homophobia* (Cleveland: United Church Press, 2009).

for friendship, support, and intimacy. Communities of faith deserve pastoral leaders who know themselves and who care about the wholeness of their own lives.

Third, every pastoral caregiver needs a trusted colleague, friend outside of the church, pastoral counselor, or other professional with whom they can have conversations about the dynamics that emerge in the context of pastoral care. Without such networks of support, caregivers put themselves and others at greater risk

Communities of faith deserve pastoral caregivers willing to invite them into conversations that are meaningful, sometimes uncomfortable, and intended to increase the trustworthiness of a community's care. Conversations about the intersection of pastoral care and sexual ethics are important for the health and wholeness of communities of faith.

Discussion Questions

1. In what ways do you experience pastoral care as a place of healing *and* a place that carries the potential for boundary-crossings in ways that may damage others?

2. How do you understand and think about pseudo-intimacy? In what ways does pastoral care invite persons into sacred spaces that carry with them the potential for deep healing and deep betrayal? What kinds of things do you watch for in yourself or others that illuminate this dynamic?

3. In what manner do the intersections of various oppressions (for example, oppressions that are grounded in race, gender, class, sexual orientation and gender identity, physical or cognitive abilities, or emotional vulnerabilities) show up in your life or in the lives of those around you? In what way do these oppressions have an impact on pastoral care?

Recommended Readings

Blodgett, Barbara J. *Lives Entrusted: An Ethic of Trust for Ministry*. Minneapolis: Fortress Press, 2008.

Celenza, Andrea. *Sexual Boundary Violations: Therapeutic, Supervisory, and Academic Contexts*. Lanham, MD: Jason Aronson, 2007.

Heyward, Carter. *When Boundaries Betray Us.* Cleveland: United Church Press, 2000.

Lebacqz, Karen and Ronald G. Barton. *Sex in the Parish.* Louisville: Westminster John Knox, 1991.

McClintock, Karen A. *Preventing Sexual Abuse in Congregations: A Resource for Leaders.* Herndon, VA: Alban Institute, 2004.

Ritter, Kathleen and Craig O'Neill. *Coming Out Within: Stages of Spiritual Awakening for Lesbians and Gay Men.* San Francisco: HarperCollins, 1992.

Tigert, Leanne M. *Coming Out Through Fire: Surviving the Trauma of Homophobia.* Cleveland: United Church Press, 2009.

10

Ministry with Adolescents
Tending Boundaries, Telling Truths

Robert C. Dykstra

A pivotal scene midway through Laurie Halse Anderson's best-selling young adult novel, *Speak*, begins with the protagonist Melinda ("Mel") Sordino, a high school freshman, waiting at a city bus stop outside her school in a raging Syracuse snowstorm. The bus will take her to meet her mother, who manages a clothing store downtown and who insists it is time that Mel, a reluctant shopper, picks out some new clothes. As she stands in the swirling storm, Mel's intriguing art teacher, Mr. Freeman, pulls up in his Volvo and asks if she could use a ride downtown, which, he says, is on his way home.

FINDING SANCTUARY

Mel has experienced a painful introduction to high school life, the result of anonymously having called the police to a teen party at the end of the summer in a moment of justified panic after she was sexually assaulted there. Then, experiencing second thoughts about having summoned them, Mel escapes undetected just as the cops arrive. But from the perspective of every other kid busted for drinking at the party, including Mel's long-time girlfriends, none of whom knows of her assault, she has become a pariah forever banished to social isolation. Mel responds to the trauma of the acquaintance rape and her subsequent rejection by peers by, in a sense, *not* responding, that is, by maintaining a complete vigil of silence for months on end. She stops speaking. She bites her lips until they bleed in order to keep from talking, from telling. Her parents, her former friends, and her teachers appear not much to notice or care.

But Mr. Freeman is different. Melinda finds in him and his art class what Anderson describes as "sanctuary."[1] Mr. Freeman begins the first day of class by saying, "Welcome to the only class that will teach you how to survive. . . . Welcome to Art," and then turns to write the word "SOUL" on the chalkboard: "This is where you can find your soul, if you dare. Where you can touch that part of you that you've never dared look at before. Do not come here and ask me to show you how to draw a face. Ask me to help you find the wind."[2] He insists that art should *mean* and *do* something, and it becomes clear in his teaching that not every work of art succeeds in this. Art requires effort and skill.

As in every other of her classes, Mel remains silent in Mr. Freeman's. He does not press her to speak for months on end. But he notices her. He appears to sense there is a reason for her silence and somehow seems to honor her own timing in whatever her search for healing or hope. He observes Mel's attempts to let her art speak for her soul. He guides and encourages her when her work falls short. His art room becomes her silent sanctuary.

For some months into the school year, Mel's encounters with Mr. Freeman are limited to that particular classroom sanctuary. Now, however, at the bus stop in the snowstorm after school, he stops to ask if she could use a ride.

Risky Business

In my seminary course on the pastoral care of adolescents, novels such as *Speak* make for intense classroom discussion and debate. Coming to that point in the book where Mr. Freeman offers Melinda a ride downtown in the snowstorm, invariably the most common initial response—especially from women, though men often notice too—is a sense of heightened anxiety for Melinda. At age fourteen, she is already a victim of acquaintance rape and now, in Mr. Freeman's offer, is vulnerable to potential abuse from an adult man, albeit the one teacher she truly respects. Perhaps as a sign of the times and the result of unrelenting headlines over two decades that have underscored the prevalence of childhood sexual abuse, many—even most—students report having assumed that Mr. Freeman will in fact abuse Mel when she accepts his offer of a ride.

This reaction demonstrates heightened sensitivity to ways authority figures—including, of course, ministers—can abuse the power of their offices. It speaks as well to the absolute necessity of maintaining appropriate personal and sexual boundaries with those in one's care. The burden of vigilance in this regard falls exclusively on the minister, and not on the young person, in one's

1. Laurie Halse Anderson, *Speak* (New York: Puffin Books, 1999), 9.
2. Ibid., 10.

professional work with children and youth (and also, as many other chapters of this book affirm, with other adults).

But as our discussion goes on, some students complicate this initial picture by wondering whether Melinda will ever become capable of moving from a status of *victim* to one of *survivor* without taking the risk of trusting offers of help from concerned others. These students speculate that just as there are risks for her in accepting Mr. Freeman's offer, there may also be risks in refusing it. She has been traumatized, after all, and really could use some help. She needs, at some point, to find a trustworthy adult in whom to confide.

In addition, students note that they identify with Mr. Freeman. They anticipate the day, or have experienced it already, when they too find themselves in a position to reach out to an adolescent victim of sexual or other trauma in their care. But how might they accomplish this in an era of keen sensitivity to childhood and adolescent sexual abuse? Is not Mr. Freeman making himself overly vulnerable, personally and professionally, by offering a student a ride, however honorable his intentions may be and notwithstanding the attenuating circumstances of a swirling storm? The students explore whether as youth ministers they could or should ever allow themselves, even in a snowstorm, to offer a ride to a young person in their care. If so, do the rules change on a fair-weather day?

These are realistic but sobering questions that frequently lead students to admit to a sense of paralysis at the thought of reaching out to young people in need. But the thought of becoming essentially unable or unwilling to reach out strikes them as equally unacceptable, for what then would it mean to be a minister of the gospel? Can those who serve in the name of a crucified Jesus really expect a risk-free vocation? Still, can they ever expect to thrive under the microscope of constant self-scrutiny or communal suspicion? Of necessity, all ministers—especially those working with children and youth—navigate this minefield.

All of these concerns penetrate to the heart of one's conceptions of the nature of ministry, of what ministry entails and seeks to accomplish, and of its categorical possibilities for good and its incontrovertible capacity to harm. They are questions of safety and risk, of self-care and self-sacrifice, of body in relation to soul, of how we might become, as Jesus instructed his followers, "wise as serpents and innocent as doves" (Matt. 10:16).

Safe Speech

Christian ministry is an enormously complex endeavor. But ministry to and with adolescents is uniquely fraught even beyond its usual complexities. Given that adolescence as a stage of life is identified in large measure with a child's emerging sexual maturation, young people invariably face an onslaught of accompanying questions, concerns, mysteries, pleasures, and, as in the case of Melinda Sordino, traumas related to sex and sexuality. Newfound sexual anxieties and explorations encompass every aspect—physical, emotional, social, and spiritual—of their lives. Sex is on their minds. As a result, every adolescent has need of and can benefit from talking about sex and sexuality with a discerning and informed adult.

For this reason, it is simply not an option for ministers who work with adolescents to avoid all manner of conversation with them about sex or sexuality. Silence on the subject speaks volumes. To avoid such talk would betray not only a profound pastoral insensitivity to what are among the most pivotal concerns of young people in their care, but may even constitute another form of professional malfeasance. A minister's unwillingness or inability to engage an adolescent around his sexual concerns would be like failing to engage a bereaved widow around her grief.

To be sure, hesitations of caregivers around these kinds of sensitive conversations are well founded and, given the complexities and boundary concerns already noted, in some sense even laudable. It is exactly right to approach these matters with great intentionality and at least mild trepidation. Those who minister to youth will be helped by thinking about and talking through these kinds of issues in advance with mentors and peers, with church boards and parents of teens. They can enroll in relevant courses and continue to immerse themselves in ethical and scientific books on human sexuality and on pastoral care and counseling. Just as essential, they will benefit from experiencing firsthand the healing power that derives from talking openly with their own trusted counselor or from enrolling in a program of clinical education with a skilled supervisor in order to grow more comfortable in this arena.

Youth ministers take these steps toward growing more fully into their own skins not only for themselves but for the sake of helping young people. The goal is for the church to become a relational sanctuary, not unlike Mr. Freeman's art class, in which teens, in his words, may find their souls, if they dare, and touch that part of themselves they have never dared to explore before. In this sanctuary, they discover *safety enough to speak* about sexual questions and interests often deemed unsafe and unspeakable by church and culture, and to do so specifically with their ministers and spiritual guides. While the capacity to talk directly and honestly, without shame or shaming, about most any aspect of sex or sexuality rarely comes naturally to seminarians and ministers, it is an ability that can and must be beneficially modeled, practiced, and eventually mastered.

MESSY DETAILS

Ron Taffel, a psychotherapist who has written extensively about his work with adolescents, insists that in this kind of conversation with young people it does not work, especially at first, for the adult caregiver to sit back dispassionately and ask adolescents to talk about their *thoughts* and *feelings* on sexual matters. Instead, Taffel urges, the caregiver deliberately encourages young people to share *behavioral details* of their sexual practices and experiences: "The more details you have," he writes, "the better you will be at getting through to an adolescent. . . . Details enliven the relationship. They also enhance our ability to be smart—not just another clueless adult."[3]

But he goes on to recognize how difficult this is for most adults because these details seem "too shocking, explicit, or raw to hear." He asks:

> Could you imagine talking to your parents about kids "hooking up" at a party? About blow jobs, group sex, genital piercing?
>
> Could you imagine voicing concerns about your sexuality or coming out as "bi" or gay?
>
> . . . Thirty years ago, teenagers lacked the vocabulary, the openness, and, perhaps most important, the blessing of the culture at large to bring up such subjects with their parents. That is why many mothers and fathers today cannot imagine that *their* kids would ever be willing to talk to them.
>
> They're wrong. In fact, graphic exchanges are precisely the kinds of conversations teenagers continuously have with one another. . . . *So get the details.* They allow you to enter into a dialogue with enough information to offer advice.[4]

Taffel recognizes that while obtaining specific details from youth "might seem more difficult if you're a male counselor dealing with a teenage girl or a female therapist dealing with a teenage boy," this is simply no longer a problem for most young people, who grow up having close friends of both sexes and talking openly with them about sex.[5] Instead, inhibitions across genders are

3. Ron Taffel, *Breaking Through to Teens: A New Psychotherapy for the New Adolescence* (New York: Guilford, 2005), 115.

4. Ibid., 115–16.

5. Ibid., 117–18.

much more likely to burden the therapist or youth minister than the adolescents in one's care. "If kids are asked specific questions," he says, "they will be relatively uninhibited about revealing graphic details of their lives. Today kids simply don't have deep inhibitions about discussing drugs, sex, and rock and roll."[6] Only by first engaging the mundane and messy details, he suggests, can adults ever expect to enter eventually into the kinds of conversations to which caregivers usually aspire and deem most important, those in which questions of feelings, power, self-perceptions, faith, and values come to the fore.

FULL-FRONTAL ENGAGEMENT

In his book, *Breaking Through to Teens*, Taffel provides numerous examples of what he calls this kind of direct, "full-frontal engagement" with young people.[7] One of these involves Sheila, a fourteen-year-old girl trying to decide whether to continue in a relationship with a "hot" two-letter athlete idolized by her friends. While the relationship could provide Sheila entry into the inner circle of "cool," her ticket of admission requires that she drink a lot of alcohol and "go down" on the boy in the process. Taffel acknowledges that it was not easy at first for him to ask about the explicit details of Sheila's experience. For her part, however, Sheila had no such qualms. As a result, Taffel gained specific insight into how best to help her:

> I learned that her 'hot' boyfriend would suddenly cool down. Right in the middle of making out, he'd leave the room to play videogames for a while. I learned that Sheila had to take her clothes off, but he refused to remove anything. He made sure all the other kids knew what had gone on within an hour of hooking up with Sheila. After a while, we both realized how empty Sheila felt during the experience. All of this allowed me to offer better advice. 'I know it's tempting, but I don't think you should be with him. Yeah, at first people are impressed. But it makes you feel horrible afterwards. You make *him* seem important—not you!'
>
> If [Sheila and I] had not struggled over the details, possible strategies, and specific interactions our exchange would have had little traction.[8]

6. Ibid., 119.

7. Ibid., 67–72.

8. Ibid., 119–120.

Readers initially may be inclined to respond to Taffel's injunctions by suggesting that while it may be possible and even necessary for professional therapists to get into these kinds of messy details with adolescents, ministers and other youth workers—whose vocational contexts and expertise differ from those of therapists—could never afford to do so. After all, isn't it possible that what he is proposing might, for some, become voyeuristic or lead to arousal? And what would happen if young people were to reveal things that press up against limits of confidential communication or that threaten their own or others' safety? Aren't therapists prepared to deal with such complexities in ways that ministers (or art teachers like Mr. Freeman, for that matter) are not? Shouldn't ministers focus instead on adolescents' spiritual concerns?

The anxieties expressed in these questions are both real and revealing. While it may be the case that talking (or even writing) about sex could be construed, in the broadest sense, as a sexual activity, such a claim would neither privilege therapists in their capacity to engage in such conversations nor exempt ministers from needing at times to do so. To be sure, the approaches of therapists, ministers, or art teachers are not simply interchangeable. Each vocation brings distinctive perspectives and resources to bear in how it addresses human suffering. Ministers, unlike some therapists, do not engage in long-term counseling and instead typically expect just one or at most a few meetings with parishioners. This does not mean, however, that ministers offer second-class care. To the contrary, the value and impact of even one such conversation can be enormous, especially because ministers, unlike many therapists, generally come to know the persons they counsel over a longer period of time and in broader family and community contexts. They can often assume a wider network of congregational support and draw on common worship experiences or church educational and fellowship programs to undergird what is shared in a counseling session.[9]

While ministers to youth should not expect to engage every adolescent one-on-one in what Taffel describes as messy details of the young person's sexual experiences, they need to be capable of direct and honest conversation around sexual concerns with individuals and in group settings when circumstances warrant and when called on to do so. Ministry, like therapy, propels its practitioners into situations where sexual suffering must be openly addressed. The question becomes not whether but how well those who seek

9. An excellent, more complete discussion of important boundary issues in pastoral counseling, including the value both of a limited number of sessions and of paying close attention to the space in which they occur, is found in Donald Capps, "How to Manage Boundaries," in *Giving Counsel: A Minister's Guidebook* (St. Louis: Chalice, 2001), 189–239.

to assist young people will do so. As Mic Hunter, a psychologist in St. Paul, once told me, "A therapist [and, I would add, a minister, and probably also an art teacher] *gets* to do what other people don't get to do and *has* to do what other people don't want to do." Ministry is difficult. This is one reason that ministers, like therapists, benefit from being accountable to professional colleagues, counselors, and supervisors in the details of their work.

For his part, Taffel acknowledges the discomfort (though not any potential for arousal) he used to feel in engaging adolescents in sexually revealing conversations. Therapists, too, like ministers and other adults, must practice navigating awkward conversations with youth. Regarding questions of confidentiality, Taffel provides especially helpful guidance that involves a surprising approach fully applicable to pastoral conversations with teens. He argues that even as adolescents need to earn privileges of unconditional privacy at home, proving to their parents over time that they are worthy of greater and greater degrees of trust, so must they earn increasing degrees of confidentiality in therapy. He writes, "The more a child gains the trust of his parents and me, the more privacy I can promise in our relationship."[10] Caregivers first need to be able to trust that young people are safe before they can assure them of relative privacy. Taffel is up-front with adolescents in their first meeting:

> "Tell me what you *don't* want me to reveal to anyone." Rather than promising that all topics are confidential, I continue, *"We'll talk about what you don't want me to say, and we'll figure out how to handle it together."* To this, I add the following reassurance: *"I'll never mention anything to your parents before you and I talk it over, unless I believe . . . and here's the part you already know . . . that you or someone else is in immediate danger."* [11]

Because working with adolescents is different from working with adults, Taffel reverses here usual therapeutic assumptions about privacy, moving from "everything except danger will be kept private" to *"nothing* is private unless you tell me it is—and even then, we'll need to talk about it."[12]

All this is to say that the intimacy or awkwardness of the subject matter and important questions of privacy need not circumvent a minister's engagement with adolescents around their sexual concerns. To return to Taffel's case of Sheila, to suggest that her struggle is only or primarily a sexual one that

---

10. Taffel, *Breaking Through to Teens*, 150.

11. Ibid., 151, emphasis in original.

12. Ibid., 151, emphasis in original.

necessitates intervention by a psychotherapist, and not one that engages her soul or spirit and thereby infiltrates the domain of a youth minister, is not only to miss the sensitive (and spiritually wise) mutual understanding at which she and Taffel ultimately arrive but to perpetuate a bifurcation of sex and spirit, of body and soul, that likely contributes to her problem—one mirrored in the larger church and culture—in the first place. This intricate and inevitable commingling of body and spirit is equally evident in the fictional protagonist Melinda Sordino's vigilant silence in response to her rape and subsequent rejection by peers in *Speak*. Her lips bleed to prevent her soul from crying out, even as they simultaneously signify its expression. Adolescents' sexual lives and concerns are resolutely spiritual, their spiritual lives wholly embodied.

TELLING TRUTHS

In *Passionate Marriage*, a book I frequently assign to help seminary students grow more comfortable in speaking openly of their own sexual interests and concerns, David Schnarch, a renowned sex therapist, describes how his clients initially compelled him to notice this intricate link between human sexuality and spirituality. In his early years of practicing sex therapy with couples, he says, he did not consider himself to be much interested in spiritual matters. But as he helped his clients become more sexually self-attuned and intimate in their marriages, he noticed that they also started to articulate newfound excitement about spiritual growth and freedom. As their sexual lives improved, in other words, they felt compelled to speak in terms of spirit:

> When I help people become more differentiated—especially helping them reach their sexual potential—they often bring up the topic of spirituality spontaneously. At first I was surprised because I never talked about spirituality—and still don't, unless clients raise the topic. The couples were also surprised, since many did not consider themselves to be "spiritual people." Others had a strong dislike for organized religion. . . . I couldn't explain to them or myself why this was happening. . . .
>
> Why was it that helping people differentiate—balancing our two basic urges for self-direction and communion—seemed to trigger their spiritual yearnings? My problem was that, like most people, the very notion of science turned my mind away from thinking about differentiation in terms of spirituality. I'd fallen into the common tendency to divorce science from Spirit.[13]

But then, he says, a client encouraged him to read theological works by Sebastian Moore, a Benedictine monk "who talks about desire out of fullness."[14] Schnarch writes:

> Since the early days of Western civilization, sex and spirit have been kept at a "safe" distance at best—and at worst, pitted irreconcilably against each other. Where Christian theology's view of spiritual desire is devoid of sensuality, Moore's is unabashedly erotic. His view is more in keeping with the spiritual "passion" of saints. Spiritual awakening is often assumed to involve transcending all desire—but some desires set us free. . . . This is why Moore argues that spiritual enlightenment is marked by the ability to desire more fully rather than by the absence of desire.[15]

The intricate bond between body and soul that Schnarch's clients—and a Benedictine monk—helped him to articulate is one that adolescents, too, will benefit from discovering, however assailed and fragile this connection has become over centuries of Christian teaching and Western culture and despite inherent risks in current attempts to convey it.

In *Telling Truths in Church: Scandal, Flesh, and Christian Speech*, Mark D. Jordan addresses with stunning candor and eloquence the clergy sexual abuse scandals that convulse the Christian church. He calls the church to account for its history of abuse and its use of theological words and authority as weapons to overpower the weak. But the alternative, for Jordan, is not silence. Rather, he challenges us to acknowledge that all authentic speech about God, all theology, is of necessity halting and incomplete. This is because at its heart theology is a language of love, an account of our encounter with God in which "it seems that the closest analogy in human experience . . . is erotic union." "Near love," Jordan writes, "language ignites or evaporates."[16] Thus, he says, "when the ablest Christian writers attempt to narrate their loving encounters with God, they do so by falling back on the incandescent languages of erotic passion."[17] Nearing passion, language invariably fractures.

---

13. David Schnarch, *Passionate Marriage: Love, Sex, and Intimacy in Emotionally Committed Relationships* (New York: Owl Books, 1997), 391–92.

14. Ibid., 396. See Sebastian Moore, *The Fire and the Rose Are One* (New York: Seabury, 1981); and Moore, *The Contagion of Jesus: Doing Theology as if it Mattered* (Maryknoll, NY: Orbis, 2007).

15. Schnarch, *Passionate Marriage*, 396.

16. Mark D. Jordan, *Telling Truths in Church: Scandal, Flesh, and Christian Speech* (Boston: Beacon, 2003), 66–67.

17. Ibid., 66.

I take this deep connection between the sexual and the spiritual, about which Schnarch and Jordan write, to suggest that while it is not easy to speak of things sexual (nor of things spiritual, in Jordan's sense) with adolescents in our care, in part because it is not easy to put words to love, we have no alternative than to attempt to speak them. The church will not protect its adolescents from abuse by a reactionary refusal of all manner of conversation about sex, however necessarily halting and risky that conversation will be. One lesson of the scandals is that the bifurcation of body and spirit still lingers. Another is that ministers have need to learn intently first to *listen* like Mr. Freeman and then, like Melinda Sordino, to learn anew to *speak*.

CONCLUSION

Is it wise for a youth minister to offer an adolescent a ride in a snowstorm? As a general rule, I would discourage my students from doing so. Might there be exceptions to the rule? As with most rules, the answer is almost certainly yes.

As Melinda Sordino settles into Mr. Freeman's car, she holds her freezing hands in front of the heating vent. He notices and turns the fan to high. He tells her she did a good job on a recent sketch and that he is seeing a lot of improvement in her work.[18] She responds at first, predictably, with silence. Then, for the first time, she begins to speak: "I don't know anything. My trees suck." To her consternation, even more words begin to slip out: "You said we had to put emotion into our art. I don't know what that means. I don't know what I'm supposed to feel."[19]

Such are the modest headwaters of a healing conversation—one truncated, to be sure, and not yet touching expressly on acquaintance rape or peer rejection. But the beginning of something new and hopeful in this risky business of searching out souls, if we dare.

DISCUSSION QUESTIONS

1. What are some of the risks both for adolescents and for ministers in pastoral conversations about sexual concerns? Are there risks inherent in not talking, or not being able to talk, about them?
2. Do you remember having an honest conversation with an adult about your sexual questions in your own adolescence? If so, was the conversation helpful? How did it come about? From your perspective

---

18. Anderson, *Speak,* 121.
19. Ibid., 122.

today, what did the adult do right, and what might he or she have done better, in that conversation?

3. In what ways might you hold yourself accountable both for maintaining appropriate boundaries with youth in your care and for telling truths in church about sex and sexuality in your present or future ministries?

RECOMMENDED READINGS

Capps, Donald. *Giving Counsel: A Minister's Guidebook.* St. Louis: Chalice, 2001.

Dykstra, Robert C. *Counseling Troubled Youth.* Louisville: Westminster John Knox, 1997.

Dykstra, Robert C., Allan Hugh Cole Jr., and Donald Capps. *The Faith and Friendships of Teenage Boys.* Louisville: Westminster John Knox, 2012.

———. *Losers, Loners, and Rebels: The Spiritual Struggles of Boys.* Louisville: Westminster John Knox, 2007.

Edgette, Janet Sasson. *Adolescent Therapy That Really Works: Helping Kids Who Never Asked for Help in the First Place.* New York: W.W. Norton, 2006.

Schnarch, David. *Passionate Marriage: Love, Sex, and Intimacy in Emotionally Committed Relationships.* New York: Owl Books/Henry Holt and Company, 1997.

Taffel, Ron. *Breaking Through to Teens: A New Psychotherapy for the New Adolescence.* New York: Guilford, 2005.

11

Teaching Sexual Ethics in Faith Communities

Boyung Lee

Susan, a minister of Trinity Church in a suburban town, was at a local ecumenical clergy meeting. Kirk, a nondenominational pastor, expressed serious concerns and distress about several recent teen pregnancies at a local high school. He insisted that churches must teach the kids about Christian morality, including that sexual intercourse should be done only within marriage relationships. He has been a strong voice for abstinence-only sex education in town. While listening to Kirk, Susan was grateful that she has Emily, the Sunday school director who has initiated a sexuality education program, Our Whole Lives (OWL), for the children and youth in her church. In spite of initial resistance from some parents, which she addresses individually, the program seems to be going well. Susan thinks that because of the program and Emily's leadership, her church kids appear to have healthier attitudes toward sex and sexuality. At least no one has gotten pregnant so far. Susan hopes and prays that Emily will continue to work with her throughout her tenure at Trinity Church.

Helen, a minister of St. Mark's Church, a mid-size, wealthy suburban congregation, is visited by John and Beth, a couple in their early forties, for marriage counseling. Helen is surprised by their request for counseling, as the couple appears to be happily married. Beth complains that John is addicted to pornography. Every day he spends hours in front of a computer, and now he insists that Beth join him. Beth tried a few times, but never enjoyed it. She feels that this is not a healthy way for a Christian couple to spend their time together. On the other hand, John believes that watching pornography with Beth energizes their relationship. While listening to them, Helen feels very uncomfortable because the couple's descriptions are at times too intimate, and thus she decides to refer them to a licensed marriage counselor. In fact, this is not the first couple that has talked to her about pornography problems in their marriage. Each time, Helen has referred them to professional counselors, and she will continue to do so. She feels that she cannot provide counseling on a topic that makes her feel uncomfortable.

Jeff is a divorced minister in his late thirties, serving a small congregation named First Church. He is a good looking, intelligent, and warm-hearted minister—and loved by everyone in his congregation. Having learned that he needs to keep clear boundaries with his parishioners regarding his divorce process at his previous church, he made it clear from his very first Sunday at First Church that he does not date parishioners. However, Tina, a divorced woman in Jeff's age group, does not think Jeff's policy is reasonable. Personally, she finds Jeff very attractive, and wants to develop a more intimate relationship with him. She approaches him several times, inviting him to coffee, movie or dinner. Each time he has declined her invitation, asking her to come to his office if she needs to talk to him. Finally while Jeff greets other parishioners in the narthex after the morning worship service on a Sunday, Tina asks him out for a date. Jeff pretends that he does not hear what she said. He does not want to embarrass her in public and plans to continue to ignore her sexual advances.

The above cases illustrate seemingly reasonable understandings of boundaries and clergy sexual ethics. Although we hear about some clergy members violating their boundaries through sexual behaviors with parishioners, they are the minority. Jeff clearly understands the importance of keeping boundaries. Helen, as most clergy members learned in pastoral care and counseling classes in seminary, refers her parishioners to professional counselors, rather than guiding them when she feels she is not equipped to do so. Susan supports Emily's balanced sexuality education program at her church, even against some parents' resistance.

However, each of the ministry approaches above is problematic. Susan implicitly teaches her congregation that sexuality education is only for the young and only the work of the education committee. Whether persuasive or not, Susan has a pastoral obligation to her colleagues and to all her congregants to bear witness to what she thinks it means to live in today's world as a Christian. This includes creating forums where the faithful can address controversial, potentially divisive, topics like sexual ethics.

Jeff, like many clergy, treats the maintenance of clergy sexual boundaries as something pertaining only to clergy, rather than practices important for congregants to understand and support. By taking this approach, he misses opportunities to help his congregation to understand the nature and importance of clergy sexual ethics. Even if the maintenance of appropriate boundaries sometimes falls solely on his shoulders, the corporate participation of his congregation in their upkeep is best for all concerned. Even if this particular exchange with Tina was not suitable, Jeff needs to foster such "teachable moments."

Helen immediately thinks of outside experts when confronted with a subject she finds personally uncomfortable and is not prepared to address. This is certainly appropriate, but like Jeff, she has allowed her choosing the "right" path to handle the matter to shut down her own continuing education in this regard. Undoubtedly, other parishioners struggle with similar issues, and she needs to develop a long range educational plan for herself and the congregation in this regard.

All of these responses are not uncommon in mainline churches, where I observe that the topics of sex, sexuality and sexual ethics comprise what educators call a "null curriculum." That is, their absence from the curriculum teaches something by not teaching anything. In this chapter, I propose several pedagogical strategies to move Christian sexual ethics—including clergy sexual ethics—from the null curriculum to a more explicit curriculum of the church.

Sexual Ethics: A Null Curriculum of the Mainline Church

The word curriculum is derived from the Latin verb currere, meaning "to run together." In educational contexts, this connotes a course to be run. Conventionally, "a course to be run" is narrowly identified with the printed textbooks, lesson plans, and explicit educational activities by which an institution oversees a course of study. In contrast to this conventional definition, in his book Educational Imagination, noted curriculum theorist Elliott W. Eisner introduces broadened concepts of curriculum and offers a comprehensive definition of curriculum from which the mainline churches will greatly benefit. Discussing the subject of curriculum in public educational contexts, Eisner says that each school offers students three different curricula: (1) the explicit curriculum, one that is the actual content, consciously and intentionally presented as the teachings of the school; (2) the implicit curriculum, one that, through its environment, includes the way teachers teach and interact with students; and (3) the null curriculum, those ideas and subjects in educational programs that are withheld from students.[1] By leaving out options and alternatives, the school narrows students' perspectives and the range of their thoughts and action. Maria Harris, a religious educator, describes null and implicit curricula this way:

1. Elliot W. Eisner, *The Educational Imagination: On the Design and Evaluation of School Programs*, 2nd ed. (New York: Macmillan Publishing Company, 1985), 378.

> [The null curriculum] is the curriculum that exists because it does not exist; it is what is left out. But the point of including it is that ignorance or the absence of something is not neutral. It skews the balance of options we might consider, alternatives from which we might choose, or perspectives that help us see. The null curriculum includes areas left out (content, themes, points of view) and procedures left unused (the arts, play, critical analysis). The implicit curriculum, in contrast, does not leave out areas and procedures. It simply does not call them to attention. They are there, operative in the situation but left unnoticed.[2]

Thus the explicit curriculum, which is often regarded as the entire curriculum, is only one facet of teaching. In fact, Eisner points out that the implicit and the null curricula might have more influence over students than does the explicit curriculum.[3]

Let us look at the above cases through the lens of these three curricula. Susan is proud that her church offers a progressive sex education program for the young. Trinity Church is explicit about the importance of including sex education as a part of faith formation for young people (explicit curriculum). Trinity Church's explicit choice of a very progressive curriculum implicitly but boldly states that they respect young people's desire to have more sophisticated information on sex, sexuality, sexual pleasure, reproductive choice, and other sex-related topics relevant to their lives (implicit curriculum). However, without saying a word, Trinity Church and their minister, Susan, are teaching the congregation that education in general—and sex education in particular—is only for young people (null curriculum). Although the OWL curriculum has versions for adults, Trinity Church uses the ones for children and youth alone. Moreover, Susan does not seem to be directly involved in her church's educational ministries. Her church's education programs seem to be the domain of the education director and committee. This null curriculum sends a strong message to her congregation that adults do not need education that connects their faith and their sex lives. It teaches that the church does not need to be concerned with the sexual ethics of its adult members. It encourages people to assume that the church is not a place that they should talk about sex, sexuality, and other related issues, even when these are pressing issues to some of them. The result is that without formally adopting it, Susan's church is practicing a

2. Maria Harris, *Fashion Me a People: Curriculum in the Church* (Louisville: Westminster John Knox, 1989), 69.

3. Eisner, *The Educational Imagination*, 378.

"don't ask, don't tell" policy. Whether this is their intended message or not, Trinity Church is teaching a strong value by not teaching anything to its adults about sexuality.

Similar messages and lessons are taught by Helen and Jeff through their implicit and null curricula. Helen's explicit curriculum is that family counseling and marriage therapy are an integral part of Christian lives and may include professional help. Referring her parishioners to experts, she implicitly teaches her own ethical values as clergy: she cares about their well-being more than her desire to have privileged access to their lives (implicit curriculum). However, despite the fact that several couples' marriages are in crisis due to pornography and, probably, other serious sexual issues, Helen does not create an educational venue for people struggling with these issues, wherein couples might be alerted to the dangers of sexual addictions and to the professional resources in the community designed to address them in depth. Her quiet actions with individual couples, though well-intended, loudly teach her congregation that sexuality and sexual ethics cannot be discussed in public at St. Mark's Church.

Jeff also teaches a very similar lesson to his congregation. Sexuality and sexual ethics are to be handled individually, not publically, and therefore, First Church is not responsible for teaching these topics. The church may teach the Bible and Christian traditions and practices to adults, but it does not explicitly teach Christian perspectives on issues such as sexuality. In sum, through their implicit and null curricula, these ministers have taught their congregations that sex education and discussions of sexuality are only for the young, and that adults need to handle issues related to sexual ethics personally or outside of the church.

These unintended teachings by well-intentioned pastoral leaders push the topics of sex, sexuality, and sexual ethics to the margin of the life of the church, making them a perpetual null curricula of the church. The sad reality is that many mainline ministers and church leaders do not pay much attention to their implicit and null curricula in their approaches to general ministries and to sexual ethics in particular. Therefore, in the following section, I offer pedagogical suggestions for moving sexuality and sexual ethics from the null curriculum to a more central place in the life of the church.

SEXUAL ETHICS: MOVING FROM NULL TO EXPLICIT CURRICULUM

The above unintended teachings of the three ministers on sexual ethics are closely related to general misunderstandings about faith education.[4] In most mainline churches I find three major misunderstandings: (1) education is something intended solely for the young; (2) learning happens mainly through studying a set of curriculum resources, and teaching is the province of a committee, generally made up of young or parent-aged adults under their leadership; (3) and adult faith formation happens mainly in one-on-one contexts or through personal efforts. Therefore, to move sexuality out of the null curriculum of the church, it is necessary to clarify these misunderstandings.[4] Specifically, I propose the following pedagogical tips:

PEDAGOGICAL TIP 1: HELP PEOPLE RECOGNIZE THAT CHRISTIAN RELIGIOUS EDUCATION IS A HOME FOR SEXUALITY AND SEXUAL ETHICS EDUCATION.

To have sexual ethics be central to the life of the church, we need to reorient our understanding of education. The English word "education" comes from the Latin e– (out) and ducare (to lead)—"to lead out." The root word for education tells us that education is to help people find a truth that is already within them. It is not just a teacher transmitting knowledge to the young, but, rather, it is helping learners, regardless of their ages, to remember what they know and to reflect critically on this in their present life contexts. Furthermore, education is meant to develop something new for the future. In other words, it is an activity that involves people's whole being, including their immediate and larger life contexts.

Similarly, Christian religious education seeks to help people to be in right relationship with God through Jesus Christ, and to incarnate that relationship in their lives, in addition to gaining biblical and theological knowledge at Sunday school. Thomas Groome, a prominent Christian religious education scholar, calls this an ontological activity, as it involves people's ontos, their very "being." Groome argues that good Christian religious education includes knowing Jesus in a personal relationship through faith, but it also illumines the practices of justice, mercy, and love associated with this relationship. Through informative, formative, and transformative activities, Christian religious education seeks to complement people's whole way of being in the world, including questions about who they are and how they live.[5]

Thus, sexuality and sexual ethics become necessary topics of the church's overarching curriculum. If Christian religious education is concerned about people's whole way of being in the world, helping people to have clear

---

4. For further descriptions of these misunderstandings, see my forthcoming book, *Restoring Community in the Mainline: A Pedagogical Guide to Communal Faith and Ministry* (Louisville: Westminster John Knox, 2013). Karen Tye calls these misunderstandings myths. See Tye, *Basics of Christian Education* (St. Louis: Chalice, 2000), 48–67.

5. Thomas H. Groome, *Christian Religious Education: Sharing Our Story and Vision* (New York: Harper and Row, 1980), 3–19.

theological perspectives on their own sexuality, sexual relationships, and ethics is an integral part of the curriculum of the church. Therefore, before or while faith community leaders introduce classes on sexuality and sexual ethics to their congregations, it is important to help members broaden their understanding of the scope and content of Christian religious education.

PEDAGOGICAL TIP 2: ASSESS YOUR CONGREGATION'S NEEDS, AND PRESENT SEXUALITY AND SEXUAL ETHICS IN A WAY THAT IS CLOSELY RELATED TO DAILY LIFE ISSUES.

Since sexuality and sexual ethics are not easy topics for many people to talk openly about, it is important for leaders to create a safe learning community for them.[6] Pedagogically, leaders need to present topics related to sexuality and sexual ethics in a way that their congregation feels are closely related to their daily life issues. Jane Vella, a prominent adult education scholar and activist, provides twelve principles for adult learning. Among those principles, she lists "needs assessment" as the first principle.[7]

Assessing people's needs is often confused with assessing what they want. Needs assessment can include what people want to learn, but what they want is not necessarily the same as what they need. When we present subjects like sexual ethics, we sometimes meet resistance. Some people resist because of the discomfort that subject matter like sexuality creates, and others resist, because they think the topics are not explicitly Christian. Still others acknowledge its importance but do not consider sexual ethics as relevant for their contexts. For these people, sexual ethics is not what they want to learn, but from a teacher's perspective, it is what they really need to learn. Therefore, figuring out effective and appropriate ways of teaching the subject is crucial for the success of sexuality education. This process of discernment characterizes what Vella calls needs assessment.

According to Vella, needs assessment is specifically listening to the voices of both teachers and learners: "adult learners must take responsibility to explain their context; the teacher must take responsibility to contact learners in every

6. Debra W. Haffner and Kate M. Ott, *A Time to Speak: Faith Communities and Sexuality Education*, 2d ed. (Fort Wayne, IN: Christian Community, 2005), 27. http://religiousinstitute.org/sites/default/files/study_guides/timetospeak07.pdf.

7. Jane Vella, *Learning to Listen, Learning to Teach: The Power of Dialogue in Educating Adults* (San Francisco: Jossey-Bass, 2002), 3–27. For a detailed description of needs assessment, see pp. 5–8 and 57–70. Vella's twelve principles are: (1) needs assessment; (2) safety; (3) sound relationship; (4) sequence and reinforcement; (5) praxis; (6) respect for learners as decision makers; (7) learning with ideas, feelings, and actions; (8) immediacy; (9) clear roles and role development; (10) teamwork; (11) engagement; and (12) accountability.

way possible, see them at work if possible, and be clear about what she can offer them."[8] This means that teachers should listen deeply to people's stories and meet them where they are. In this sense, it is understandable why Vella defines needs assessment as the "participation of the learners in naming what is to be learned."[9]

Spending time with congregants through formal and informal contacts, learning about their life circumstances, identifying their fluency and comfort level in sexual ethics, assessing their learning styles, listening to their pressing issues and concerns, praying with them, and so on are all possible ways of assessing their needs. Through these contacts, we can identify why some are resistant to sexuality education and what will be the most appropriate ways to introduce sexual ethics to them. Ministers are in a very privileged position to collect this data because, through an official pastoral care format like visitation, we have much easier access to our parishioners' lives than other professionals.

> PEDAGOGICAL TIP 3: HELP PEOPLE TO HAVE A SHARED OWNERSHIP OF
> THEIR LEARNING ABOUT SEXUALITY AND SEXUAL ETHICS.

Beyond collecting data through personal contacts, it is important for congregations to feel that they own the learning process and its contents. Vella says that adults learn better when they feel respected as decision makers about their learning.[10] Even when the program on sexual ethics is initiated by a pastoral leader, if the members of the church feel that they are the co-creators of the curriculum, their involvement in the program is increased. For this, I propose the following methods as ways to create a communal ownership:

Anonymous Personal Story-Telling. Invite your congregation to anonymously submit their own stories about how they as Christians understand sex, sexuality, and sexual ethics. They can write about their own journey, about how they came to terms with their own sexuality, and sexual ethics. Also, invite them to identify the issues in sexuality and sexual ethics with which they are personally struggling, and what topics about which they feel uninformed and want to know more. These narratives can provide the teacher with ideas about the specific topics that might well be addressed and the level of intensity appropriate to the class.

---

8. Ibid., 5.
9. Ibid., 4.
10. Ibid., 71–84, 129–148.

Media Library on Sexuality and Sexual Ethics. Ask your congregation to submit an annotated list of media that expresses their own views of sexuality and sexual ethics. They can be movies, music videos, YouTube clips, songs, or writings. Using pop media to frame sexuality and sexual ethics gives several advantages. First, for people who do not want to share their personal stories in public, using pop media to express their own views or struggles gives them a level of anonymity and objective perspective. Second, since not everyone learns best through lectures and discussions, using different genres of pop media provides an easier access to people with different learning styles.

Share a Survey and Learning Bibliography.[11] Once your class on sexuality and sexual ethics has launched, ask the participants via e-mail for a set of three or four questions that are later forwarded to the entire group of participants. Invite them to describe (1) their involvement in sexuality-related work and projects such as a local sexual violence prevention work, and so on; (2) their hopes for learning after attending the first class, when the "syllabus" for the course was introduced; and (3) their reflection on their best learning experiences in sexuality education, particularly experiences that helped them to form a Christian sexual ethic.

These methods are designed to help your congregants to be the subjects of their own learning about sexuality and sexual ethics, and they also serve as needs assessment tools. Needs assessment and shared ownership of the learning process stand in reciprocal relationship to one another.

PEDAGOGICAL TIP 4: BRING DISCUSSIONS OF SEXUALITY AND SEXUAL ETHICS
EDUCATION TO WHERE PEOPLE ARE.

Although people form their identity as Christians and learn Christian values and behaviors through being a part of a community that embodies Christian values in its worship, fellowship, and service, I observe that most clergy and faith communities do not see these venues as teaching moments. Creating an educational program that considers the three dimensions of the curriculum—explicit, implicit and null—means that everything we do as a faith community can be and should be regarded as a teaching moment.

People who only come to Sunday morning worship service will get interpreted messages on Christian sexual ethics through the sermon, music, prayer, and other elements of worship that are carefully planned to present different dimensions of sexuality and sexual ethics issues. Those who learn

11. Adopted from ibid., 247–249.

better through interpersonal relationships will also learn about the subject by participating in a church's special or ongoing fellowship programs, such as a fellowship meal followed by film discussions that address another dimension of sexuality. While we study Christian sexual ethics, the church can also focus on a service project in connection with a local shelter for survivors of sexual or domestic violence, or with a teen pregnancy support center. The point here is that if we think that education is much bigger than learning through books in a classroom context (a currently dominant model), many more people can benefit from our educational ministries, and in turn, it will create cohesiveness in our life together as a community of faith.

CONCLUSION

Among many possible ways to teach sexuality and sexual ethics in the church, I have focused on four fundamental pedagogical principles that can also be applied to teach different subjects. It is my conviction and belief that a good education that is faithful to its original meaning, will follow a just process and create justice for all. As long as we approach sexuality and sexual ethics in compartmentalized and ghettoized ways in the church's education ministries, our teaching will only reach a select few. Sexuality and sexual ethics should be a shared way of living in faith communities rather than topics of isolated study. For that, I hope that ministers and faith community leaders approach their ministries with an educator's consciousness.

DISCUSSION QUESTIONS

1. Reflect on your own approach to issues related to sexuality and sexual ethics. What are the explicit, implicit and null curricula in your current ministry context?

2. How does your church talk about or teach sexuality and sexual ethics? Who is the audience? Who is missing? In what format is it taught? Reflect on ways to reach out to more people, and to make it more central to your congregation's life. What will be the obstacles and stumbling blocks?

3. Based on your knowledge of your congregants, what will be the appropriate ways to conduct a needs assessment for the teaching of sexuality and sexual ethics?

4. Reflect on the obstacles and stumbling blocks that you identified, and compare them with your implicit and null curriculum. Do you see any associations between them? If not, does your list suggest any

insights in terms of creating a shared ownership of your sexuality and sexual ethics education?

RECOMMENDED READINGS

Haffner, Debra W. and Kate M. Ott. *A Time to Speak: Faith Communities and Sexuality Education*, 2nd ed. Fort Wayne, IN: Christian Community, 2005, http://religiousinstitute.org/sites/default/files/study_guides/timetospeak07.pdf.

Lee, Boyung. "Teaching Justice and Living Peace: Body, Sexuality, and Religious Education in Asian-American Communities." *Religious Education* 101, no. 3 (Summer 2006): 402–19.

McClintock, Karen A. *Sexual Shame: An Urgent Call to Healing*. Minneapolis: Fortress Press, 2001.

———. *Shame-Less Lives, Grace-Full Congregations*. Herndon, VA: Alban Institute, 2011.

Measor, Lynda. *Young People's Views on Sex Education: Education, Attitudes and Behaviour*. With Coralie Tiffin and Katrina Miller. New York: Routledge, 2000.

Religious Institute on Sexual Morality, Justice, and Healing. "10 Ideas for Breaking the Silence Around Sexuality." http://www.religiousinstitute.org/acting-out-loud/10-ideas-for-breaking-the-silence-around-sexuality

Taverner, William J., ed. "Faith, Religion, and Sexuality Education." Special issue, *American Journal of Sexuality Education* 6, no. 1 (2011).

12

Touch Not Mine Anointed

F. Douglas Powe

Too frequently, we hear or read about stories of sexual impropriety in African American congregations. One of the most visible stories in the past few years took place at New Birth Missionary Baptist Church and involved Bishop Eddie Long. At one point, New Birth had over 20,000 members and was one of the most influential congregations in the country. In 2010, four males filed suit against Long for "using his power to influence them into sexual relationships with him."[1] When the allegations first came out, the bishop told the New Birth congregation that he would fight the allegations tooth and nail. In fact, when he preached the Sunday immediately following the first allegations he said, "I've got five rocks and I haven't thrown one yet."[2] Long used the Bible story of David and Goliath to set himself up as an underdog character like David, even though he was the person with the power in the congregation. Long eventually settled with his accusers out of court, and it is assumed, as a part of the undisclosed settlement, that the parties are not allowed to discuss any part of the case.[3]

The fallout from the case is widespread. Vanessa Long, his wife, filed for divorce, causing Long to step down from the church for a period. Long and his wife did eventually reconcile, and she dropped the divorce suit. Dr. Bernice King, the daughter of Dr. Martin Luther King Jr., left New Birth shortly after the allegations. New Birth experienced a decline in membership after the allegations and public scrutiny from around the United States.

1. Edecio Martinez, "Bishop Eddie Long Settled So He Didn't Have to Go on Record, Says Lawyer," *CBS News*, May 27, 2011, http://www.cbsnews.com/8301-504083_162-20066740-504083.html.

2. "Bishop Eddie Long: Minute-by-Minute Recap of Long's Comments Sunday," *Atlanta Journal-Constitution*, September 27, 2010, http://www.ajc.com/news/news/local/bishop-eddie-long-minute-by-minute-recap-of-longs-/nQkX9/.

3. Edecio Martinez, "Bishop Eddie Long Settled."

The impact of this one case upon the African American Christian community and the wider community should not be underestimated. It played out like a soap opera for those inside and outside of the African American community. Much has been written about this drama, but I am hoping to use it as a starting point for challenging African American congregations to think about the importance of congregational healing following ministerial misconduct as it relates to evangelism. To this end, I will briefly outline two points: (1) the reasons I believe the Davidic narrative is paradigmatic for some African American clergy in leadership; and (2) seeking a holistic way forward that includes the Davidic narrative, but promotes accountability. Specifically, I develop the notion of the prophetic resistance needed for the community to move forward toward healing and justice. An evangelistically healthy congregation must balance anointed leadership with prophetic accountability.

DAVIDIC NARRATIVE

Eddie Long's infamous line, "I've got five rocks and I haven't thrown one yet," is emblematic of his attempt to portray himself as the underdog and not the aggressor. He hoped to alter emerging church-wide and public perceptions by offering an interpretation that appeared to be rooted in a biblical narrative. Long is right in turning to the Davidic narrative as a way of understanding African American clergy leadership and the implications for evangelism. He is wrong in the way he articulates the narrative. Broadening the Davidic narrative gives a more holistic picture for understanding the connection between identifying with David and African American clergy leadership.

CHOSEN

In this portion of the Davidic narrative (1 Sam. 16:1-13), David is chosen by God to be the king of Israel. Samuel is sent to the house of Jesse and calls in each of Jesse's sons until David (the youngest son) finally comes in from the field and is chosen by God. Samuel anoints David. The language of being chosen has significance in Israel's history and also for the African American community, which has adopted many of the Hebrew narratives as their own.

Dwight Hopkins describes the adoption of Hebrew narratives from a black liberationist perspective as a "rereading of the Bible" in favor of the downtrodden.[4] James Cone's black liberation language is even stronger in his earlier works, wherein he argues that God sides with blacks.[5] My point

4. Dwight Hopkins, *Introducing Black Theology of Liberation* (Maryknoll, NY: Orbis, 1999), 23.

is that the idea of contextualizing the Hebrew text by connecting it to the African American tradition as a means for understanding the current situation a community faces is not something new within the African American community. In terms of a liberation model, the ability to contextualize Scripture helped African Americans to make it through the perils of slavery. The challenge in many African American congregations comes when a community narrative—such as, God has chosen the Hebrew people—is interpreted as applying unambiguously to individuals, meaning the understanding of what it means to be chosen is no longer primarily a communal perception.[6]

This is particularly true for the many African American congregations that tend to be hierarchical and dominated by male clergy. In her book, *How Long? How Long?*, Belinda Robnett writes, "Gender was a defining construct of power relations and shaped the structure of the [civil rights] movement. Men and women clearly had differentiated access to structural and institutional power. Dr. King, for example, had access to the primary institutional hierarchy, or formal leadership, track of the Black church."[7] Her point is that gender and power within African American congregations are often inextricably connected.

African American male clergy are often perceived as God's anointed and, therefore, granted greater power than those who were not "chosen" by God. In her *Religious Dispatch* blog, Sarah Posner posits that Long and others interpret Psalm 105:15—"touch not mine anointed"—as evidence that God has chosen them and not others.[8] The positives related to this ideal of being chosen are the respect and authority given some African American male pastors. The challenges related to this ideal of being chosen are the respect and authority given to some African American male pastors. To use biblical language, it is a blessing and a curse, because the way in which the authority is used has implications for the ecclesial community. For example, a pastor can "strongly encourage" parishioners to do whatever is asked because he is seen as God's chosen.[9] It is not that showing respect for the pastor is bad, but when it becomes an unearned right or an unquestionable expectation based upon an

5. James Cone, *God of the Oppressed* (Maryknoll, NY: Orbis, 1975), 33.

6. I am not claiming that a communal of understanding of being chosen is not problematic. I discuss issues related to a communal understanding in "Is Liberation the Starting Point for African American Theology of Evangelism?" *Union Seminary Quarterly Review* 62, no. 1 (2009): 1–16.

7. Belinda Robnett, *How Long? How Long? African-American Women in the Struggle for Civil Rights* (New York: Oxford University Press, 1997), 19.

8. Sarah Posner, "Eddie Long Plays Victim," *Religion Dispatches,* September 26, 2010, http://www.religiondispatches.org/dispatches/sarahposner/3419/eddie_long_plays_victim/

understanding of the pastor being chosen, it can create conditions in which there is little check against abuse (for example, Eddie Long).

On the flip side, such authority enables pastors to make decisions that may move the congregation forward. A pastor can decide unilaterally that the congregation will get involved in fighting for a just wage for all workers and that the church will offer resources toward this end. Pastors can use their authority for furthering the community's outreach. Even in this instance, however, they must be careful that they do not cross the line towards abuse.

The bottom line is that, in this portion of the Davidic narrative, there is a shift in the object of the adjective "chosen" from a communal to more individualistic referent. The resultant implications for the way a pastor uses authority means autocratic leaders can point to the Bible as the source of their leadership style. For African Americans looking for strong leadership, congregations led by individuals like Long can be a Mecca of sorts. The numerical and financial success of these congregations supports the pastor's claim of being chosen by God, and more people are attracted to the congregation. This can be an evangelistic Mecca when things are seemingly going well, but can quickly turn into a mirage when things start going wrong. In cases like Eddie Long, the downward spiral impacts not only New Birth but also congregations trying to live out discipleship in other ways. I will return to this point later in the essay.

CHARISMA

African American clergy who identify with David tend to be charismatic. I believe Long identified with David immediately after the allegations because David was charismatic. Even before David became king, the people were attracted to him. In 1 Samuel 18:6-7, the text depicts the Israelites dancing and singing about how David shines brighter than Saul. There is something special about David that attracts other individuals.

David is a warrior's warrior. David is the one who defeated Goliath. In the same vein, many charismatic pastors are perceived as celebrities. These pastors are the embodiment of success and "spirituality" at the same time. In other words, the combination of earthly success and being anointed from on high sets these pastors apart from others. Jonathan L. Walton, in a CNN interview with Rick Sanchez, makes this point about charismatic leaders like Long: "It creates a paradigm where all the women want the pastor and all the men want to be like

---

9. One could argue that the parishioners want to do certain things for pastors (I am not speaking of inappropriate things), and I am not saying that is wrong. I am suggesting that a pastor can use influence in a way that makes some parishioners feel like they must do it as a part of being obedient to God.

the pastor."[10] Obviously Walton is exaggerating, but we do not want to miss his point.

Marcia L. Dyson, in her article, "When Preachers Prey," provides even further insight into the phenomena described by Walton. She writes:

> We may even view the minister as we would a glamorous entertainer or celebrated professional sports star. I have witnessed sisters who rush for those seats in the first three rows in the sanctuary—to be close to the *preacher* [emphasis mine]. We become sanctuary cheerleaders, rooting the minister on. Later we swell the reception line, wanting our Sunday best acknowledged by a hug from the man of God. "You're sure lookin' good there, sistah" is the admiring refrain many of us look for from the minister. Often women press notes into his palm: "Call me tonight, please. I can only confide in you."[11]

Dyson describes how some preachers are perceived like sports superstars or great entertainers. It is something about these figures that draws folk to them, particularly women. These preachers have a certain charisma about them; as such, even if they are married, other individuals are drawn to them sexually.

Dyson correctly points out the negative side of this attraction. Speaking autobiographically, she talks about a preacher who came on to her when she was going through a tough time in her marriage. She did not give in to this preacher's attempts to seduce her, but she did not return to that congregation and stayed away from church for two years. It is extremely problematic for preachers to use their charisma for sexual gain because it often destroys the faith of those victimized, as well as that of others who hear about such matters.

While the charisma of a pastor may initially attract individuals to a congregation, it is this same charisma that can destroy a congregation if misused. It not only destroys the faith of many in the congregation but, depending on how widely known the story of indiscretion is communicated, confirms for those outside of congregations why the church is "no good." The preacher is no different than a hustler on the street trying to get one over on people.

10. "RD on CNN: Eddie Long's Manly Protestantism," interview of Jonathan Walton by Rick Sanchez, *Religion Dispatches*, September 22, 2010, http://www.religiondispatches.org/dispatches/professorsdesk/3399/rd_on_cnn__eddie_long_s_manly_protestantism/.

11. Marcia L. Dyson, "When Preachers Prey," *Essence* 29, no. 1 (May 1998): 120.

Lost is any sense of the church as a place of healing or well-being. The church becomes like any other institution trying to take advantage of those it can. Unfortunately, many preachers do not see that they are misusing their charisma toward this end, nor do they see the damage they are doing inside and outside of the congregation. This physical, mental, and spiritual damage has a long-lasting impact.

COERCED

The final way that I believe some African American clergy identify with David is by attempting to alter the narrative's conclusion. As the story unfolds (2 Sam. 11:1-15), David uses his position of authority as king to call Uriah's wife Bathsheba to the palace to sleep with him (an act we understand today as sexual abuse). It is bad enough that he sleeps with another man's wife, but David has Uriah killed by placing him on the front line with no support. When things go awry in congregations, many preachers, like David, will try to coverup their misuse of power by altering the narrative. There are often multiple strategies employed to alter the direction of the plotline in order to avoid the prospect of being held accountable.

For example, at the end of 2011, Long stated he was stepping down to work on his marriage, but he came back after just a few weeks and, in a bizarre ceremony, is crowned a king by a supposed rabbi named Ralph Messer. Anthea Butler describes Long's coronation as "one more chapter in his quest to remain in a dead pulpit attached to a dead megachurch."[12] Those, like Long, who resist being held accountable for their actions contrive to rewrite the events surrounding their effort to stay in power.

This manipulation of the events often extends to how they control the victims. Christa Brown writes, "It is inherently manipulative for any pastor to use a congregant, even an adult congregant, for his own sexual ends. In some states, such conduct may even be considered a felony, just as it would if a psychologist or physician were to sexually exploit a patient."[13] Brown's point is that many pastors who are involved in sexual misconduct manipulate parishioners by developing a narrative to fit the pastor's sexual needs.

Brown describes a pastor who manipulated his disciples by telling them he had to check them out "spiritually, scholastically, socially and sexually."[14]

12. Anthea Butler, "Watch the *New Birth* Throne: Eddie Long Declared 'King' by 'Rabbi,'" *Religion Dispatches,* February 1, 2012, http://www.religiondispatches.org/dispatches/antheabutler/5641/watch_the_new_birth_throne:_eddie_long_declared_'king'_by_'rabbi'/.

13. Christa Brown, "Eddie Long: The Real Scandal is Even Bigger," *Religion Dispatches*, September 27, 2010, http://www.religiondispatches.org/archive/3429/eddie_long:_the_real_scandal_is_even_bigger.

This deceptive narrative seemed truly beyond question not only to the victims but also to others around the pastor who never questioned his inappropriate actions.[15] The ability of some pastors who are engaged in inappropriate behavior to manufacture a false or misleading interpretation of it allows them not only to fool the victims but also those who should be holding congregational leaders accountable to their pastoral obligations.

The impact on congregations of this confusion is often a split between those who buy into the alternative (deceptive) narrative and those who seek a narrative that will hold the pastor accountable. When pastors are not held accountable for sexual abuse, those seeking the latter tend to leave their congregations, if not the church altogether, and many with no ecclesial affiliation remain unchurched. Those who buy into the alternative narrative will often stay and even defend the narrative, even when presented with evidence to the contrary. This is why some congregations will experience sharp decline in membership and little growth but not completely fall apart.

I have suggested that some African American clergy identify with the Davidic story from the perspective of being chosen, charismatic, and coercing the narrative. These congregations often experience decline as a result of their inappropriate behavior. This decline is not only internal, but also impacts those outside of the church who, as a result of this betrayal of trust and of the truth, do not perceive the church as a safe space for moving them toward wholeness, particularly sexual wholeness.

PROPHETIC RESISTANCE

I started this chapter with the scriptural reference: "Touch not mine anointed." This text is rarely read in context; it says, "Touch not mine anointed, and do my prophets no harm" (Ps. 105:15). The prophet has high authority that should be respected in the same way as the one who is anointed. In the Davidic paradigm that I am suggesting, it is important to include the prophetic voice that speaks against abusing those without power.

Right after David attempts to contrive the narrative to fit his needs, Nathan, the prophet of God, calls David to accountability through a parable (2 Sam. 12:1–23). David may be anointed, but Nathan has as much power as David. Unfortunately, this is where the parallel breaks down between David and many African American clergy. Although Nathan-like figures may call pastors to accountability, church leaders often do not follow David's lead and

14. Ibid.
15. Ibid.

admit to wrongdoing. In many instances, they simply continue to proclaim their innocence or settle out of court and make no statements (for example, Eddie Long).

When there is no accountability, the ecclesial community cannot experience the healing it needs. Those outside of the church do not see it as a safe space for seeking healing. If some African American clergy are going to identify with David, then they need to buy into the whole narrative and not just the parts they like. African American congregations have to become safe places for those who are truly seeking healing and an affirmation of their humanity.

Kelly Brown Douglas picks up on the importance of an affirmation of humanity and the prophetic resistance needed for the community to move forward toward healing. Douglas specifically develops a sexual discourse of resistance against homophobia.[16] I believe her ideas can be expanded in ways that move ecclesial communities toward a better understanding of developing a prophetic response. For example, Douglas is interested in "exposing the relationships among race, sex, and power."[17] I would add gender to the list, and believe that a discourse around gender, race, sex, and power is an important step in moving the community toward a healing prophetic response.

Let me suggest a few ideas, based upon Douglas's work, for moving African American congregations toward prophetic resistance. First, Douglas argues that the real enemy is injustice.[18] All too often, some congregations lose sight of the real enemy and get sidetracked by ancillary matters. For example, the Long case became more about the accusers seeking financial gain than it did about the possible injustice of sexual misconduct. If African American congregations are going to be safe spaces where all are welcome, then we must address the real enemy of injustice, even when it challenges our very core. This signals to those outside of the congregation that this is a place and space where I can go for healing.

Second, a discourse on resistance can help African American congregations to understand how they are perpetuating hegemonic power.[19] The civil rights movement focused on examining the ways in which some Anglos used power over African Americans to deny their humanity. In congregations, we have to do the same and examine how some are preventing us from moving toward healing for all in the community. This will require an open dialogue, bringing

16. Kelly Brown Douglas, *Sexuality and the Black Church: A Womanist Perspective* (Maryknoll, NY: Orbis, 1999), 106.

17. Ibid.

18. Ibid.

19. Ibid., 107.

together those inside and outside of the congregation. It has to be an ongoing dialogue, one in which all sides are open to listening and not simply giving talking points. I believe doing this also signals to those outside the congregation a willingness to move toward healing.

Obviously, a lot more can be said on how a congregation moves toward prophetic resistance, but starting with addressing the real enemy and examining the way power is used will make a difference. The prophet Nathan did both of these in the parable: he told David and was able to convict David of his wrong-doing. It is my hope that, by having such a conversation, some congregations will become convicted and engage both the inside and outside communities in new ways—ways that will lead to healing and justice!

CONCLUSION

Many African American congregations are struggling today, and I believe one reason is an inability by some to help move those inside and outside of the community toward healing. In this chapter, I outlined some of the challenges facing the African American church in prophetically resisting distortions of power by pastoral leaders, as well as some of the benefits of doing so. Congregations that are willing to resist giving in to abuse by those who are "anointed" will become safer spaces, able to deal more faithfully with issues of injustice confronting the entire community. And this prophetic resistance may be a balm for evangelistic health, moving struggling African American congregations to a path of thriving.

DISCUSSION QUESTIONS

1. In your congregation, how is the authority of the pastor validated or affirmed through the use of biblical narrative? Does that narrative allow room for prophetic resistance? To whom is the pastor accountable, other than God?

2. What ideas for promoting congregational healing do you discover in reading Nathan's conversation with David in 2 Samuel?

3. What are some ongoing efforts that your congregation can do to promote healing for the entire community affected by the sexual misconduct of a ministerial leader?

4. Do you agree that accountability in the form of prophetic resistance to the unchecked power of a pastor can lead a congregation from struggling to thriving? How is this form of truth-telling related to evangelism?

RECOMMENDED READINGS

Brown, Christa. *This Little Light: Beyond a Baptist Preacher Predator and His Gang.* Cedarburg, WI: Foremost, 2009.

Douglas, Kelly Brown. *Sexuality and the Black Church: A Womanist Perspective.* Maryknoll, NY: Orbis, 1999.

Dyson, Marcia L. "When Preachers Prey." *Essence* 29, no. 1 (May 1998): 120–22.

Dyson, Michael Eric. "When You Divide Body and Soul, Problems Multiply: The Black Church and Sexuality." In *The Michael Eric Dyson Reader*, 219–37. New York: Basic Civitas Books, 2004.

Pinn, Anthony B., and Dwight N. Hopkins. *Loving the Body: Black Religious Studies and the Erotic.* New York: Palgrave MacMillan, 2004.

13

Mission and Sexuality

Steven Charleston

We don't need a generation of Christians who believe that the aim of Christianity is personal happiness. Nor do we need a generation of Christians who believe that the aim of Christianity is sexual purity. Rather, we need a generation of Christians who are on a mission from God.[1]

The statement above was part of a blog I discovered while researching Christian attitudes toward mission and sex. It was written by Pat Hannon, associate dean of the chapel at Indiana Wesleyan University. It was intended for his campus community as part of an answer to a very simple question he posed: what does sex have to do with mission? Good question. If mission is not about making us happy in our own comfort zone by seeking to transform the world into our image, and if it is not about our imposing our own values of sexual behavior on others, then what is Christian mission about when it engages us in areas of human sexuality? The answer can be found in how we define mission and how we understand sexuality.

For centuries the church has sought to balance human sexuality with the call to mission. Sex and mission have been intimately connected ever since Jesus saved an adulterous woman from stoning. The teachings of the church have consistently engaged the sexual ethics and customs of the cultures in which Christian mission has participated. Mission is not value neutral in regard to sexuality but reciprocal in how it both has shaped and been shaped by sexual conduct.

The relationship between mission and sex begins with the recognition that they are both integral parts of human life. "The church does not have a mission," write Stephen B. Bevans and Roger P. Schroeder in their book,

---

1. Pat Hannon, "Missional Sexuality," *Faith On Campus* (blog), January 31, 2012, http://faithoncampus.com/missional-sexuality/.

Prophetic Dialogue: Reflections on Christian Mission Today, "but the mission has a church."[2] In other words, mission is not a noun but a verb, not a thing we take into the world as a fixed message but an experience we share in living out what we believe. "If mission precedes the church," they argue, "and constitutes it as such . . . mission will be understood as part of Christian life."[3]

The same can be said of sexuality. It is a part of life, a part of who we are and what we do as humanity. Therefore, the intersection of Christian mission and sexuality occurs not only in theologies and theories but also in the very fabric of our everyday lives as communal creatures living in a shared history.

This encounter has never been easy. Sex and mission have a long and often painful history. As the early Christian community began to include a wide variety of cultures within its life, it carried a great deal of sexual baggage with it. The sexual mores of ancient Israel that were interwoven with the very earliest Christian communities quickly engaged the Roman and Hellenistic cultures as the faith spread around the Mediterranean. Compromises and conflicts marked the development of Christian theology that resulted from these engagements, perhaps most clearly in the writings of St. Augustine. His legacy, however, only continued the process as Christian mission moved into Europe, Russia, and India. Over time, the sexual content of mission became fused with European colonialism. As the religious evangelism of Europe spread out to cover the globe, it took the sexual behavior of the colonizers with it.

Anglican scholar Kevin Ward has sketched this intertwined relationship between European sexual practice and missionary expansion in a way that graphically illustrates the deep historical roots of these two forces:

> The colonial encounter can itself be understood as a violent sexual intrusion (both in literal and metaphorical terms). The colonised were subject to unwelcome 'desire' on the part of the colonizer. . . . This involved not only the abuse of women for sexual gratification but also the entrapment of women in a colonial economic system. . . . In such cases, the relationship between coloniser and colonised was a denial of the humanity of the colonised.[4]

2. Stephen B. Bevans and Roger P. Schroeder, *Prophetic Dialogue: Reflections on Christian Mission Today* (Maryknoll, NY: Orbis 2011), 16.

3. Ibid.

4. Kevin Ward, "Gay People as Missionaries: An Interrogation of the Silences" (unpublished paper), http://www.anglicancommunion.org/listening/book_resources/docs/kevin ward.pdf.

The first step in any contemporary mission activity across cultural borders should be to remember, recognize, and reflect on this kind of powerful human experience. The sexual exploitation of others in a mission context is not ancient history but an ever-present possibility when cultures, genders, and ministry roles are brought together in the intimacy of spiritual interaction. Mission is not an objective activity but a deeply subjective translation of one value system into contact with another. Mission and sex have had a bad reputation historically, and even if this reputation is not fully deserved, it is, nevertheless, a reality that we need to acknowledge, a lesson we need to learn.

To illustrate how this lesson remains a challenge for Christian mission, let us consider two contemporary mission encounters and examine how subtle these lessons may be.

Case One. Church of the Redeemer, a largely European-American, suburban congregation has become aware of the growing population of immigrant families from India in their neighborhood. Many of the members of Redeemer work with Indian colleagues in the technological industries that employ the majority of people in this mid-sized California city. The parish decides to make a special effort to welcome Indian families. The clergy and lay leaders are careful to make sure that this outreach is not misunderstood as an attempt to "convert" their guests but only to offer hospitality. The plan is to host a pot-luck—a "welcome to the neighborhood" supper—on a Saturday evening, with no intentional Christian content. The leaders are proud of their sensitivity to the cross-cultural dynamics of past missionary history and look forward to a fun experience. However, on the evening that several Indian families arrive, the planners are distinctly aware of a chill in the room between the hosts and guests, even though they have welcomed the newcomers with warm smiles and hugs. They are confused because, in their estimation, they did not do anything to press their religious views but treated their Indian neighbors as they would anyone else from their own parish community.

Case Two. A church youth group has been preparing to go on a special mission trip to a Native American reservation. The teens will be accompanied by adult leaders. As part of the preparation, the pastor has made sure that all those going on the trip have had an orientation to the historical and cultural sensitivity she believes they will need to be appropriate guests on the reservation. They have discussed the old missionary attitudes and the racist history that have colored the relationship between the Native community and Europeans. The mission group is clear that it is going only to offer support to Native people as "equals" and that a big part of the expectation is that the group will "learn more than they can teach." The parish leaders are confident that they have entered into this mission relationship in a respectful manner, but are hurt and surprised when, after only a few days on the reservation, they are invited to leave because they have offended the elders with what is vaguely described as "loose moral conduct."

Neither of these two cases seems to be inherently insensitive. The leadership has, in fact, been conscientious in their planning, precisely because they are aware of how Christian mission has violated other cultures in the past. In this contemporary context, the leaders have sought to be careful not to push "conversion"; they have sought to avoid racial stereotypes that would make others feel they were being condescended to; they have tried to learn the lessons the past has taught them about how appropriate cross-cultural mission should be carried out. They have done all of these things well and for good reasons, and they are understandably upset and surprised when things seem to go wrong. What has happened? What mistakes have they made? In both cases, the answer involves the hidden dimension of sexual values.

In the first instance, the good people at Church of the Redeemer tried too hard to treat their Indian guests as if they were part of the family. The warm hugs at the door as people entered were designed to show how welcoming the community could be, but unintentionally those embraces crossed over the invisible space set by traditional Indian custom between genders and age groups. The hugs were too intimate. Rather than making the Indian families feel at home, these familiarities violated the values of interpersonal contact dictated by Hindu custom, especially for the older generation of Indian parents or grandparents.

Sexuality is a spectrum. It involves not only physical contact between persons but also the social and psychological worlds they inhabit. Sexuality is not just about sex but also about who we are raised to be, who we think we have become, and what we believe we are to do. It may take very obvious forms, such as prohibitions against what is considered immodest clothing, but it can also take subtle forms, such as prohibitions against forms of touch. In Thailand, for example, it is considered offensive to lay hands upon another person's head, an intimacy taboo that would make the Christian "laying on of hands" for healing problematic.

Part of mission planning involves not only considering past missionary activity but also the occasional, almost unconscious experiences involved in these interactions, such as greeting and/or leave taking. These simple actions can convey subtle, sexually-laden content that can easily escape even the most conscientious cross-cultural planners. It may be worth remembering that inappropriate encounters between persons often begin with the subtle, apparently innocent engagement of gesture, touch, and personal space.

The second case underlines this point. When the youth group went to the Native American reservation, they also planned ahead to be culturally sensitive. They intentionally reminded themselves of the colonial past that had so marred early-Christian missions. They tried to adapt to the traditional Native culture and were careful in every interaction they had with their Native American hosts. But still the relationship unraveled. Why? In this instance, it was not what the group did or did not do in interaction with the "others"—the Native American host community—but rather what the group did only among themselves, without being aware they were stepping on any culturally sensitive toes. One of the hallmarks of some Native American social-sexual value systems is modesty, not only in the manner of dress but also of behavior. A teenager in short shorts and a halter top being outwardly talkative and overly informal may seem relatively harmless to a Euro-American, but this same behavior can cross the line for very traditional Native elders.

There are times when sexuality comes down not to an action but simply to a *presence.* A woman standing still in a sun dress without a hat in some areas of the Vatican or Riyadh will still attract the negative response of the community there, even if she never moves or says a word. A pastor sitting alone in a closed room with a parishioner who feels the presence of clerical authority may easily slip over into power dynamics that are sexual even if that was never intended.

When we speak of the subtle cues that are contained in the social or sexual interaction between persons of different cultures, we must be aware that those cues can be transmitted just in being who we are. What is normative public presence for us may not be for others. Therefore, mission becomes negotiation. At times, we may have to negotiate our ability to be authentic to our own values while being acceptable to the values of others. The reaction received by the youth group was not because of something they did or did not do; it was just for being who they were. They had spent time considering how they might be perceived for the *past,* for the history of mistakes that were made between the church and other cultures, but they had failed to think how they might be seen in the *present,* as unintentional signalers of negative cultural messages. Compromise for the sake of mutual respect is the name of the game in the borderlands of sex, mission, and culture.

Given these two illustrations of just how subtle and delicate the balance between sexuality and mission can be, it is fair to ask: How can any Christian person or group find a way forward? How can we carry out mission in a way that maintains appropriate boundaries and respects cultural differences? Part of the answer may lie in how we understand ourselves as missionaries, as agents of mission. If we know what we don't want to be (the stereotype of the insensitive colonizer sexually abusing others), how do we find an image, a language, to describe what we do want to be?

In her book, *Godbearing: Evangelism Reconceived*, Elaine Robinson gives us a choice. She redefines the practice of mission as the role of Godbearing, of embodying the message we seek to convey:

> Godbearing, as the fruit of the Spirit blossoming within us, points us toward a threefold orientation or attitude toward life: 1) *bearing God* or bearing the renewed image of God within, 2) *bearing witness* or bearing faithful witness to God, and 3) *bearing suffering* or bearing with Christ the world's suffering. To be a follower of Christ means that we reorient or redirect our lives to be agents of life and love. We become planters of seeds and sowers of healing and wholeness.[5]

The reorientation Robinson describes is the negotiation process required in the praxis of sexual values and mission action. "Godbearing" allows us language to speak of the three fundamental elements of that process: (1) a way to embody our message in an authentic presence that is also respectful of others; (2) a way to reach out in witness with others that invites them in but does not violate their integrity; and (3) a way to share in a common experience that transcends both cultures with a universal message of hope, healing, and wholeness.

The effective exercise of mission within the fluid context of human sexuality and cultural values requires that we keep these three principles before us at all times. Are we a Godbearing presence, even if we never say a word? Are we making a Christlike witness when we do act or speak? Are we truly sharing in this experience with others in a way that transforms us both through the life and love of God? These become the formative questions that shape our planning and exercise of mission. They help us to disclose the deeper aspects of our values, attitudes, and behavior. They call us to be even more attentive to exactly the same criteria in the lives of those we encounter. But most importantly, they invite us to understand the nexus of sex and mission for what it can actually be: a transformative encounter.

Robinson says that "the reality of human life is that we find ourselves struggling against forces that undermine wholeness."[6] What she describes as the mission of Godbearing is the process by which we achieve wholeness.

5. Elaine A. Robinson, *Godbearing: Evangelism Reconceived* (Cleveland: Pilgrim, 2006), 85.

6. Ibid., 77.

And wholeness, according to the World Council of Churches (WCC), is a defining characteristic of mission. As the WCC's document "Together Towards Life: Mission and Evangelism In Changing Landscapes" describes it, Christian mission must strive for healing and wholeness as it "sees a human being as a multidimensional unity . . . the parts that have become estranged need to be reclaimed."[7] As human beings, we become whole when we do not feel that there is a part of us that must remain hidden. We are whole when we are not afraid that we will be exploited. We are whole when we are free to share ourselves completely, in trust and in safety. We are whole when we can celebrate ourselves as being created in the image of God.

As Christians, our mission is not only to experience this depth of wholeness in our lives but also to do all that we can to help other human beings experience this gift, this abundant life, in their own experience. The transformative nature of our sexuality is not that it gratifies us in isolation but that it bonds us in community. Godbearing means taking up the identity we each have as sexual beings and living that identity out with dignity, responsibility, and integrity. It also means recognizing the humanity of others through compassion, justice, and respect. Mission and sexuality are both integral aspects of shared life. Living them out through the gospel is, as Bevans and Schroeder describe the spirituality of inculturation, "tremendously hard work and will shape and stretch those who engage in it in ways almost infinitely beyond imagining"[8]—for it requires us to suspend judgment, practice listening, and learn the lessons of diversity. But ultimately, the effectiveness of mission is determined by the depth of this awareness. The wholeness we seek emerges when we have such an appreciation of the values, customs, and preferences of the other that we begin to enter into their worldview. We begin to see the world through their eyes, and this experience, as the reciprocal power of mission in action, transforms "us" as it transforms "them." The encounter becomes not the one-way street of earlier colonial forms of evangelism but the life changing reorientation of Godbearing. In essence, it becomes radical hospitality.

We do not always associate sexuality with hospitality, but viewed through the lenses of mission, that is very much what it becomes. Intimacy implies an inviting in. If intimacy is mutual, respectful, and consensual, then it is a welcoming of the other into the most personal places of life for both parties.

---

7. World Council of Churches Central Committee. "Together Towards Life: Mission and Evangelism in Changing Landscapes." 2012, http://www.oikoumene.org/en/resources/documents/wcc-commissions/mission-and-evangelism/together-towards-life-mission-and-evangelism-in-changing-landscapes. See esp. secs. 33, 43, 48, 77, 90.

8. Bevans and Schroeder, *Prophetic Dialogue,* 95.

It is a negotiation. It is an exploration. It is a sharing of awareness. Therefore, the nature of the transformation that occurs when mission is carried out in the highly nuanced arena of human sexuality is the core of what Christian theology describes as hospitality. It is what the people at Church of the Redeemer sought to extend. It is what the youth group sought to encounter. Hospitality was the goal of their mission. Hospitality was the means of their mission.

Radical hospitality takes us in the direction of Godbearing because, as Robinson says, "'Radical' means more than our common usage of 'extreme;' it signifies getting to the roots or to something more basic or essential."[9] That essential element of mission, which is intentional enough to be deeply aware of sexual values, is characterized by Joon-Sik Park as a new form of classic Christian evangelism:

> For evangelism done in the context of hospitality, an intentional and genuine effort to cross significant racial, ethnic, and socioeconomic boundaries is an essential and integral part. . . . Evangelism in the context of hospitality recognizes the equal worth of every person and does not accommodate the gospel to discriminations based upon cultural and socioeconomic differences.[10]

Unlike the violation of boundaries practiced by intrusive forms of evangelism, mission as Godbearing creates a climate of radical hospitality that recognizes difference as the potential for mutual transformation. It celebrates the diversity among us. It calls us to have zero tolerance for either imposing our own values or rejecting those of others out of hand. It demands a level of maturity that sees sexuality as a spectrum, not a personal piety. It requires a sophisticated attentiveness to communication, negotiation, and cross-cultural learning. It implies a process, not a fixed position.

Mission is a practice of radical hospitality. It is openness to being transformed by an exchange of values that can be both comforting and challenging. Mission is Godbearing in our simple act of being present to the other, in our willingness to be permeable in sharing our witness with others, and in our participation in the transformation of the world by a Spirit that is beyond all of our limited definitions. If there is such a thing as a fusion of mission and sex, then it is in this realm of mystery, where mission, like human

---

9. Robinson, *Godbearing*, 80.

10. Joon-Sik Park, "Evangelism and the Practice of Hospitality," in *Considering the Great Commission: Evangelism and Mission in The Wesleyan Spirit*, ed. W. Stephen Gunter and Elaine Robinson (Nashville: Abingdon, 2005), 149–50.

sexuality, is a drive that brings us to a wholeness that we can never discover alone but only when we are willing to discover it with another.

Discussion Questions

1. What lessons can and should be learned from the historic experience of Christian missions that resulted in sexual abuse, racial prejudice and colonial exploitation? How do those lessons apply to the contemporary exercise of cross-cultural mission?
2. As a mission planner, what can you do to be attentive to the spectrum of cultural values in regard to human sexuality? How can you help ensure that even subtle value systems are taken into account?
3. How do you understand evangelism? How does it reflect what has been described as "Godbearing" as personal example, shared witness, and public transformation?
4. In what ways is "radical hospitality" an expression of Christian mission and in what ways does this concept speak to the inclusion of sexual values in the process of planning for shared ministry?
5. If wholeness requires compromise, negotiation, and a mature respect for the values of others, then how do you see that kind of dialogue unfolding? How would you guide such a process if you were a mission planner? Are there limits to Christian compromise?

Recommended Readings

Bevans, Stephen B., and Roger P. Schroeder. *Prophetic Dialogue: Reflections on Christian Mission Today.* Maryknoll, NY: Orbis, 2011.

Knight, Henry H., III, and F. Douglas Powe Jr. *Transforming Evangelism: The Wesleyan Way of Sharing Faith.* Nashville: Discipleship Resources, 2006.

Robinson, Elaine A. *Godbearing: Evangelism Reconceived.* Cleveland: Pilgrim, 2006.

World Council of Churches, Pontifical Council for Interreligious Dialogue, and World Evangelical Alliance. *Christian Witness in a Multi-Religious World: Recommendations for Conduct.* 2011, http://www.oikoumene.org/en/resources/documents/wcc-programmes/interreligious-dialogue-and-cooperation/christian-identity-in-pluralistic-societies/christian-witness-in-a-multi-religious-world.html.

World Council of Churches Central Committee. "Together Towards Life: Mission and Evangelism in Changing Landscapes." 2012, http://www.oikoumene.org/en/resources/documents/wcc-commissions/ mission-and-evangelism/together-towards-life-mission-and-evangelism-in-changing-landscapes.

14

Preaching and Sexual Ethics

John S. McClure

The *Listening to Listeners Project*, a major empirical study of sermon listeners, supported a research team who interviewed 263 sermon listeners in twenty-eight congregations of various sizes, locations, denomination, and racial-ethnic composition across the midsection of the United States. One of the most striking results of this massive study was the discovery of the importance of the *relationship* between the preacher and the sermon listener.[1] Listeners testified that when they believe they have a *good*—healthy, responsive, mutual, affirming—relationship with their preacher, they understand better, invest more in what is said, and feel predisposed to respond to the message in positive ways. For many, the relationship with the preacher was closely associated to their relationship with God.

A key element in all human relationships is sexuality. Among other things, sexuality involves the managing of power, vulnerability, intimacy, boundaries, roles, bodily display, and sexual feelings. Because the preacher is also in a professional role and is often speaking about matters of deep personal, spiritual, and psychological concern, the preacher-listener relationship also includes many of the dynamics that are found in other arenas of church life, such as pastoral care, counseling, ritual leadership, advice-giving, spiritual and casual conversation. The ways that sexuality is managed (or not managed) in those situations are carried by listeners into the sanctuary on Sunday morning and nested within the preacher-listener relationship.

At the same time, especially for Protestant Christians, the pulpit is the center of the symbolic life of the church community. The pulpit is where the core theological narrative of a congregation is negotiated in relation to authoritative texts and traditions. The presence or absence of themes bearing on sexuality within this core narrative becomes an important part of the way

1. Ronald J. Allen, *Hearing the Sermon: Relationship, Content, Feeling* (St. Louis: Chalice, 2004).

sexual ethics is treated within a congregation. Where these themes are present in constructive ways, congregations are given permission to include their own sexuality in the ways they think about, speak about, and embody the narrative of faith.

Attention to human sexuality by preachers can help to foster healthy, trustworthy relationships both in and out of the pulpit. First, I will focus on personal sexual ethics, encouraging preachers to develop a healthy personal self-awareness of the role of their sexuality in the preaching event. Second, I will consider professional sexual ethics, particularly the ways in which one's role as both a professional minister and an ordained pastor translates into dynamics of power that every preacher must understand when preaching. As official (and paid) interpreters of scripture and tradition, and as those who typically "control the microphone," preachers have significantly more power than congregation members. Preaching can express—through embodiment, performance, voice, manner, and theme—genuine care for persons as sexual beings. Although this is not the place to enter exhaustively into the impact of the social construction of sexual behavior on the pulpit, we must keep in mind the influence of cultural sexism on our understanding of clergy sexuality and power. The dynamics of power and sexuality for women in the pulpit are quite different than they are for men.

Personal Sexual Ethics and Preaching

We can think of personal sexual ethics as an ethical framework that is not explicitly tied to one's professional role. Personal ethics are behaviors and practices that all Christians should have. In other words, all Christians should have an awareness of their own sexuality and of the kinds of signals (listed below) that should help them set appropriate limits on and properly nurture their sexual behavior.

In their book, entitled *Sex in the Parish*, Karen Lebacqz and Ronald G. Barton summarize interviews with pastors regarding sexual ethics.[2] Most of the pastors interviewed identified personal sexual ethics as an essential element of their pastoral practice. In other words, these pastors insisted that developing a healthy sexuality and good sexual self-awareness and boundaries in one's own personal life would serve them well in the parish. Although Lebacqz and Barton show how this perspective is, in many ways, naïve, particularly because it fails to take into account the unequal power dynamics that exist within a professional relationship, it is clear that discerning how to care for one's self as a sexual being

---

2. Karen Lebacqz and Ronald G. Barton, *Sex in the Parish* (Louisville: Westminster John Knox, 1991).

and achieving personal knowledge and self-awareness of one's sexual self are tremendously important. It makes good sense that preachers who place their bodies, voices, and deepest thoughts in front of others each Sunday morning will benefit profoundly by increased self-awareness.

Although many things might be included in a list that constitutes healthy sexual self-awareness, Lebacqz and Barton provide a useful list of the kinds of signals that pastors might use to tell them "when they are getting into trouble."[3] While I believe that all of these have implications for preaching, I have italicized those that are of particular importance for the preaching event:

- *the "publicity test": what would others think?*
- physical arousal—one's own or the other's
- inordinate sexual fantasy
- *sexual gestures or body language*
- *sexual innuendo in verbal exchange*
- intuition, instinct, or not feeling right
- *wanting to share intimacies that are not called for*
- a parishioner wanting too much time or attention
- *wanting to shift the focus to sexual subjects*

Lebacqz and Barton go on to state that some of these signals are "internal mechanisms for foreseeing trouble. Others are tests that can be used after an initial 'feeling' alerts the pastor to the fact that something is wrong."[4]

There are, of course, many cultural dynamics involved in establishing one's personal sexual ethics. In a patriarchal culture, where men are socialized as aggressors and women as self-protectors, some internal signals may inevitably differ by gender. Although oversimplified, Lebacqz and Barton boil this cultural difference down to the fact that men will generally need to identify signals that help them "know when *they* want to step over the line," whereas women will more typically need to identify "when *the other person* wants to step over the line."[5] Although these are stereotypes, and are not true in every case, they do point to the baseline need to identify at least two kinds of culture-bound signals for all of us: signals of sexual interest or aggression, on the one hand, and signals of sexual harassment or intrusion, on the other.

In many instances, however, we can be internally sensitized to these signals yet unaware of their presence in the event of public communication. It has

3. Ibid., 65.
4. Ibid.
5. Ibid., 132-133.

become clear to me that one of the great benefits of video-recording sermons is that it can help us become aware of signals that we are giving externally that we may not be aware of internally. Many of these signals are, in fact, culturally pervasive. They "go without saying" and are found in everything from dress codes to gestures, postures, facial expressions, uses of space, vocal pitch, patterns and rhythms, proximity to microphones, and so on.

Exploring personal ethics in relation to the pulpit involves engaging several key categories of questions:

Feelings: How do I deal with sexual feelings when preaching or preparing a sermon? How do I deal with the desire to flirt, sexually impress, or attract? How do I deal with feelings of sexual aggression or need for intimacy?

Boundaries: Am I aware of sexual advances during sermon feedback at the church door and beyond? Am I feeling the need (in the pulpit and beyond) to protect myself from someone's sexual interest or advances?

Use of Sexual Themes and Language: Does the way that I use language reflect a healthy approach to human sexuality? How willing and comfortable am I to talk about sexuality from the pulpit? Is there unnecessary sexual innuendo or under-currents in my pulpit speech?

Self-Disclosure: Do I use self-disclosure in my preaching to create or to share intimacies that are not called for or to bolster my own sexual image? What forms of self-disclosure in the pulpit might be considered flirtatious?

Personal Integrity: Is there a healthy relationship between the sexuality I express in private and the sexuality I express or teach in the pulpit?

Clothing: Does the way that I dress express my sexual identity in a healthy and even robust way?

Embodiment: Do I use my body in a way that promotes a healthy sexuality in the pulpit? Do I use gestures, vocal intonations, or postures to signify sexual display, aggression, or attraction?

These are simply some of the questions that preachers might consider when thinking about some of the ways in which their own personal sexual ethic translates into the preaching context. Several vignettes might be discussed with such questions in mind:

- In order to appear more authentic, Jon likes to wear very tight jeans and a shirt unbuttoned to mid-chest when he preaches. He sits on a barstool with legs uncrossed and speaks intimately into a handheld microphone, holding the microphone close to his lips, speaking softly, sometimes whispering. During his sermons, close-ups of his body and face are projected on an overhead screen. He is offended when a woman in the congregation complains that he seems to be "coming on to" the women in the congregation.
- A pregnant preacher is delighted as she preaches advent sermons about Mary and Elizabeth's pregnancy and birth experiences. She is troubled, however, about how her openness about her experience with these texts seems to be unexpectedly encouraging church members to touch her stomach on the way out the church door.
- A pastor is consumed by pornography in his private life. In a sermon on Ephesians 5:22—"wives submit to your husbands as to the Lord"—he argues that for a woman to submit is "just the natural way we're wired as men and women."
- Sally is confident in her sexuality, and intentionally dresses boldly as a woman. She is worried, however, about all the comments she gets about her wardrobe, especially her shoes.
- Carol is a self-described "hugger" and intentionally uses hugs at the church door to loosen up her congregation of the "frozen chosen." She is troubled, however, that one man, a leader in the church, puts his hands on her side too near her breast or slides his hands too near her rear while hugging.
- In a sermon illustration, Jim describes his high school dating relationships with some bravado and a knowing wink as "following the usual pattern: hanging out with cheerleaders in the back seat of daddy's car." At the door, one of his sermon listeners says, "I never had much respect for guys like you in high school."

PROFESSIONAL SEXUAL ETHICS AND PREACHING

Professional ethics highlights the differences of power that exist between preacher and parishioner. The professional is in a fiduciary role of authority within the community of faith, and crossing sexual boundaries is an abuse of power and a violation of the sacred trust invested in that authority. Because the preacher represents the sacred, the violation of this trust can also have significant repercussions on the trust that a person has for God.

There are, however, significant differences in how this power plays out for men and women in the church. It is far more likely, therefore, that a female minister will experience sexual harassment from staff members and parishioners than will a male minister. In other words, sexuality is often used to curb the power of women rather than to bolster it. This introduces different power dynamics into the preacher-listener relationship. It suggests that men will more typically need to attend to the ways in which their preaching expresses or legitimates sexual "power over" others. Women, on the other hand, without falling into self-victimization—"sexual harassment or attraction is my fault"—will more typically need to attend to the ways in which they, as preachers, do in fact become victims of sexual harassment or sexualized resistance or "push-back" from church members, male and female.[6] Again, this "difference" is loaded with cultural baggage, and certainly men and women preachers need to consider both sides of this power differential. Nevertheless, preachers, whether male or female, wield significant power to interpret the ways of God toward humanity.

Professional sexual ethics requires us to make decisions regarding the pastoral theology we bring into the pulpit. We should learn to preach in a way that will help the sexually vulnerable in our midst experience God's love and empowerment. And we should find ways to "do no harm"—or as little harm as is possible—to those who are vulnerable in our midst.[7] For instance, years ago, after preaching what I considered to be a prophetic and challenging sermon about "forgiving seventy times seven," I received a phone call from a woman in the congregation who had recently escaped a violent domestic relationship. She informed me that my sermon could potentially have talked her into staying in her situation, in which case she might not still be alive. Although not intending harm, my sermon might have caused harm. I needed to attend more carefully to her vulnerability, the vulnerability of those in similar circumstances, and to the ways in which my own power both blinded me to her situation and reinforced the interpretation I had given.

The same dynamics are true in our choices of illustrative material. Elsewhere, I have interpreted sermon illustrations as constituting a large part of the sermon's "cultural code."[8] For instance, it is easy, and often makes us

---

6. See ibid., 241.

7. See Marie M. Fortune, *Love Does No Harm: Sexual Ethics for the Rest of Us* (New York: Continuum, 1995).

8. See John S. McClure, *The Four Codes of Preaching: Rhetorical Strategies* (Louisville: Westminster John Knox, 2004). See also McClure, "The Other Side of Sermon Illustration," *Journal for Preachers* XII, no. 2 (Lent 1989): 2–4.

feel "one of the gang," to adopt cultural stereotypes about human sexuality. As preachers, it is valuable for us to take a "culture inventory" annually to assess the "homiletical culture" in which we embed the gospel of Jesus Christ. This self-assessment then allows us to think about ways to broaden that culture, thinking about families in new ways, mitigating sexual stereotypes, identifying instances in which women or men are treated as objects or without subjectivity, and re-thinking the theology that is implicit in the way culture is portrayed in our sermons.

Coercive ritual is another way that professional and pastoral power is sometimes exercised inappropriately from the pulpit. In their book, *Facing Shame: Families in Recovery*, Merle Fossum and Marilyn J. Mason make use of the metaphor of the "zipper" to speak about sexual shame and the violation of sexual boundaries. For persons with a healthy sexuality grounded in self-respect, the zipper around their physical self is "internal." *They* establish and control the boundaries around their sexual selves. For a person whose sexuality has been violated, perhaps through incest, childhood sexual violence, rape, or domestic violence, the "zipper" becomes "external." *Others* have dominated and confused the control of boundaries.[9] If we modulate this metaphor to the level of worship and preaching, we enter the realm of coercive ritual. The preacher as ritual leader has the power to take hold of the "zipper" to our intellectual, emotional, and sometimes physical selves. Without our consent, and by virtue of her special power as ordained clergy, she may—intentionally or unintentionally—coerce us to do something we don't want to do or have not considered or planned to do. When worship services and preaching are filled with coercive rituals—"take out a pen and write down . . ."; "turn to your neighbor and give a hug and say . . ."; "now hold hands with the person next to you and . . ."; "take five minutes to share one personal fear with the person in the pew behind you . . ."; and so on—we may imitate and enact shame, and sometimes sexual shame. Coercive rituals can bolster the idea that the preacher as ritual leader is someone who has his hand on my "zipper."

The nature of pastoral power is also communicated through voice and gesture. Elsewhere I have written about how the "grain of the voice" can establish the shape that our relationship with God takes from the pulpit.[10] This relationship is signified by many tones of voice: persuasive, collegial, moralistic,

9. Merle A. Fossum and Marilyn J. Mason, *Facing Shame: Families in Recovery* (New York: W.W. Norton, 1989), 70–84.

10. See John S. McClure, "The Grain of the Voice: Inventing the Soundscape of Religious Desire," in *Mashup Religion: Pop Music and Theological Invention* (Waco, TX: Baylor University Press, 2011), 109–122.

wise, insightful, responsible, anxious, troubled, longing, hopeful, angry, violent, fearful, sexual, mysterious, sentimental, and so on. There is an old cartoon of a young child seated with his mother in the front pew of the sanctuary just beneath a circular pedestal pulpit. The child has a frightened look on his face as the preacher rants and rages, sweat pouring down, spittle spraying the first few pews. The mother whispers to her son: "Don't worry, he can't get out of there." This little cartoon says much about the ways that the tone of voice and body language of preachers can demonstrate how we are to understand power—both their power and God's power. Preachers can consider how their voice and body language are reinforcing cultural norms and stereotypes about "power over" others sexually, and in other arenas of life. In situations where listeners may have been victims of childhood or adult sexual violence, violent self-presentations may reinforce and sanction sexual abuse.

On the positive side of the equation, our professional and pastoral ethic encourages us to give expression to at least three theological realities. First, we can invite sermon listeners into noncoercive and nonviolent relationships with God and all of God's people. Second, preachers can work to express what Nancy Ramsay calls a "fierce tenderness" for the wounded sexual being of many.[11] This love is fierce because it ceases to be a "bystander" when it comes to sexual ethics. It challenges listeners with absolute clarity to respect sexual boundaries and to commit to providing genuine sanctuary for those who have experienced the crossing of those boundaries. This love is tender because it appreciates and honors the sexual vulnerability of everyone, including oneself. It realizes, as Wendy Farley has shown, that divine compassion, expressed and offered freely by the community of faith, is the only force that can in any way re-create what has been de-created by sexual violence or by violating sexual boundaries through abuses of pastoral power.[12] Third, a professional ethic can give expression to a firm and persuasive love for those socialized into forms of sexuality that are life-denying and harmful (to self and others). This will involve preaching sermons about many important themes in which sexual behavior and practices are embedded: sexual and domestic violence, pornography, dating, love, marriage, childhood, sexual orientation, family, adultery, and so on.

It is important to have a good referral system in place as a backdrop for some of this preaching. Preaching sexual themes invokes a range of responses

---

11. Nancy J. Ramsay, "Preaching to Survivors of Child Sexual Abuse," in *Telling the Truth: Preaching about Sexual and Domestic Violence,* ed. John S. McClure and Nancy J. Ramsay (Cleveland: United Church Press, 1998), 58–70.

12. Wendy Farley, *Tragic Vision and Divine Compassion: A Contemporary Theodicy* (Louisville: Westminster John Knox, 1990).

and sometimes brings to the preacher's office door sexual predators and sexual wanderers, as well as those who earnestly seek help. In most situations, it is not the pastor's role to enter into counseling regarding intimate sexual behavior, and it is crucial to develop a network for referring persons who come to discuss these issues.

Exploring professional ethics in relation to the pulpit invites us to engage several new categories of questions:

Theology: How can I better express a theology that is nonviolent, noncoercive, and compassionate in nature? How might I rethink the ideas that I preach—God's power, forgiveness, sin, salvation, and so on—in order to keep from harming those in my congregation who may be victims or survivors of sexual or domestic violence? How can my preaching communicate the evil inherent in sexual abuse or harassment? How can my preaching persuade those socialized into unhealthy or dangerous sexual practices to seek transformation?

Power: In what ways might my preaching be either expressing or legitimating non-consensual, coercive, or life-endangering "power over" others? Am I experiencing harassment that involves a sexualized interpretation of my self-presentation in the pulpit (innuendo based on my appearance or pulpit presence)? How can I avoid engaging in coercive ritual? How can I modulate my tone of voice to give voice to faith that is nonviolent and noncoercive? What changes in body language might make my preaching more mutual and affirming and less fearful?

Homiletical culture: How can I avoid exclusive or harmful sexual stereotypes in my sermon illustrations?

Several vignettes might be discussed with these questions in mind:

- Jim preaches an aggressive sermon entitled "Power over the Enemy" in which, at one point, he shakes his fists in the air and shouts that we have to quit being "wimpy, girly, impotent, effeminate" Christians and, in the power of the Spirit, go "on the attack against the tempter and deceiver!"
- Susan is an associate pastor and has been preaching once a month. One Monday morning after preaching, Susan's phone rings and it is one of the prominent women in the congregation. She chastises Susan for looking too provocative for the men in the church when she preaches. She says that she has spoken to several church members

who are bringing a petition to the church board to keep her from preaching any more.

- A preacher is preaching a sermon on 2 Corinthians 6:14. In order to illustrate the problem of allowing oneself to be "unequally yoked with those who are unbelievers," the preacher tells the story of a well-known college football hero who, as a Christian, decided to break off an engagement with a young woman because he had discovered that she had engaged in extra-marital sex before they met.

CONCLUSION

To summarize, it is important that we, as preachers, learn to think as intentionally as possible about: (1) how we understand our own sexuality and sexual boundaries in relation to preaching; (2) how we understand the fiduciary trust and dynamics of power involved in preaching as a part of our ministry of preaching; and (3) the positive and proactive possibilities for developing a pastoral sexual ethic that will extend care, compassion, and the courage to change to many of our listeners.

DISCUSSION QUESTIONS

1. As you review a video recording of yourself preaching, make note of your body language and what kinds of signals you might be (un)intentionally conveying to the congregation. Practice being more intentional about your sexual self in the pulpit.

2. What are three ways that your preaching can express God's "fierce tenderness" for the vulnerable and for those who are victims or survivors of sexual abuse?

3. Take a "cultural inventory" of your sermons over the past year, listing stereotypes and depictions of human sexuality. How can you broaden the "homiletical culture" in which you embed the gospel message to include a more inclusive range of healthy sexual covenants (families, relationships, and so on)?

4. How can your preaching encourage the congregation to be active in seeking the sexual health of its members and the larger community?

Recommended Readings

Fortune, Marie M. *Love Does No Harm: Sexual Ethics for the Rest of Us*. New York: Continuum, 1995.

Lebacqz, Karen, and Ronald G. Barton. *Sex in the Parish*. Louisville: Westminster John Knox, 1991.

McClure, John S., and Nancy J. Ramsay, eds. *Telling the Truth: Preaching About Sexual and Domestic Violence*. Cleveland: United Church Press, 1998.

McCullough, Amy Peed. *Her Preaching Body: A Qualitative Study of Agency, Meaning, and Proclamation in Contemporary Female Preachers*. PhD diss., Vanderbilt University, 2012, http://etd.library.vanderbilt.edu/available/etd-03222012-104750/unrestricted/HERPREACHINGBODY.pdf.

Rutter, Peter. *Sex in the Forbidden Zone: When Men in Power–Therapists, Doctors, Clergy, Teachers, and Others–Betray Women's Trust*. New York: Fawcett Crest, 1991.

15

Public Worship and Human Sexuality

Don E. Saliers

When Christian congregations gather to worship, people enter a space and time that intensifies language and gesture. The assembly comes to hear, speak, sing, and touch in God's name. In that set of actions are also found the ambiguities of human bodies interacting and the necessary interplay of human senses: sight, sound, taste, smell, and touch. Public worship is always a place where the words used depend radically on that which is nonverbal for their meaning and point. It is a place of eros, of desire for belonging and care, as well as a desire for contact with God. From the gathering rites of greeting and welcome, through the intimacies of sacramental actions, singing together, and blessing, the principal desire and intention is to remember and to enact love of God and neighbor "as oneself."

Public worship of God contains a distinctive form of restrained eros. Eros is a complex term signifying a deep attraction to someone or something. In ordinary speech and popular U.S. culture, the word "erotic" narrows to mean sexual desire. Reflecting on worship and ritual practice in churches requires that we bear the more expansive set of meanings in mind. We can thus properly speak of an erotic desire for God that involves love and care for the neighbor as oneself. One way or another, the human body and our senses are central features of the congregation's participation in and experience of worship. The worship leader's body language and understanding of human emotional responses is an integral part of this participation.

Faithful pastoral and liturgical leadership requires awareness of the ambiguity that can flow from desire in the context of worship. Leaders must resist erotic distortions. For pastors and laity, mutual physical presence, ritual bodily behaviors, and bodily participation are potential sites of sexual confusion and misconduct.

When the Christian assembly gathers for communal worship, questions of sexuality may seem far removed. We are not accustomed to reading the interaction between clergy and congregation from this point of view. Most Christians tend to separate holiness and church time from matters of human sexuality. While understandable, such a separation can lead to a dangerous lack of awareness and emotional confusion. "Sacred space and time" is often a place where repressed feelings of sexual desire and attraction can be awakened. Christian worship and liturgy may thus evoke confused erotic responses generated by the desire to be loved by God while loving neighbor and self.

Because worship deals with the relationship between God and our lives in their totality, sexuality is present. By "totality," I mean the fullness of physical, emotional and mental aspects of being a human person, that is, embodiment. God is both the creative source of our human vital energies and the one who knows the human heart. God desires relationship with our embodied selves and makes our "hearts restless," as St. Augustine observed. Both our vitality and all the desires of our hearts—the whole of one's life in the world—are present in every worship occasion.

In this essay, I explore how features of public worship, especially in its non-verbal dimensions, relate to sexuality and ethical responsibility. We begin with some reminders about relationships between the verbal and nonverbal dimensions of worship. After considering some performative aspects of leading public worship, I turn to interpersonal relationships between leaders and the assembly and especially to how cultural images and attitudes may or may not affect perception and even preoccupation with sexual energy and desire. Then, we explore the positive spiritual dimensions of eros and sexuality. Finally, we ask about pastoral norms—such as truth-telling and resistance to harm—that may guide and direct our attention to encouraging and practicing healthy eros in congregational worship patterns.

VERBAL AND NONVERBAL DIMENSIONS OF CHRISTIAN PUBLIC WORSHIP

Every pubic worship service typically consists of texts from Scripture, hymns and songs, prayer, ritual actions, and proclamation. At the same time, verbal language in worship is always interacting with sight, sound, touch, smell, movement, and a local cultural style of speaking and hearing. Some traditions are much richer than others in nonverbal symbols, such as the cross, bread and wine, oils for anointing, lighted candles, vestments, and arrangements of furnishings and architecture. The nonverbal environment can be simple—as in most Baptist or Reformed traditions—or quite elaborate—as for example, in Orthodox or high Anglican sanctuaries. The environment itself contains nonverbal "languages" that affect how words are heard and interpreted and what ranges of meaning may be operating in the communication between leaders and people. In this way, the words used in worship depend in large measure on the non-verbal dimensions of particular practices in specific communities. Whatever the style or tradition, worship gathers a community and focuses the whole self before God.

A great deal of emotional energy is bodily released in singing, praying, preaching, and touching, as well as in acts of healing. In more liturgical traditions, all the senses may be stimulated by sight, sound, smell, taste, and touch, particularly when the sacraments are celebrated regularly. Yet, even in more verbal traditions, the body is still a crucial focal point where facial expression, gesture, and tone of voice convey more than the words express on the surface. For these reasons, we must remain conscious of the fact that Christian public worship will inescapably involve human sexuality and its ambiguities more than first meets the eye, the ear, and human hands.

Habits of expressing mutuality in a particular tradition or congregation will also have a profound effect on congregational participation. Some congregations pass the peace with great enthusiasm, with lots of hugging and touching. Other practices, such as foot washing or regular healing with "laying on of hands," become accepted habitual features in some assemblies. The celebration of Holy Communion can be an intimate serving, receiving, and eating. In these and other cases, physical expression is essential to the ritual behavior, inviting holy intimacy as well as potentially inappropriate intentions and actions.

Performative Dimensions of Christian Pubic Worship

Perhaps even more significant for the erotic communicative power of words and gestures is the fact that every utterance is "performative." That is, words are spoken with tones of voice, rhythm, pitch, facial expression, and a range of bodily postures and gestures. In preaching, for example, the same words can have profoundly different effects, depending upon their delivery. A sermon on the "love of Christ" when delivered loudly, with an edge of anger and judgment in the voice, is very different from the same sermon delivered in a more contemplative manner. More to the point, a seductive manner of speaking can easily be misconstrued. A prolonged touch may also encourage forms of sexual ambiguity.

Persons who bring unresolved personal problems, such as abusive or unhappy marriages, may be subject to projecting their sexual needs onto one another. Around the globe, statistics about patterns of sexual abuse in the church are alarming. Some estimate that in the United States, one in five adult women is a survivor of some form of child sexual abuse.[1] Most churches rarely acknowledge these matters until a crisis arises. This is why forms of bodily communication (and miscommunication) in the congregation need to be thought about carefully. Innocent, caring gestures can be misunderstood as inviting something more than ritual participation.

Cultural Images We Carry into Worship

In contemporary North American media and advertising, the ubiquity of sexually oriented images of women and men play a significant role in how we "see" one another. Television advertising, fashion magazines, and popular movies all constantly shape how the human body, especially of women, is perceived. Feminist theorists have noted the problems of the "male gaze" that often carries sexual fantasies. Some recent ads have featured female fantasies about men as well. It is unfortunate that cultural shifts have made distinguishing "the sensual" (of the senses) and "the sexual" difficult for many persons. Industries that commercialize sensual images as sexual create an atmosphere of distortion and distraction. Forms of imagination that lie hidden in our minds can easily play into the ambiguities of nonverbal language. This is why dress, hairstyles, makeup, and being attractive are all in the perceptual field in worship—both for the leaders and for congregants. Body language plays a central role in the sexual signals we send or restrain. We will return to the matter of practicing restraint and resisting sexual distractions in the final section of this essay.

In our present culture, public figures must be attractive. Congregations, particularly among wealthier constituencies, want their leaders to "look the part." Being attracted to healthy looking, well-dressed religious leaders is a natural response, but it can complicate the art of leadership. A caring and compassionate action or disposition becomes more ambiguous for an emotionally vulnerable person when it comes from an attractive worship leader. Restraint in clothing, makeup, and manufactured appearance is prudent.

Christian worship comes very close to the vulnerable centers of our lives: the desire to belong, to be loved, to be intimately known by a caring God and community. These spiritual-physical desires are mediated by human means in worship. In this sense, worship aims to hold life up to truth, grace, and goodness and to present alternatives to a range of romanticized views of human

---

1. The National Center for Victims of Crime, http://www.victimsofcrime.org/media/reporting-on-child-sexual-abuse/child-sexual-abuse-statistics

relationships. For persons with unresolved emotional problems and accumulated tensions—ranging from destructive self-criticism to unmet sexual needs within their primary relationships—the context of worship can intensify such problems and needs.

EROS AND SEXUALITY HAVE POSITIVE SPIRITUAL DIMENSIONS

We need not deny that the human desire for God has sexual overtones. Scripture itself has employed the language of desire to speak of the relationship between the seeker and the divine life. In the Psalms, the Prophets, and Song of Songs, the desire for God and for belonging to a community of love and justice are given in sensual images. Relationships between God and Israel, between God and the church as the Body of Christ, as well as between God and human persons, as we read in the Song of Songs, are all celebrated in the language of seeking, longing, desiring. "As the deer longs for flowing streams, so longs my soul for you, O God," sings Psalm 42:1.[2] Nuptial imagery of the Bride and Bridegroom, such as in the Song of Songs and book of Revelation, are part of traditional Christian language of prayer. Moreover, God is imaged as the lover of humankind—"God's steadfast love endures forever" (Ps. 118:29; see also Ps. 136) and "God so loved the world" (John 3:16). Women mystics, such as Teresa of Avila and Dame Julian of Norwich, wrote fiercely without fear of the love of God incarnate in the fleshly body of Christ.

What are the consequences of this deep desire for God on the liturgical assembly and in our "life together"? Christian faith and worship is grounded in the desire to love God and neighbor as we love ourselves. The Eucharist (Holy Communion) is permeated with bold images and actions of tasting, seeing, and enjoying God's love embodied. The sharing of bread and wine in the name of Christ is an act of double intimacy. Here, we exchange "the bread of heaven" and the "cup of salvation" through the means of touch, gesture, and taste. The hymn, "Taste and See the Goodness of the Lord" (based on Psalm 145), may be sung even while we take pleasure in the human communication of belonging and embrace.

All major ritual occasions in worship carry deep emotional power. They are associated with the human desire to belong, with birth, death, reconciliation and forgiveness, sickness and recovery. Denial of or simply repressing the sexual energies implicit in the worshiping assembly is not the point. Rather, the question is how we are both to welcome and use such energies for good, not for ill. The way forward is found in reflecting on the concrete reality of

2. Unless otherwise noted, all scripture quotations are taken from the New Revised Standard Version.

who is desired in worship, *who* is loved, and *who* is doing the loving. Faithful worship always asks *how* we are to love and how worshiping God alters the nature of the relationship between those united in Christ. Awareness of the forms and patterns of Christian worship where sexual energy is at play can be both positive and negative.[3] By asking the question, "Who is the Lover and whom the Beloved?," we establish a frame for analyzing what can go wrong and what can prove grace-filled and faithful. For example, in preaching and praying, the leader should make clear that, however drawn into the needs of others we become, God is the primary source of love and that humanity and the body of the Church are "beloved" in ways that transcend the pastor's efforts to care.

Truth-Telling and Resistance to Harm

In light of all these factors, the church seeks disciplined practices of truth-telling and resistance to injurious sexual attitudes and behaviors. As God incarnate in Jesus embodied unconditional and impartial love, so must those who care for the church. To have a passion for God and for the way of love and justice signified in worship, a person must be grounded in the pattern of life in Jesus Christ. Discipleship requires cultivating virtues and practices of deep respect that resist self-preoccupation and violating the image of God in others.

Those who lead have a key role in establishing and guiding the congregational ethos regarding human sexuality. At the same time, leaders cannot control every response. This is where honest and consistent discussion of these issues must be part of the educational pattern in local churches. Handling the ambiguities in sexual responses to leadership is not always natural to us. Some knowledge of the process of transference and projection is required in order to discern when the necessarily sensual dimensions of worship have become sexualized. Self-serving feelings, such as craving attention and physical response, can be worked on and refined in therapy,[4] but counter-practices are

---

3. Two insightful works that can form the basis of such study for clergy and congregations are Margaret A. Farley, *Just Love: A Framework for Christian Sexual Ethics* (New York: Continuum, 2006) and Cristina L. H. Traina, *Erotic Attunement: Parenthood and the Ethics of Sensuality between Unequals* (Chicago: University of Chicago Press, 2011).

4. There are teachers, both inside and outside the church, who know both the deeper spiritual traditions of desire and the tensions of our mixed motives and the play of the psyche—including our tendencies toward self-deception. Good spiritual direction as well as pastoral counseling must be encouraged for leaders of worship (clergy or lay) who struggle with inappropriate feelings of attraction. Therapeutic skills are called for in difficult cases that clergy accountability partners should not undertake on their own.

necessary in order to modify and refine unexpected sexual fantasies or impulses that may arise naturally as people journey toward greater wholeness.

When a pastor's sincere empathy evokes from someone in the congregation a longing to be sexually comforted by the pastor, honest acknowledgment is necessary. Clergy need to develop awareness of tendencies in their parishioners toward sexual attraction without loss of the positive erotic dimensions of vital leadership. All the nonverbal dimensions of worship come into play here. Leaders are called to reflect more carefully on matters of facial expressions, tone of voice, gesture, touch, forms of eye contact, and, especially, on our own and others' tendencies to romanticize empathy and interpersonal warmth. Becoming aware of how others' romantic fantasies may arouse our own is also a crucial step for worship leaders.

Three practices deserve special mention. *Custody of the body* means care in avoiding indiscriminate touch and seductive modes of physical communication. Giving and receiving physical touch, as in pre-service greetings or the passing of the peace, are occasions for restraint, particularly if feelings of attraction begin to dominate the ritual actions.

Custody of the eye is equally important. Gazing into a parishioner's eyes with tenderness is a natural part of pastoral warmth. But such exchanges can easily be misunderstood, especially if accompanied by remarks that are too intimate or suggestive of more than genuine pastoral care. Sustained looking at another's body or manner of appearance is a sign of preoccupation. Both the leaders and the congregation need training in knowing how to read body language, as well as controlling any tendencies to gaze at the other's body. Worship does require looking at one another. At stake is what we do in looking. Perhaps the older phrase—"beholding one another"—connotes the sort of respect the gospel proposes. For example, Jesus' encounter with the woman in a synagoge shows truthfulness and respect as a model (Luke 13:10-17).

Reading ambiguous behavior is a third crucial practice to be learned and sustained. Worshipers come with a wide range of needs, hurts, and life circumstances. Most clergy get into difficulty when they are not aware that a person is misunderstanding or misconstruing sexual features of clergy behavior. Worship leaders cannot possibly know all such dynamics, but can at least become skilled in reading the behavior of those who may target the worship leader with sexual needs and ambivalences. This is also part of attentive pastoral care and counseling outside the liturgy.

Because the actions at Holy Communion can carry a high level of personal intimacy, custody of body, touch, and eye is especially important. Over-personalizing the giving of the cup and the bread can be problematic, for both presider and recipient. Ministers who serve can intentionally focus on "seeing Christ" in every one who comes to receive. Here, impartiality is crucial. Being overly effusive or especially attentive to some and not to others stands in tension with the giving and receiving of the sacrament of the Lord's table.

All the interpersonal actions of worship should be done in the name of the triune God of mercy, justice, and holiness, not in the name of entertaining or calling attention to the physical virtues of the presiders. The most relevant primary practice in leading worship is to infuse the acts of communication with a sense of mystery that embraces all human frailties that are present with profound respect and healing.

In preparing for worship, the leader holds the whole congregation in mind, discerning what will build up mutual love and care for them rather than imposing his or her needs and desires. The aim is not sexual repression but liberation and freedom from the cultural captivities that sexualize others. Presiding well in word and sacrament acknowledges and addresses such cultural captivities. Worship respects boundaries while radicalizing compassion. It celebrates the incarnation of God ("the Word became flesh and lived among us" [John 1:14]); those who lead are commissioned to show in attitude and behavior that worship confers holiness on all relationships.

CONCLUDING REFLECTIONS: PRACTICES AND VIRTUES

Leading worship faithfully and with integrity requires a continually unfolding self-knowledge, which is both profoundly experiential and permeated with wisdom about human sexuality. The true goal in leading worship is to learn with one another how to "love as God loves."[5] Cultivating this virtue is a continual process, since congregations and their leaders are always changing under the impact of various life circumstances and are subject to cultural images and forces.

We all may wish that we lived in a different era, with less attention to exploitative images of the human body. But most of us do not live in a culture of restraint and holiness. Many Christians sincerely try to repress the fact that we have already internalized the world of images that exploit the human body. But this will not work. We need to practice resistance to these distortions, rather than repress them, and give more attention to mutual respect and personal integrity. These two virtues, along with others explored here, are part of what faithful worship offers us.

5. See Roberta C. Bondi, *To Love As God Loves: Conversations with the Early Church* (Minneapolis: Fortress Press, 2003).

There is no guarantee that those who come to worship will be formed deeply enough to avoid acting inappropriately with regard to matters of sexual distortion. Thus, we speak of communal and personal disciplines. The question is how to work with impulses and inappropriate states when they arise. In Christian liturgy, what should we gaze upon? To what should we attend? It is the mystery of God incarnate. God risks coming to us in a human form that is itself always culturally embodied. But if the central reality of worship is adoration, praise, and the continual unfolding of the power of God to rescue us from our addictions and our self-preoccupations, then there is a foundation for personal and communal discipline. Such practices of restraint and self-examination are themselves born in and lead to a noncoercive, nonpossessive love. Understanding ourselves as sexual beings who are accountable to God and to the community leads to a form of life that addresses episodes of narcissism, as well as unexpected erotic attractions.

The biblical story of Mary anointing Jesus' feet with perfume with her hair and tears is a powerfully sensual scene (John 11:2, 12:1-3). Like the disciples, many people react negatively because it is so daring. Consideration of such actions opens us to the vulnerability created by gender issues and to the ambiguity of sensual contact. Jesus knows this as a blessing. Worshiping congregations may also draw negative responses to the vulnerability produced by foot washing. Yet this act is practiced chastely by several traditions, echoing Jesus' own action before the last supper. Ignoring the sexual energies at work in leader-assembly relationships is not helpful. Instead, we need practices of resistance to the distortions of desire in the whole range of verbal and nonverbal modes of communication, with practiced attention to mutual respect and sexual boundaries. These virtues, along with the classical biblical ones named in 1 Corinthians 13—faith, hope and love—are intrinsic to the adoration and praise of God in Christ. In this way, all pastoral efforts in dealing with specific issues of sexuality are born of respect for the *imago Dei* that Christ comes to restore.

Dealing with the ambiguities of sexual energy in worship cannot be achieved solely within the worship service itself. Disciplined and caring leadership is only part of the story. The more important means of dealing with these issues will take place outside the liturgy, especially in planning, preparing the congregation, and discernment in evaluation. Only when there is an integrated sense of the relationship between teaching, spiritual formation, good pastoral care, and the community's sense of common worship will we have a chance of addressing and healing some of these profound issues thrown at the church in contemporary life.

A concluding reference to Jesus and his followers in the poignant episode recorded in John 21 seems fitting. The scene is the post-resurrection encounter with the disciples fishing by the sea. Jesus invites them to breakfast and to questions about love. Addressing Peter he asks three times, "Do you love me?" And Peter replies with increasing intensity, "Lord, you know I love you." Each time, Jesus directs that love and desire away from self-preoccupation to the ones his followers are to serve: "Feed my sheep," "tend my lambs." This is the sign of Christian desire, in which we come to fall in love with God-in-Christ, and thus make our desire congruent with his desire to feed, reconcile, touch, and love the poor and the hungry. For we are to learn again and again to love as God loves.

Discussion Questions

1. Where in the course of worship in your congregation is there likely to be the most intimate human contact or communication? What intentional practices of truth-telling and resistance to harmful behaviors mediate this intimacy?

2. In worship planning, what attention is paid to the role of gender images in the readings, prayers, and hymns? How do the worship planners attempt to interpret and set a theological context for understanding these images, perhaps in contrast to culturally pervasive messages about sexuality and the erotic in popular media?

3. How is sexual embodiment "performed" through rituals and acts of public worship in your congregation? What power dynamics influence the way in which this embodiment might be perceived?

4. When you as a worship leader perceive that your persona, words, or actions are being misinterpreted or misperceived in sexually unhealthy ways by a congregant, what are some concrete steps you might take to redirect those sexual energies and attention back to God?

5. How informed and pastorally aware are your sermons and communal intercessions in regard to matters of sexual abuse?

Recommended Readings

Cooper-White, Pamela. *Shared Wisdom: Use of the Self in Pastoral Care and Counseling.* Minneapolis: Fortress Press, 2003.

Fortune, Marie M. *Is Nothing Sacred? The Story of a Pastor, the Women He Sexually Abused, and the Congregation He Nearly Destroyed*. Eugene, OR: Wipf & Stock, 2008.

Gabbard, Glen O., and Eva P. Lester. *Boundaries and Boundary Violations in Psychoanalysis*. New York: Basic Books, 1995.

Saliers, Don E. *Worship as Theology: Foretaste of Glory Divine*. Nashville: Abingdon, 1994.

———. *Worship Come to Its Senses*. Nashville: Abingdon, 1997.

Traina, Cristina L. H. *Erotic Attunement: Parenthood and the Ethics of Sensuality between Unequals*. Chicago: University of Chicago Press, 2011.

PART IV

Pastoral Leadership

16

Pastor/Parishioner Relationships
Love, Power and Vulnerability

Jeanne Hoeft

Kathy is a young woman who was appointed to a church in a small town. She has been there for nine months and everything seems to be going very well. The small but stable church is responding well to her leadership. Kathy grew up in a small town and enjoys the lifestyle. She is making friends, though she at times gets lonely. On Thursday, after a meeting at church, Jason, a church member, asked her if she would like to go out to dinner with him the following evening. Jason has lived in town all his life, except when he left to go to college. He runs a small computer business and has been a great help to the church when it comes to improving technology. Kathy and Jason work together well and she finds it easy to relate to him. She looks forward to the dinner and getting to know him better. On Friday, he picks her up; they go out to dinner; they have coffee and dessert at her house; and then Jason returns to his home. They both find the evening completely relaxing and enjoyable.

Many pastors and religious professionals think of clergy sexual misconduct as sex outside of marriage. The scene above does not describe a pastor having sex, and yet, it could be considered a form of misconduct. The situation above calls into question the nature of a pastor's relationship with a parishioner. Understanding, preventing, and responding to clergy sexual misconduct requires the church to attend to the relational needs of all human beings and the exercise of power within relationships. The church often gets sidetracked by the sexual aspects of sexual misconduct and misses the underlying issues of power. Sexuality and sexual morality are certainly within the circle of the church's concerns, and they are aspects of sexual misconduct, but the reason that clergy have a "fiduciary" responsibility is because of the unequal distribution of power in a relationship between pastor and parishioner. Monitoring power is a necessary component of building healthy relationships between pastors and congregants.

CREATED IN AND FOR RELATIONSHIP

Relationships are the "stuff" of life. Many contemporary theologians emphasize the relational quality of God and creation as central to the Christian faith. Human beings exist in an interdependent of web of connection in which no one stands completely independent of other human beings. We need one another. We need the earth and all other living creatures in order to survive. Love, a central feature of the Christian faith, in and of itself requires relationship, the lover and the object of that love. To love and be loved is perhaps our most basic need. We need to be both the giver of love and receiver of love. Love always operates in both directions, in giving and receiving. Our human need involves the fullness of that dynamic. Though sometimes the Christian faith seems to emphasize giving love—love God, love neighbor, love self—we know how to love by virtue of having received love. Loving relationship is essential to fullness of life for individuals and communities. Since relationship with others constitutes life itself, and the need to love and be loved is a core aspect of human existence, maintaining our relational life engages much of our attention and energy, even if only subconsciously.

The importance of social connection and support in human life cannot be overemphasized, but we must also attend to the wide variety of relationships that hold us. Our lives depend on everyone—from the person we will never meet who grows our food, to the acquaintances we see regularly at the grocery store or speak to on the phone, to the social media friends we chat with about our comings and goings, to the friends with whom we share our thoughts and feelings, to our most intimate partners who know our deepest secrets. While all relationships involve giving and receiving, there is a qualitative difference between our relationship with the grocery store clerk and our intimate partner. As finite creatures, most of us fumble through our relational lives trying to do our limited best to shape a life according to the values we hold. At times, out of fear, desperation, or worse, our needs are distorted into relationships of harm.

In this mix, are the multiple pastor and parishioner relationships within a congregation. For pastors, there is a difference between relationships with parishioners, with friends outside of the church, and with an intimate partner. Pastors may have many relationships that fill social needs to a point, including those appropriate relationships with members of the congregation, but they often fail to attend to their own need for more intimate and emotionally close relationships. Sometimes the many ways that parishioners share their deepest thoughts and feelings with a pastor can give him a *feeling* of having close relationships, but the pastor should not be sharing his feelings in the same way as the parishioner. These interactions can give a superficial sense of being close to someone and obscure the pastor's need for mutually authentic close relationships. Though some incidents of clergy sexual misconduct occur at the hands of predators seeking to exploit vulnerable persons, most of the time it happens when a pastor loses touch with his own emotional needs and turns to inappropriate ways to fulfill them. Pastors must give attention to the different kinds of relationships they establish and practice careful self-awareness about their human need for emotionally close relationships.

BOUNDARIES

Boundaries enable strong, healthy, loving relationship in all its forms, whether between intimate partners, coworkers, friends, or parent and child. Contrary to an understanding of boundaries as that which constrains, Marie Fortune indicates that there is "joy" in boundaries because they enable relationship.[1] Boundaries, like a county line on a map, mark the place where one ends and the other begins. Personal boundaries establish the necessary distinction between self and other enabling me to say, "This is me and this is not me." Bodies are a rather basic distinction between persons; less evident are the distinctions we set internally between our own thoughts and feelings and the thoughts and feelings of others. Personhood develops in the ongoing internalization of our experiences with others. These experiences accumulate and go through a kind of sorting, merging, rejecting, and reshaping as they make us who we are. At times, in the midst of this process, we are not always clear to what extent a thought or feeling has become authentically "mine." I may not be sure that a particular thought—a thought of someone I admire, for instance—is my own fully internalized thought when it is still on the surface or at the beginning of the internalizing process.[2] I may be tempted by the fact of my admiration to take on the thoughts and feelings of another person and lose track of my own sense of self, especially when I am stressed or otherwise vulnerable. The internal "me" and "not me" is never as clear as the notion of boundaries seems to project;

---

1. Marie M. Fortune, "The Joy of Boundaries," in *Boundary Wars: Intimacy and Distance in Healing Relationships*, ed. Katherine Hancock Ragsdale (Cleveland: Pilgrim, 1996), 78–95.

2. For a rich description of this process as a kind of transference taking place in the context of ministry see Pamela Cooper-White, *Shared Wisdom: Use of the Self in Pastoral Care and Counseling* (Minneapolis: Fortress Press, 2004).

there is always a bit of slippage. Nevertheless, with self-reflection over time, we can come to know ourselves as distinct, though not fully separate, persons.

Healthy loving relationships require boundaries that are appropriately permeable. They must allow a certain level of giving and receiving, of influencing and being influenced by the other. Boundaries that are too permeable threaten relationships, as the two merge into one and the difference or uniqueness between the two ceases to exist. If a pastor becomes an ordinary member of the congregation, then she is no longer pastor. Boundaries that are impenetrable threaten relationships because they let nothing pass between the two—no interaction, no influence, and no love. If a pastor sets rigid invulnerable boundaries in which the pastor is not at all willing to receive and does not allow for interaction with members of the congregation, then the possibility for ministry with that congregation will diminish to the point of being impossible. The key to healthy, life-giving relationships is to find the appropriate amount of permeability for each permutation of relationship. A primary factor in determining the appropriate amount of boundary permeability in relationships is the distribution of power. The more equitably power is distributed, the more permeable boundaries can be. In our most intimate relationships of love and mutuality, we can more safely make ourselves open to one another. However, even in our closest relationships, boundaries open and close as personal situations shift and change.

POWER

Power, the capacity for influence, is at play in every relationship and in every interaction. Drawing on process theology, James Poling identifies power as "the energy of the relational web itself."[3] The movement across the boundaries of relationship is the movement of power. The give and take in a relationship, like speaking and being spoken to, reflects the movement of power, in that the actions of one produce an effect in the other. However, the nature of the effect or influence depends on the context in which the interaction is carried out and the nature of the relationship between parties. Power is ascribed to persons, to positions, or to groups in a complex network of cultural norms and meanings, social institutions and structures, and personal characteristics. One's ability to influence others may be based on economic status, role, or physical size. In the context of the church, the pastor, by virtue of the office, theological education,

3. James Newton Poling, *The Abuse of Power: A Theological Problem* (Nashville: Abingdon Press, 1991), 25.

and often charisma, has more power and influence than do other members of the congregation.

However, power is a dynamic, not a substance, so the dynamics of power in congregations are not simple or static. As philosopher Michel Foucault said, "Power is everywhere."[4] The movement of relational power is operating through the web of social interactions and cultural meanings in multiple ways all at once. In the context of a committee meeting that is deciding the church budget (including the pastor's salary), power is more evenly distributed than when the pastor is visiting one of those committee members in the hospital. As a patient in the hospital, one is more dependent on others and less able to affect the environment. As someone becomes more vulnerable, he is more easily influenced and less likely to be able to influence others. Pastors have been entrusted with the care of the vulnerable. Persons open themselves up to pastors, sharing their deepest struggles. Pastors are often present in times of crisis, like death and illness, and at times of great change, like births and marriages. In this way the pastor represents the body of Christ—the whole community of faith—as she offers support and guidance on behalf of the congregation. In order for people to become this vulnerable with a pastor, they must be able to trust that the pastor will use his power with their best interests at heart. They must be able to trust that the pastor will not violate them by exploiting their vulnerability or use it for the pastor's own benefit.

Power is neither good nor bad in and of itself; it is simply an aspect of relational existence. However, the way that power is exercised or enacted can be life-giving or life-diminishing. When power is used appropriately in a situation where one is more vulnerable than the other, it can bring strength and agency to the one in need. When it is used coercively or unilaterally, it can do great harm. The way in which we use power in relationship becomes one of the factors determining the extent to which a relationship functions for the wellbeing of all.

Relational Dynamics in Ministry

The complexity of relational dynamics between a pastor and congregation offers pastoral ministry one of its greatest possibilities and poses one of its greatest challenges. Most incidents of clergy sexual misconduct between adults happen not when a predator seeks out a victim but when a pastor gets lost, fearful, lonely, or self-aggrandizing in the midst of a complex web of

---

4. Michel Foucault, *The History of Sexuality: Volume I: An Introduction,* trans. Robert Hurley (New York: Vintage Books, 1990), 93.

relationships that make up her work. Misconduct begins well before a pastor finds himself sexually involved with a parishioner. The nature of pastor/parishioner relationship evolves one decision at a time. It is easier to say that sexual involvement between a pastor and parishioner is wrong than it is to recognize the potential of that involvement in each seemingly small decision along the way.

The scene from ministry that opens this chapter is meant to suggest that sexual misconduct can best be understood in the developing and changing relational web of ministry. Kathy and Jason seem to be developing a friendship. They have much in common—education, values, and interests—and their personalities seem to find good connection. Neither Kathy nor Jason is particularly vulnerable at this time, except perhaps to the extent that each feels the loneliness of being single in a social world focused on couples and in a small town where outlets for recreational social engagement may be few. In large cities, there are many more opportunities for putting relational distance between pastor and parish, but small towns offer less chance for anonymity and bring a very public role for pastors.

In the larger social context, Kathy and Jason may experience a relatively balanced exercise of power, though that might be mitigated to some extent by differences in gender, economic status, or other factors not included here. However, in the context of the church, Kathy can exercise more power than can Jason, by virtue of her role, status, authority, education, and the information she holds about other persons in the congregation. When Kathy and Jason went to dinner alone, that signified a potential shift in their relationship and an increasing amount of boundary permeability. When she invited him into her home afterwards, that was an additional opening of boundaries. This might not be considered sexual misconduct, but it is necessary at this point to watch the shifting boundaries and movements of power in this relationship.

Since the relationship began in the context of the church where Kathy is a pastor and Jason a parishioner, Kathy must reflect carefully on her own needs for friendship and intimacy, so that she might choose wisely in caring for herself, for Jason, and the rest of the congregation. Small towns and rural areas present a challenge for clergy as they seek to develop friendships outside of the congregation. Often there are few people in town who are not closely affiliated to or actual members of the church. There is not likely to be other clergy from the same denomination from whom a pastor could find peer support, and often the other churches may be from such different theological traditions that they provide little common basis for developing friendships. It is often the case that the people in town who share a pastor's interests, values, and commitments are actually members of the congregation. Single young clergy, like Kathy, find this situation quite challenging. They often have to be content with establishing a couple of close friendships in the area where they live. Kathy may need to look beyond her own town for developing friendships or romantic relationships. A regularly scheduled visit to the nearest metropolitan area can be helpful, as can regular visits to the nearest town where there are other clergy. Social media, when used carefully, can also be a way to stay connected to friends away from town. Ministry in small towns and rural areas requires a kind of intentionality and planning for developing a network of supportive meaningful relationships beyond the congregation.

If this relationship is to be a good friendship within the ministry of the church, Kathy may need to tighten her boundaries a bit and monitor carefully the movements of vulnerability and power. For instance, a friendship of this type might include lunches and conversations about church, town, public events, and personal history of the kind that is easily shared in public; but it would not include confiding about struggles in the church or personal information shared in confidence. If Jason became more vulnerable in any way, if he became sick or in need of pastoral care, Kathy would need to monitor closely the use of her position and role, shoring up her boundaries a bit so that she can become the one to sustain and guide Jason during difficult times. There is a giving and receiving in this kind of relationship, but Kathy, by virtue of her pastoral role, needs to be clear that what she receives must be appropriate to her professional role and that Jason's personal needs take precedent to her own.

Kathy should also remember that this is not only a relationship between herself and Jason; it is a relationship that involves the whole congregation and, in small towns, can involve the whole town. Pastors are public persons, meaning they have a role or hold an office that comes with a strong communal and societal expectation. Society looks to clergy for guidance, wisdom, and calls to moral accountability. In a sense, clergy are not simply leaders of congregations; they are leaders for the whole community. In large metropolitan areas where there are many clergy, pastors experience more choice in their level of public involvement; but small towns often have high expectations for civic leadership for their local clergy. With this public role comes power and a high level of public scrutiny, which clergy are often unprepared for. Kathy cannot proceed naively assuming that her "private" life is her own. With her ordination, she has made a commitment to consider the effect of her actions on the community.

The perception of others about Kathy's relationship with Jason affects the web of relations that form this community. For instance, if it is generally perceived that Jason is a "special" friend of the pastor's, then, when Jason speaks out on an issue in a committee meeting, Kathy will need to be attentive to the perception that she will automatically support Jason's position and that Jason will always support Kathy's position. Other members of the congregation may well wonder if she tells Jason things that she does not tell them. Close friendships between pastor and parishioner can lead to many power struggles within a congregation and have many times deeply divided and damaged the ministry of the community of faith.

Could a relationship like the one developing between Kathy and Jason move toward a more intimate relationship in a way that would not be misconduct but a healthy romantic relationship, life-giving not only for them but the congregation? Where does friendship end and dating begin? When does dating begin to include a sexual aspect to the relationship? In contemporary times in the United States, we do not have clear cultural lines between these forms of relationship. Because relationships are complex and always involve multiple layers of vulnerability and power dynamics, there are no clear-cut rules.

Clergy sexual misconduct is a problem rooted in the harm that can be done in helping relationships because of the power differential; that power differential between pastor and parishioner is always there in the context of the church, whether they are friends, dating friends, or lovers. If dating is seen as a step toward an increasing mutual vulnerability and more boundary permeability between two persons, it is problematic in the context of pastor and parishioner, because power cannot be mutually exercised in that context. The difficulty is that people often do not know, or admit, that they are dating until they are. The lines between kinds of relationships are fuzzy and shifting, but they must be attended to at all times. Pastors must become adept at naming the relational shifts, especially in the context of the congregation. The closer and more intimate we become, the more potential there is for harm.

If Kathy and Jason were to pursue a closer relationship, it would take much discernment and conversation. Kathy would need to consult her mentors in ministry and spend much time in self-reflection, perhaps engaging a counselor to help her sort out her own motivations. It would have to involve ways to mitigate the power difference within the congregation, including an agreement that she would always need to "keep confidences" from him, a step back on Jason's part from involvement in church leadership, perhaps even his moving to another congregation and identifying someone else as his pastor. Kathy may also want to inform her pastor-parish relations committee or supervising pastor about the nature of her relationship with Jason. These kinds of relational shifts in the context of ministry require a high level of emotional functioning and spiritual depth on all parties.

In general, pastors are tempted to deceive themselves as to their capacities for this kind of relational engagement, often resulting in unnecessary hurt and pain for many people. One sign that a move of this kind is problematic is the inability to increase emotional distance and hesitance to consult those who will hold us accountable. If Kathy is hesitant to talk to a mentor or counselor about this and cannot put the required distance between her and Jason while she seeks more clarity, then she should take that as a sign not to proceed toward more intimacy with Jason. It is essential that pastors confide in someone who will be honest with them and hold them accountable to living in ways consistent with their values. Regrettably, a more common experience is that pastors find themselves simply sliding down a slope toward inappropriate and harmful relationships with little awareness of the decisions they are making along the way.

CONCLUSION

In the best of ministry, pastors are indeed fulfilling some of their social needs through relationships with members of the congregation. Caring and authentic relationships are necessary for carrying out the mission of the church. They take time, trust, and careful attention to nurture. There is certainly a kind of friendship between pastor and parishioner, but the question is how close can those relationships be and still allow the pastor to function as pastor? Life-giving ministry requires authentic relationship, which entails vulnerability and openness between pastor and congregation with an eye toward how power is being exercised in each moment. Attending to shifting boundaries and dynamics of power is not something that the pastor does only in relation to sexual desire; rather, it must become second nature in all her relationships.

DISCUSSION QUESTIONS

1. As you reflect on your own sense of boundaries and delineating between yourself and others, under what circumstances are you most vulnerable to overly rigidifying or loosening those boundaries?
2. Reflect on a group interaction in which you were involved. What are the ways that power was ascribed and exercised during the group interaction?
3. What kind of friendships do you think are appropriate between pastors and members of their congregations? How could a

congregation communicate expectations and create structures that can support appropriate friendships in ministry?

Recommended Readings

Cooper-White, Pamela. *Shared Wisdom: Use of the Self in Pastoral Care and Counseling*. Minneapolis: Fortress Press, 2004.

Doehring, Carrie. *Taking Care: Monitoring Power Dynamics and Relational Boundaries in Pastoral Care and Counseling*. Nashville: Abingdon, 1995.

Fortune, Marie M. *Sexual Violence: The Sin Revisited*. Cleveland: Pilgrim, 2005.

Poling, James Newton. *The Abuse of Power: A Theological Problem*. Nashville: Abingdon, 1991.

Ragsdale, Katherine Hancock, ed. *Boundary Wars: Intimacy and Distance in Healing Relationships*. Cleveland: Pilgrim, 1996.

17

Pornography and Abuse of Social Media

Joyce Ann Mercer

Digital technologies can be a powerful tool for ministry. Recently, in Northern Virginia, an ecumenical advocacy organization supporting affordable housing sought to mobilize five hundred church members for an impromptu meeting with local politicians and mortgage bankers. Their use of social networking sites such as Facebook, along with email, Twitter, and text messaging, successfully allowed pastors and organizers to get the word out to their diverse constituencies quickly, efficiently, and at little or no cost. Meanwhile, all over the United States and the globe, campus and youth ministers use social networking sites and text messaging to send photos, inform youth and parents about upcoming events, and even offer brief online pastoral care with a generation of young people who are "digital natives." Today, there exists a vast, rapidly growing variety of Internet-enabled digital technologies, including social networking sites, chat rooms, email, instant messaging, online groups and organizations, digital gaming technologies, and massive multiplayer online role-playing games (MMORPGs, such as Second Life). In this chapter, the terms "Internet" and "digital technologies" function as shorthand references to this expanse. Churches continue to develop creative ways to use this array of technologies as constructive resources for ministry. At the same time, however, these same ministry-enhancing digital communications modalities can raise issues of professional sexual ethics for church leaders in ways unimaginable before the digital revolution. Consider the following two scenarios, drawn from real-life situations in ministry.

Kayla, a twenty-six-year-old female seminary student, regularly "friends" members of the youth group from the church where she is assigned for field education on her Facebook page. On this popular social networking site, Kayla stays in touch with youth in the church and posts announcements of upcoming youth group activities, as well as photos from the group's activities. She uses digital social networking to keep up with what the youth are doing; it is an easy way to find out about their sports events, band concerts, birthday celebrations, and school plays. The youth know they can always reach Kayla because she is just a tweet, text, or Facebook message away. And by reading their online postings, she often learns about problems or needs not brought to her in face-to-face conversations, allowing her to extend pastoral care. In fact, Kayla must continually make decisions about how to treat the information she accesses online. Just last week, she learned through a chain of Facebook posts that the parents of a boy in her group were separating because of one parent's extramarital affair. Kayla also uses Facebook to stay in touch with her own family and friends, including college friends, whose posts regularly appear on Kayla's "wall" and who do not relate to her in her ministerial role. Her Facebook page contains personal photos, including a few from her college years showing her in sexually suggestive poses or less modestly dressed.

Harry, an ordained minister, enjoys the way email allows him to stay in touch with people from a church he previously served. One of those former church members, Cindy, a woman who had been a major supporter of Harry's ministry and a lay leader, initiated some flirtatious emails with Harry. Harry responded with flirtatious emails of his own, enjoying the sexually charged energy he felt with their correspondence. Soon, the two regularly composed and shared with each other by email sexually explicit stories. Harry also began using images from Internet pornography websites to enhance his story-writing and his pleasure, enjoying the unencumbered sensuality he felt able to express with Cindy as he made up stories to send her. Their cybersex relationship was physically exciting to both of them, with none of the messy, disappointing, and difficult elements of their respective marriages. The two managed to keep their cyber-affair secret from their spouses until Cindy's husband discovered and read some of their email exchanges. Cindy and her husband divorced a year later. Harry, while remaining married and vowing to discontinue this particular cyber-affair, continues to access and view Internet pornography several hours a week. Sometimes he uses the office computer for this purpose. He sees his actions as a harmless personal preference, since his pornography use involves neither "real" people nor children and, as he sees it, cannot offend anyone since it is not public.

These two scenarios, at first glance, may appear distinct from each other. Kayla's case seems to center on a problematic lack of awareness about the possible boundary issues involved in combining personal and professional uses of social networking sites. But she is open and public about her use of the Internet as a tool for ministry and is not trying to hide her communications or deceive anyone. The primary ethical question in Kayla's situation concerns her fiduciary responsibility to care for those with whom she is in a ministerial relationship (the youth) in the way she has set up her use of social networking. Harry's case, in contrast, involves abuse of power through the intentional use of the Internet for the purpose of his own sexual gratification, without regard for harm to others. And unlike Kayla's use of digital communication, which was public, Harry's cyber-affair and pornography use involved secrecy and deception. Despite differences, these two scenarios share a number of common features and raise similar questions for professional sexual ethics. In what follows, I will explore five areas of concern: relaxing of professional boundaries; confusion from the collapse of distinctions between real and virtual worlds; the absence of privacy, anonymity, and confidentiality in uses of digital technologies; the intensification of intimacy and disinhibition common to social networking; and the challenges posed by these technologies for good self-care by ministers.

Boundary Issues

Social networking, email, internet chat rooms, and blogs, by design, invite users to experience digital spaces as casual, participatory environments in which the role distinctions and formal boundaries that structure many in-person encounters are relaxed.[1] While this leveling effect may be highly desirable for social relationships, in the context of ministerial relationships, it can result in blurred professional boundaries. In both Kayla's use of social networking sites and Harry's engagement in cybersex, digital technologies "aid and abet" the confusion of boundaries. Ministerial leaders need to consider carefully how to manage the relaxing of boundaries these technologies invite.

The minister is always the one responsible for maintaining appropriate professional boundaries. Even if the virtual context (*social* networking) and language ("friend me!") invite blurring or relaxing of roles, ministers still remain responsible for upholding the integrity of the ministerial relationship. Elizabeth Dresher tells about an Episcopal priest-friend who always envisions herself wearing her clergy collar when she logs onto her Facebook site.[2] That way, even when interacting with people who may be in family or social relationships with her, her priestly identity guides her participation on the site. Similarly, M.L. Daniel and Marie Fortune, quoting a local pastor, recommend as a best

---

1. M.L. Daniel describes this helpfully in her recorded webinar, "What You Need to Know: Healthy Boundaries and Social Networking in Ministry," FaithTrust Institute, 2012, http://www.faithtrustinstitute.org/training/events/701A0000000WT4DIAW.

2. Elizabeth Dresher, unpublished remarks during a presentation for the Practical Theology Group's session of the American Academy of Religion annual meeting, November 19, 2012, Chicago, IL.

practice for ministers using social networking the following guideline: "I don't post anything on my Facebook page that would not be acceptable to my mother and my Bishop."[3]

Kayla, when directing a communication to a personal friend or posting a personal photo on her social networking website, does not cease to stand in her role as youth minister. Her responsibility for boundary maintenance suggests either modifying the content of her Facebook page or establishing a separate personal page on a different social media website for use exclusively with friends and family outside of her ministry. The overriding concern is maintaining the integrity of the ministerial relationship, whether in virtual or physical contexts.

Churches are still figuring out the ethical responsibilities of ministers in relation to the "second selves" of persons to whom they have a professional obligation. Similarly, the issues raised by the minister's own web-based persona constitute relatively new ethical terrain. When people of faith encounter an online persona of their minister, they still bring to that encounter the expectation that ministers will act in the best interests of those they serve.

THE REALITY OF THE VIRTUAL WORLD

Contemporary uses of digital technologies make clear that any strict division between cyber reality and physical reality cannot be maintained today. The idea that the social space of the Internet is a "virtual"—as opposed to an "actual"—reality *seems* to suggest that activities taking place in cyberspace are somehow less significant, even less true. Such a distinction is a vast oversimplification.[4] Digital technologies bring any number of phenomena, including cybersex and interactive pornography, to which persons respond as if they were physically proximate. Cybersex refers to the experience of engaging in sexually intimate behavior in an online or virtual environment. Cybersex can take place entirely as an exchange of words, or may involve visual images and/or sound. Participants experience and respond to the presentation of selves and the intimacy of Internet relationships as *real*, even though bodies are not present to one another in material space. These relationships "become real in their consequences."[5]

---

3. M.L. Daniel and Marie M. Fortune, "Faith Community Considerations: Social Networking," FaithTrust Institute, 2011, http://www.faithtrustinstitute.org/resources/articles/clergy-ethics.

4. "The reality of virtual things emerges from interactions with the representations, not a quality of the things themselves. . . . As representations they exert real influence that allows people to respond to them as if they were real." Dennis D. Waskul, Mark Douglass, and Charles Edgley, "Outercourse: Body and Self in Text Cybersex," in *Net.seXXX: Readings on Sex, Pornography, and the Internet,* ed. Dennis D. Waskul (New York: Peter Lang, 2004), 17.

In fact, describing cybersex relationships as virtual—with this term's overtones of "less than real"—obscures the significance of these relationships. There is actual desire, pleasure, longing, and sexual release in the bodies of those engaging in cybersex. The threshold between virtual and actual sexual experience becomes thin. Harry's online relationship with Cindy included sexual and emotional involvement of a caliber that must be described as an abuse of the power of the ministerial relationship (Cindy was a congregant in Harry's former church). Furthermore, it was also a breach of emotional and sexual fidelity to their spouses. Yet, Harry justified his involvement as not being a problem since it was "only online." Similar misconceptions surround the use of pornography.

Pornography consists of sexually explicit materials produced for the purpose of sexual arousal that eroticize humiliation, violence, subjugation, abuse, or degradation, usually for monetary gain. Pornography objectifies and fragments, exploits and harms (vulnerable) persons in its production and use.[6] These features of harm, exploitation, and subjugation distinguish pornography from "erotica." The latter might include, for example, a film or a book with healthy sexual content that does not involve the exploitation or objectification of a person in order to produce it, and in which the pleasure experienced by users does not depend upon depictions of sexuality fused with violence, humiliation, or other dehumanization. Erotica viewed by a person or a couple who experience sexual pleasure from it can enhance pleasure and a sense of wholeness in persons. Pornography, by contrast, fragments sexual pleasure from the rest of personhood by seeking the achievement of that pleasure through the dehumanization of others.

Research on behavioral addictions and online pornography suggests that digital technology use reshapes neural pathways for experiencing desire and pleasure in ways that permanently alter the brain. When a person engages in activities motivated by pleasure, such as eating chocolate or viewing erotic images, the brain releases dopamine, a neurotransmitter that "rewards" the person with pleasurable feelings. The behavior acts as a trigger for the reward; the reward motivates the behavior. Normally, over time, dopamine release

5. Ibid.

6. For this definition, I am drawing upon denominational statements on pornography from the Presbyterian Church (USA), *Pornography: Far from the Song of Songs* (Louisville: Office of the General Assembly, 1988), http://www.pcusa.org/resource/pornography-far-song-songs/, and United Methodist Church, "Pornography and Sexual Violence," in *The Book of Resolutions of The United Methodist Church 2008* (Nashville: United Methodist Publishing House, 2008), http://www.umc.org/site/apps/nlnet/content2.aspx?c=lwL4KnN1LtH&b=4951419&ct=6869411&notoc=1.

tapers off in response to the trigger, because it is no longer necessary to motivate behavior (for example, a person is motivated to eat, care for infants, and so on, even in the absence of high doses of dopamine that reward the behavior). A person accessing sexual content on the Internet triggers a response in the brain's reward center (release of dopamine) and activates an association between pleasure and that external trigger. But when accessing sexual text and imagery *in the rapid succession made possible by digital technology*, the novelty and speed of triggers intermittently combine to create a situation in which dopamine rapidly and continually floods the brain instead of tapering off over time. This results in a vicious cycle in which ongoing dopamine release makes the activity triggering it take on more and more significance—that is, it becomes associated with high reward.[7] As that activity becomes more central, other domains, such as work, family relationships, or recreation, become increasingly less important. As neural pathways become patterned over time by this flooding of dopamine, this process effectively rewires the brain's reward center, so that the learned triggers (pornography, hot chatting, and so on) become *necessary conditions* to the brain's experience of desire and its pleasures. Internet cybersex and pornography thus closely parallel experiences of substance use and addiction, because users become habituated to elevated levels of dopamine and experience withdrawal symptoms in the absence of these levels.

Cybersex addiction constitutes a problem for clergy on many levels. When addicted, persons continue to use a substance (such as alcohol or other drugs) or engage in a behavior (such as gambling, shopping, or cybersex), even when doing so creates significant problems in their lives. Clergy addicted to Internet sex risk their marriages or partner relationships, careers, and health in order to engage in this behavior. Addictions are marked over time by the need to increase the amount or intensity of use of the substance or behavior in order to achieve the same pleasurable effect. With cybersex addiction, users not only must access an increasing quantity of cybersex content over time, but they must also seek out higher levels of intensity in content (for example, increasingly violent depictions of sex). Cybersex addiction draws users into an obsessive focus on the object of their addiction, to the detriment of other life domains. Important social, occupational, and recreational activities are given up because of this focus on Internet sex. Cybersex addicts come to prefer engagement in virtual sexual relationships at the expense of other forms of family or church

---

7. Mayo Center medical researchers Bostwick and Bucci find that with internet pornography and cybersex, like drug use by addicts, "repeated exposures (to the trigger event) do not extinguish dopamine release." J. Michael Bostwick and Jeffrey A. Bucci. "Internet Sex Addiction Treated with Naltrexone," *Mayo Clinical Proceedings* 83, no. 2 (2008): 229.

relationships. Cybersex addiction involves clergy in compulsive, secretive sexual behavior that takes up more and more of their time and energy.

The most significant ethical problem cybersex addiction poses for clergy lies in the dehumanization it entails for both the addicted person and those depicted in Internet sexual material. In cybersex addiction, desire becomes distorted by its attachment to pleasure premised on the objectification of those who are depicted in pornographic imagery. The frequent sexualization of violence in cybersex texts and imagery desensitizes users to the effects of violence against women and nurtures the attachment of users' desire to situations involving violence, subordination, or degradation of persons. Cybersex addiction distorts real-time relationships by forming users into people who view others (most often women or children) merely as objects for self-gratification, rather than as persons made in the image of God.[8]

PRIVACY, ANONYMITY, CONFIDENTIALITY

Even though technology experts continue to warn of the limits to privacy in digital technology, both Kayla's and Harry's situations show that many people tend to act as if information and communications on the internet are confidential and private. Different types of digital technology vary, but there is little real privacy in the world of digital communication.[9]

Should clergy treat as confidential personal information they learn through social networking or by reading someone's blog? In a recent conversation with an ecumenical group of clergy, no single consensus emerged in response to this question. As religious professionals continue to sort out the ethics of virtual communication in pastoral relationships, erring on the side of caution (that is, not communicating to others information from online sources without permission of the person involved) seems to be the best way of avoiding a problem in handling information obtained from social media.

---

8. Kelly Oliver puts it well when she writes, "The pornographic way of looking or seeing takes the object of its gaze for its own pleasure or as a spectacle for its own enjoyment without regard for the subjectivity or subject position of those looked at. The pornographic way of looking reinforces the power and agency of the looker while erasing or debasing the power and agency of the looked-at." Kelly Oliver, *Women as Weapons of War: Iraq, Sex, and the Media* (New York: Columbia University Press, 2007), 2.

9. As Lori Andrews, a law professor and expert on technology and privacy issues, makes clear, "Everything you post on a social network or other website is being digested, analyzed, and monetized. In essence, a second self—a virtual interpretation of you—is being created from the detritus of your life that exists on the Web." Lori Andrews, *I Know Who You Are and I Saw What You Did: Social Networks and the Death of Privacy* (New York: Free, 2011), 19.

What *is* increasingly clear is that there is no private or anonymous use of digital communication. In fact, many forms of digital technology invite the false sense that one is engaging in a private, one-to-one exchange or that the exchange is automatically limited to a small group. If a Facebook user with around a hundred friend contacts has her privacy controls set to allow posts and photos to be shared with "friends of friends," content intended to be accessed by a small group may travel to nearly 17,000 others.

Ministers should not expect content they post on the web to be confidential. Kayla's flirtatious personal photos and communications to college friends containing sexual innuendos, while not directed toward members of her youth group, may nevertheless make their way to these youth. Kayla's behavior risks the integrity of the ministerial relationship. Ministers also should not necessarily expect their online viewing to remain anonymous. Thus, clergy like Harry, who regularly accesses online pornography, need to be aware that this activity probably will not remain completely private over the long run. It should go without saying that the use of sexually explicit materials that exploit persons, particularly women, whether accessed at home or at church, fall outside of the boundaries of appropriate conduct expected of ministers. Harry's use of the *church* computer for this purpose creates an additional compromise of professional sexual ethics. Harry brings pornography into both a physical and a virtual location (the church office and the computer's online access history) that could be accessed intentionally or accidentally by persons in the faith community, potentially jeopardizing ministerial relationships.

ADDED INTENSITY

The amplified intensity of interaction in digital spaces distorts relationships. In Kayla's case, her ability to "drop in" virtually on youth group members at almost any moment of their lives, and their ability to do the same with her implicitly, distorts the levels and quality of close connections. For Harry, this amplified intensity happened in sending and receiving carefully composed stories with erotic content as the exclusive focus of the relationship. It also happens with digital interactive pornography use. Interactive pornography refers to pornographic imagery that can be manipulated by the user and is thus interactively—rather than passively—engaged.

Digital communication, including gaming, generally involves a focused, narrowing down of attention that supports an idealized sense of connection and intimacy with the other, a feature that can contribute to marked disinhibition, in which participants in online relationships often share deeply intimate, close details of their emotional experience, real and fantasized. Understandably, for some people, such hyper-intimate, idealized relationships can become more appealing than relationships with ordinary, real-time persons. Participants can craft their own images, leaving out less desirable elements. In cybersex, there are no domestic squabbles to negotiate and no crying babies to break the mood. These dynamics thus create the potential for such online relationships to interfere with face-to-face, intimate relationships.

CHALLENGES TO SELF-CARE

The cases of Kayla and Harry illustrate some real challenges digital technologies bring to healthy self-care. How does the expectation of continual availability pose a risk to the integrity of professional ministerial relationships? What needs—and whose needs—are being met by the sense of deep connection imagined when ministers can "follow" the daily details of congregants through posts, location tracking, and photos? What does Harry's choice of frequent use of online pornography mean for his overall sexual health and wholeness? Such questions point to the challenges Internet communication poses for ministers' self-care.

An important part of self-care is Sabbath—the ability to structure time in ways that bring a balance to work and rest. Most of us in the United States spend increasing amounts of our time online. Smart phones threaten to erase the division between spaces where we work and those where we do not. Ministry, by definition, is a public profession that has always involved a high degree of availability: the crisis call that comes in the middle of the night or the occasional funeral that needs to happen on the pastor's day off are part of the reality of ministry. Digital communication can easily move such events from the category of occasional, crisis-driven need, into the category of routine expectation. Furthermore, online technologies may subject ministers to the myth of indispensability: "I have to keep my phone on in case of a text, email, or call, because someone might need to reach me." Under these terms, it becomes difficult, if not impossible, to embrace grace-filled practices of a more mindfully present, centered life in the Spirit.

Lastly, using online pornography necessarily involves a minister in a secretive effort to address his or her needs in an unhealthy way. Most denominations express expectations and standards for ministerial conduct in policy documents. For example, the Evangelical Lutheran Church in America states, "Ordained ministers are expected to reject sexual promiscuity, the manipulation of others for purposes of sexual gratification, and all attempts of sexual seduction and sexual harassment, including taking physical or emotional advantage of others."[10] Such expectations clearly rule out pornography use as acceptable clergy conduct.

BEST PRACTICES

Digital technologies offer great promise for ministry when used with care and intentionality. They also bring ethical issues to the foreground. Some guidelines specific to digital technologies and professional sexual ethics for ministry are:

- Treating all forms of digital communication, including email, as public.
- Taking into account the power imbalance in ministerial relationships, in matters such as "friending" some persons and not others on social networking sites. Commonly recommended best practice for ministers using these sites is to respond to requests from members of the faith community to become a contact instead of initiating requests to "friend" congregation members.
- Taking regular "technology Sabbaths," suspending the use of computers, smart phones, and other digital devices.
- Use as a criteria for what is appropriate to say, post, or access online whether such communication would be appropriate if spoken publicly at a vestry or session meeting.
- Having a policy regarding the use of social networking sites and other digital communication by church leaders and members that clarifies how information on these sites is understood and how the sites will, and will not, be used.

DISCUSSION QUESTIONS

1. Does your church have a policy guiding its use of the internet and digital technologies? How should such a policy address professional sexual ethics?
2. What kinds of power do ministers, both ordained and lay, exercise when engaged in relationships mediated through digital technologies? In what ways is this like, and unlike, face-to-face relationships?

10. Evangelical Lutheran Church in America, "Vision and Expectations: Ordained Ministers in the Evangelical Lutheran Church in America," 2010, http://www.elca.org/Growing-In-Faith/Vocation/Rostered-Leadership/Ordained-Ministry/Vision-Expectations.aspx, Part III.

3. How might the church best respond to ministers who use online pornography or are involved in cybersex relationships, and why is this a best response?

4. How can churches foster creative, healthy uses of digital technologies by church leaders and members alike?

Recommended Readings

Adams, Peter J. *Fragmented Intimacy: Addiction in a Social World*. New York: Springer, 2008.

Cooper, Al, ed. *"Cybersex: The Dark Side of the Force,"* Special issue, *Sexual Addiction & Compulsivity*. Philadelphia: Brunner-Routledge, 2000.

Creed, Barbara. *Media Matrix: Sexing the New Reality*. New South Wales, Australia: Allen and Unwin, 2003.

Daniel, M.L., and Marie M. Fortune. "Faith Community Considerations: Social Networking." FaithTrust Institute, 2011. http://www.faithtrustinstitute.org/resources/articles/clergy-ethics.

———. "Social Networking and Healthy Boundaries in Ministry: Asking Critical Questions." FaithTrust Institute, 2011. http://www.faithtrustinstitute.org/resources/articles/clergy-ethics.

Graham, Elaine L. *Words Made Flesh: Writings in Pastoral and Practical Theology*. London: SCM Press, 2009. See esp. Part V, "New Technologies and Post/Human Futures."

Lofgreen, Connie A. "Clergy and iPorn: Sex Addiction in the Faith Community." In *The Storm of Sex Addiction: Rescue and Recovery*, 143–52. Omaha, NE: Starpro, 2012.

18

When Leaders Fall

Adam Hamilton

It was ten minutes before worship was to begin, and I was walking to the sanctuary, my sermon manuscript in hand, when one of our lead staff approached and told me that we had a personnel issue we needed to talk about after worship. I could tell by the look on her face that it was serious, and I asked her, "What's going on?" She said, "I have reason to believe that two of our pastors have become involved in an affair." I was shocked. These were two of the most gifted young clergy that I knew. As I walked onto the chancel to begin worship, I turned and saw that assisting me in worship at the service was one of these two pastors.

Every year the media is filled with stories of the infidelities of prominent people in our society—pro-golfers, late night talk show hosts, governors, members of congress, and, yes, preachers. Statistics are difficult to find, but one poll of 1,050 evangelical pastors found that 30 percent admitted to an inappropriate sexual relationship with a parishioner at some point in their careers.[1] I pray that number is high, but whatever the number, the fact is that every leader will struggle at some point with temptation, and many will wrestle with the temptation towards sexual misconduct. None of us are immune. Put us in the wrong set of circumstances at the wrong time in our lives, and we will struggle. This is why even Christian leaders must develop healthy boundaries in their lives and ministries.

In this chapter, I'd like to begin by looking at how to lead your congregation through the challenge of the moral failure of a ministerial leader. Then we'll consider how and why sexual misconduct of this kind happens with leaders and a few things you might do to prevent it from happening to your

1. Richard J. Krejcir, "Statistics on Pastors," Francis A. Schaeffer Institute of Church Leadership Development, 2007, http://www.churchleadership.org/apps/articles/
default.asp?articleid=42347&columnid=4545.

team. Finally, we'll look at strategies for how you can personally resist this temptation.

I. LEADING YOUR ORGANIZATION THROUGH SEXUAL MISCONDUCT OF A KEY LEADER

You have two competing obligations as a church leader in the case of the moral failure of one or more of your leaders. On the one hand, you are concerned for the individuals and their families who have been involved in the affair. Their lives are in crisis. On the other hand, you are responsible for the health of the church and the impact the news of the affair will have on everyone in your congregation. Because the church and her leaders represent God, because they call the church members to live for God, because members turn to their leaders for spiritual guidance, help and counsel, the fall of a leader will leave many confused, hurt, and feeling betrayed. For some, it may undermine their faith.

In our situation, with the bishop responsible for the process of discipline, the question for our church became: How do we help our congregation through this crisis? It seemed to us that we had four options: (1) say nothing and allow the rumor mill to take over with misinformation, leaving our congregation confused and hurt; (2) be evasive and acknowledge that these pastors had left our team "for personal reasons." This option seemed only slightly better than the first and would still leave a lot of questions, fostering distrust. We believed it lacked transparency and would not help the congregation work through the pain of losing two pastors in this way; (3) the "scarlet letter" approach—a blunt condemnation and distancing ourselves from the pastors; (4) approach this crisis with transparency, honesty, and compassion.

In this fourth option, which we chose, we would acknowledge that two of our pastors had become involved in an extramarital affair. We would help our congregation and staff work through the grief and feelings of betrayal. And we would ask our congregation to see these pastors through the lens of the gospel—a gospel that offers grace and redemption.

Our aim was to demonstrate the two competing demands of integrity in this situation. We wanted our congregation to know that we took seriously the integrity of our leaders. And we wanted our church to model integrity in how we respond to people who are broken and who have sinned. We could either be the Pharisees of John 8, with our stones in hand ready to destroy the adulterers, or we could follow Jesus, who looked with love upon the woman caught in the act of adultery and offered her mercy. On the one hand, there was a question of the integrity of our staff and leadership. On the other hand, there was a question of our church's integrity and faithfulness to the gospel of Jesus Christ.

In our case, things happened fast. On Monday, the pastors were placed on leave by the bishop. Weddings would immediately have to be reassigned. Pastoral and administrative responsibilities had to be handed off to others. I met with several of our key lay leaders and lead staff to discuss together how we should move forward. It was determined that we would pursue a course of transparency, integrity, and grace.

On Tuesday, I met with our staff and key lay leaders, expressing briefly what had happened, acknowledging the feelings that come when a pastor falls, and then calling us as a church staff and leaders to model for our congregation how Christians respond to a crisis like this—taking seriously the breach of integrity and at the same time expressing the compassion and grace of Christ for broken people. This was a painful and traumatic meeting, and we gave them time to meet in small groups to talk through their feelings.

On Wednesday, I sent an email to the congregation briefly describing the situation, the fact that the bishop was suspending the pastors pending the outcome of a discernment process, and that it was unlikely that they would be reassigned to our church. I invited them to worship and indicated I would be addressing the situation and inviting our congregation to see these events in the light of the gospel of Jesus Christ. I recognized the seriousness of what had happened and the consequences of this. I called them to be the church—to love broken people—and reminded them that these pastors and their families would need the love of the church. Then I wrote: "In being transparent and addressing this with you I hope our church models one side of integrity. But in offering grace and mercy and love to all who sin, including pastors, I hope we model the other side of integrity."

Over the weekend, I spent five minutes before the sermon addressing what happened and how seriously we take the integrity of our leaders. I described the process the bishop was leading and what we do as a church to minimize and prevent sexual misconduct of our staff. Following this, I preached a simple gospel sermon about temptation, sin, repentance, and grace. The sermon was not about the pastors who had fallen but about the rest of us. We looked at how we all struggle with temptation, how sin makes empty promises but only delivers pain. And we looked at the gospel of Jesus Christ, who came to seek and to save those who are lost.

I ended with the story of the woman caught in the act of adultery in John 8:3-11. I told our congregation that this was a defining moment for us as a church. We had already been clear that we take seriously the integrity of our pastors. Would we be a congregation that "shoots its wounded"—gossiping and speaking judgmentally about the pastors who had fallen, stones in hand ready to condemn? Or would we see them as Jesus saw the woman brought to him by the Pharisees, with compassion and mercy in his eyes?

This event had the potential to be the most traumatic event in our church's twenty-year history. I've seen churches handle this kind of situation very differently—with one of the other three options—and struggle for months or years. No matter how you handle a situation like this, some will feel you mishandled it. We had some families leave the church, feeling we should not have publicly addressed this. Others stayed but felt the same way. But the vast majority of our people felt we had handled this well; they felt compassion for the pastors and gratitude and respect for our transparency, the fact that we took it seriously, and that we approached it with grace.

Bear in mind, publicly addressing this does not feel like grace to those who were involved in the affair. Did we do the right thing? I believe we did what was best for the church. The congregation and others would eventually learn of it, and had we not handled this openly, I believe a lack of transparency and disclosure would have compromised our integrity and prevented healing from happening sooner.

Each situation is unique. I think our approach in this situation allowed the church to quickly move beyond the trauma. It helped us work through the situation in a way that was open, honest, and redemptive. It clarified that we take seriously this kind of breach of ministerial ethics. And it restored confidence in our ministerial leaders.

II. Why Leaders are Susceptible

Let's consider for a moment a few of the things we do to try to prevent sexual misconduct among our leaders at the Church of the Resurrection.

We have developed guidelines, policies, and principles to which we ask our staff to adhere. This includes a staff covenant that each of us sign, which is reviewed annually regarding our expectations. Among our policies meant to help staff avoid misconduct is a rule against traveling out of town alone with another staff member of the opposite sex. We suggest that if anything looks like a date or could be construed as a date, then we avoid it. We have other rules we've set up, and these are important, but the reality is that all the rules in the world will not prevent sexual misconduct.

Twice a year, I gather our staff together to offer what some call the "sex talk." This is a frank talk about how affairs happen in the workplace, warning signs, and the real consequences of inappropriate relationships among our staff. We don't focus exclusively on sexuality; we talk about all kinds of temptation. I'd like to share with you a little of the content of that talk.

I begin by reminding our staff that as human beings we're all wired with a drive for companionship; we yearn for feeling close to other human beings. This is not a bad thing. We also all have a sex drive–a desire for physical intimacy. Again, God gave us these as gifts. The challenge is a third drive we all also share–one that tends to distort the good gifts of God—that is, the sin drive. When the sin drive meets the sex drive and the intimacy drive, we find it easy to be drawn into relationships that will ultimately bring pain.

Adding to the challenge for church leaders is that we represent God and goodness and compassion, which has its own attractiveness to others. Church leaders are also at risk because often we work more hours than we should. We sometimes struggle with feelings of isolation, and we want people to like us.

Most of us can identify with the tendency Paul described in Romans 7 when he wrote, "I do not understand my own actions. For I do not do what I want, but I do the very thing I hate. . . . For I do not do the good I want, but the evil I do not want is what I do. . . . So I find it to be a law that when I want to do what is good, evil lies close at hand" (Rom. 7:15, 19, 21).[2]

All of us have known this same tension. This is why Jesus tells us to pray daily, "Lead us not into temptation." It is why each of the New Testament authors addresses temptation and the lure of sin. As the great old hymn says, "Prone to wander, Lord I feel it, prone to leave the God I love." This is *our* story.

So, here's one way sexual misconduct can begin in the workplace: you work closely with someone, and you enjoy their company and they yours.[3] It is exciting to share the work of the Lord and to dream about changing the world. You collaborate and there is joy in that. But then you go home. You're late *again*. You try sharing the exciting things you're working on; your spouse is supportive but, understandably, she or he doesn't want to spend the entire evening talking about your job—even if it is at the church.

The next day, you are back to work with your fellow staff member collaborating about your work. Your colleague never seems to tire talking about these things, and once more you feel satisfied at the end of the day—even energized—because you worked together on things in which you believe. You go home that night, and it's time to take out the trash.

Over time, you find yourself feeling drawn to your coworker. The relationship includes banter back and forth that, if you were in junior high, you might actually call flirting. Somewhere in here you have the first sense that this

2. Unless otherwise noted, all scriptural quotations are from the New Revised Standard Version.

3. Predators follow a different path. Marie Fortune draws a distinction between wanderers (as described here) and predators, who engage in grooming behaviors as they find potential victims. Marie M. Fortune, *Responding to Clergy Misconduct: A Handbook* (Seattle: FaithTrust Institute, 2009), 23.

may not be so smart—it is just a little feeling inside, a red flag. Do you listen to it—we might rightly recognize that it is the voice of the Holy Spirit—or do you dismiss it as nothing?

At some point, you admit to yourself that you are attracted to this person. You think about what it would be like to be with this person. Walter Wangerin, author and Lutheran pastor, in his book, *As For Me and My House*, speaks of this as the "moment of the maybe."[4] We begin to mull this over, and we wonder, "What if . . .?" Wangerin notes that when we play with "maybe," we're on our way to "yes."

The "moment of the maybe" is when sin is gestating, being rationalized and legitimized. It is a time of self-deception. When we're pondering "the maybe," a strange thing happens to our powers of reasoning. They become distorted. We imagine somehow that it will all work out okay if we say yes. We set aside the thought of guilt or shame, how we teach or preach about marriage, or what happens to our spouse or children, or her spouse and children. Here, I remind our staff of the old blues song written by Oris Mays, "Don't let the devil ride, he'll want to drive, don't let the devil ride."

There are a hundred small steps between "maybe" and "yes"—a touch, a hug that lasts a moment too long, the sharing of personal things, little white lies. But one large step that is very hard to recover from is sharing your feelings of attraction with the other. Either the other is surprised and uncomfortable, or they reciprocate—and where does that end? I tell our staff, *never* share those feelings with the other; it is a short step from sharing those feelings to acting upon them.[5]

At some point, you've got to see clearly what you are doing. If you enter into the relationship, how does it end well? You cannot carry on the deception forever. And when it is discovered, what will the consequences be? The dreams you once had in your life will be over. There will be pain. Things will not continue as they have been. All is not lost. God is the God of the second chance. But that path will be harder and more challenging than you imagine, and you may find that you are taking this path alone.

I share this with our staff in the hope of helping them to recognize the warning signs and to clearly understand the consequences, and then to find the strength to no longer say "maybe" but to say "no." I have to believe that there are some of you reading this chapter who can relate to this. You are in the

---

4. Walter Wangerin, Jr., *As for Me and My House: Crafting Your Marriage to Last,* expanded ed. (Nashville: Thomas Nelson, 1990), 196–97.

5. However, sharing these feelings with someone appropriate (for example, a counselor or trusted friend) can help diffuse the power of the secret attraction, as discussed in "4. Reveal," later in this essay.

midst of the struggle right now. So let's conclude by looking at how we resist temptation.

III. The Five "Rs" for Resisting Temptation

There are a few things that have saved me from pursing the path that begins with "maybe." These are the 5 "Rs" of resisting temptation. There are no silver bullets to resisting, but it's doing these kinds of things that keeps us on the right path.

1. **Remember** who you are. You are a child of God, a follower of Jesus Christ, a leader in the church. You may be someone's husband or wife, someone's mother or father. Is the thing you are struggling with consistent with who you are? Every morning, I wake up, and the first thing I do is slip to my knees next to my bed and say a short prayer, "Lord, once more today I give my life to you. Help me to live for you and honor you. Make me the man you want me to be."

2. **Recognize** the consequences of your actions. There are certain questions I ask myself when I'm feeling tempted in any area of my life. Will I feel better or worse after doing this? Will I feel more human or less? Will I be proud or ashamed? Will I be freer or will I be enslaved by doing this? Who will be hurt by my actions? If the thing becomes known, what will happen to the church, the people who trusted me? I try to use my imagination to think of the worst possible things that could happen were I to pursue the temptation I'm experiencing. Again, I ask, "How does this end well?"

3. **Rededicate** yourself to God. This is a bit like what you were taught in school if you ever find your clothes on fire—"stop, drop, and roll." When you are being tempted, you simply stop, drop, and pray. Often, when we're struggling with "the maybe," we stop praying. I find that prayer is like taking a cold shower when you're tempted. The power of the temptation dissipates.

4. **Reveal** your struggle to a trusted friend. Part of the power of temptation comes from its secretiveness. When you tell the secret to someone holding you accountable, it loses some of its power. When that person will ask you, from time to time, how you are doing in the area in which you were struggling, it helps. This is why James tells us, in 5:16, to "confess your sins to one another, and pray for one another, so that you may be healed."

5. **<u>Remove</u> yourself from the situation.** When Jesus speaks about sin in the Sermon on the Mount, he tells us that if our eye causes us to sin, we're to pluck it out, or if our hand causes us to sin, we're to cut it off. He is using hyperbole, but he's seeking to make this same point: remove yourself from the situation. Better to enter the kingdom with one hand or one eye than to have both hands and both eyes and lose the kingdom. This may be as simple as making sure you don't spend time alone with the individual to whom you are drawn. But in some cases, it may mean leaving the church you are serving to serve elsewhere. Better to serve in another church than to destroy your life and your congregation.

Okay, let me end by reminding you of two big ideas I've tried to communicate in this chapter and which I sought to share with our congregation through our crisis. The first is simply that the aim of the Christian life is sanctification. Paul describes this in 1 Thessalonians 4:3-5, and 7:

> It is God's will that you should be sanctified: that you should avoid sexual immorality; that each of you should learn to control your own body in a way that is holy and honorable, not in passionate lust like the pagans, who do not know God. . . . For God did not call us to be impure, but to live a holy life. (NIV)

Christians are asked to live a life worthy of our calling. We're called to honor God with our bodies. We're called to take seriously our wedding vows and those of others. We're called to model for others what the Christian life looks like. The second big idea is this: We'll all be tempted as human beings. We'll struggle, and sometimes we'll fall. But the last word for Christians on this matter must be grace.

There will be people who fall in the church. There will be leaders who lose their way. There are consequences when this happens—both personally and in our ministry. But the church's primary business is forgiveness for sinners. We serve a Lord who was accused of being a friend of sinners, drunkards, adulterers, and prostitutes. He called a woman who had been divorced five times and was now living with a man to be his first missionary to the Samaritans. He invited a thief to be his apostle. He told parables about prodigal sons whose fathers welcomed them home with open arms even after they had squandered their inheritance. And from the cross, his dying words were, "Father, forgive them; for they do not know what they are doing" (Luke 23:34). He is the God of the second chance. That is the gospel we live to proclaim!

So, resist the temptation. **Remember** who you are; **recognize** the consequences of your actions; **rededicate** yourself to God; **reveal** your struggles to a friend; and **remove** yourself from the situation. But if you have sinned, there is grace, and we, as churches, must be places where we show that grace to our wounded and broken.

Discussion Questions

1. Consider possible distinctions between professional sexual misconduct and other forms of sexual immorality: Did the two errant pastors discussed in this chapter abuse the power of the ministerial office? Was there a breach of fiduciary duty?

2. How may recognizing the "competing demands of integrity" inform your decision making as a ministerial leader? What risks are involved in following each of the four options this congregation faced?

3. Compare and contrast the situation of the Church of the Resurrection with that of Vienna Presbyterian (see *Washington Post* article, below). In each case, how did the senior pastor choose to practice transparency, integrity, and grace? How did these actions contribute to congregational health and healing?

4. Consider a time when you utilized any of the "Five 'Rs' for Resisting Temptation." How would you modify this list of suggestions, if at all?

Recommended Readings

Fortune, Marie M. *Responding to Clergy Misconduct: A Handbook*. Seattle: FaithTrust Institute, 2009.

Gaede, Beth Ann, ed. *When a Congregation Is Betrayed: Responding to Clergy Misconduct*. Herndon, VA: Alban Institute, 2006.

Hopkins, Nancy Myer, and Mark R. Laaser, eds. *Restoring the Soul of a Church: Healing Congregations Wounded by Clergy Sexual Misconduct*. Collegeville, MN: Liturgical, 1995.

James, Peter G. "Religious Hypocrisy." Sermon delivered at Vienna Presbyterian Church, Vienna, VA, March 27, 2011. http://www.viennapres.org/fileadmin/media/sermons/print/2011-03-27 Religious Hypocrisy.pdf.

Ruth, Kibbie Simmons, and Karen A. McClintock. *Healthy Disclosure: Solving Communication Quandaries in Congregations.* Herndon, VA: Alban Institute, 2007.

Wangerin, Walter, Jr. *As for Me and My House: Crafting Your Marriage to Last.* Nashville: Thomas Nelson, 2001.

White, Josh. "Vienna Presbyterian Church Seeks Forgiveness, Redemption in Wake of Abuse Scandal." *Washington Post*, April 2, 2011. http://www.washingtonpost.com/local/vienna-presbyterian-church-works-to-overcome-revelations-of-sexual-abuse/2011/03/30/AF3hNxQC_story.html.

19

Sexual Issues in Parish Ministry

Youtha Hardman-Cromwell

Discipleship requires lifelong learning. Christians who wish to address sexual issues in the context of parish ministry must wrestle with scriptures and traditions, as well as with new insights about human sexuality emerging from the sciences, all the while analyzing contemporary practices and fostering dialogue within the church about these matters.

Consider Pastor Wilkins' experience. She opens her email on Monday morning to find this message from her youth group leaders:

> Help! Members of our group have been talking among themselves for a while about various sexual issues that have been in the news lately: same-sex marriage, infidelity scandals, pedophilia, and rape. Added to that, an unwed, former youth group member is pregnant. Last night one of the youth asked us directly if we can have time in youth group meetings to talk about these issues. We don't feel prepared to do this. What do we do now?—Ken and Barbara

How would you respond if you were Pastor Wilkins?

Being well-informed about the kinds of sexual issues that contemporary Christians—and those we seek to draw into the Christian community—are wrestling with and facing in their everyday encounters is essential to ministry. The hunger of youth groups for conversations about issues like those noted above gives witness to this need. And these topics are coming to the church not only through our young people, who are often more open and questioning about sexual issues, but also from adults—married, divorced, surviving spouses, GLBT, and otherwise single adults who are in our faith community and in the wider community. The church needs to respond appropriately and proactively. Faith leaders need to be ready to help seekers think through the situations they hear about, live with, and about which they make decisions. If the desire for open exploration is to be honored (like that of Pastor Wilkins's youth group), we need to be aware, well-informed, and ready to talk about subjects like abortion, contraception, fertility issues, masturbation, celibacy, and other issues that are likely to surface,.

All of our relationships are expressed through our body and, thus, through our sexuality. So sexuality and spirituality cannot be separated. Viewing body and spirit as dichotomous has produced a history of the church failing to deal adequately with sexual issues. Unless we as believers are knowledgeable and thoughtful about our sexual lives, it will be easy to use our bodies in ways that do not honor the fact that we are God-created and God-loved beings.

Reluctance to address the sexual issues can result in persons being misinformed and engaging in harmful and unhealthy uses of their bodies, because the church community has been silent or had only one thing to say to those who are single: "No." Each of us must make sexual choices, and spiritual leaders are called and challenged to help parishioners make them. People need help in integrating their sexual being with their beliefs, values, and relationships with God and neighbors.

As ministerial leaders, we must increase our comfort level with and ability to speak openly, honestly, and knowledgeably about sexual issues of all kinds, even of those practices which we consider detrimental. We need to prepare ourselves so that we are not surprised or express shock or revulsion by any subject that is raised by those with whom we minister. Our responsibility and call are to be supportive of every person's desire for help and enlightenment, as well as encouraging in the way we react, keeping in mind that none of us is beyond the love and grace of God. Silence or only three words of counsel—"just say no"—will not do.

Three principles have emerged from and guided my work in pastoral ministry and sexual issues, principles that could help guide Pastor Wilkins and other ministerial leaders to address sexual issues in ministry. To be effective, those who lead explorations in sexual issues must:

- Be in touch with themselves as sexual beings and the sexual dynamics inherent in their leadership roles.
- Seek an increase in knowledge and comfort level with sexual issues through a commitment to life-long learning.
- Be committed to communal deliberation and discernment using scriptures, current events, case studies, and emerging scientific information.

Self-Awareness

One of the first things leaders need to do is to be sure that we are in touch with ourselves as sexual beings. Who are the persons and what are the behaviors and things that appeal to our particular sexual libido? Are we taking care of our sexual needs outside of the ministry setting in ways that are faithful to our Christian commitments? To whom are we attracted in our church setting? How are we establishing and intentionally protecting our professional boundaries?

We also need to acknowledge our sexual and emotional wounds. Have we been abused physically or psychologically? Do we carry unresolved pain because of a particular circumstance or situation in our life, such as an alcoholic parent, a horrific divorce, the death of a child or parent, scars from adultery, premarital sex or pregnancy, rape, abortion, sexual orientation issues, or gender identity issues? We need to be particularly judicious when such issues are involved in ministry settings. In addition, we need to be aware of our limitations in counseling and refer persons who need more than prayer and presence to those who are trained in counseling. It is prudent to maintain a list of counselors and counseling services for referral when the issues are presented that exceed our knowledge and preparation.

A consciousness of the sexual dynamic that may arise in the worship context is equally important. Congregations tend to have a number of persons who are single, either in their wider life or in the congregation (that is, their significant other is not a part of the worshipping community.) For some, the good touch—physically and emotionally—that they receive in the congregation may be the only favorable, intentional touch they receive on a regular basis. If the worship experience produces an emotional high, especially if it is spirited and elicits strong emotions, that good feeling may become associated with the worship leader and may lead to romantic projections or sexual fantasies. As leaders, we are in the power position and are responsible for setting boundaries, keeping our role clear, and maintaining appropriate relationships.

A Commitment to Lifelong Learning

We all need to be life-long learners in order to provide leadership around sexual issues in our community. Continued learning is supported by a climate of greater openness to talk about sexual matters and responses to questions that are raised. This openness is to be celebrated. It leads to the development of a more precise vocabulary. For example, "homosexuality" and "pedophilia" refer to quite different phenomena, even though some confused people may still equate them. Polygamy and polyamory are related but distinct lifestyles that are based on different cultural and social understandings. Date rape and statutory rape are types of rape; both are illegal and abusive, yet they may be characterized by quite varied dynamics.

I have learned much from years of working with seminary students to help them increase their knowledge of sexual issues. Topics that lately have emerged as important are polyamory and the sexual concerns of those who have survived life changing illnesses or accidents. Young people may be more aware of polyamory than other adults. This is an increasingly practiced lifestyle that Pastor Wilkins would want to be aware of as she responds to her youth group. It appears to be a refining or development of the open marriage concept, in which neither monogamy nor polygamy is valued. Polyamory differs from infidelity because other sexual relationships are willingly condoned by those with whom one is involved; it is something to which all the parties involved agree. Adherents maintain that it is possible to be involved in multiple intimate, sexual relationships without damage to any of them. The basic premises are that participants must be honest with all the partners involved and that all relationships take work to maintain in a healthy way. A critical discussion of polyamory could serve as a door that opens into a discussion of healthy relationships and their distinction from abusive relationships and relational violence of all kinds.[1]

Some young people may be dealing with health-related issues that potentially impact sexual life, such as diabetes, cancer survival, loss of limbs or the use of them, and other physical situations that may prevent usual sexual interaction.[2] When these conditions exist, they may negatively impact levels of self-esteem and result in distress or depression. In their relationships, persons and their partners need to have the expectation and learn how their gift of sexuality can be experienced in positive ways despite their challenging physical conditions. To be a lifelong learner in this area of knowledge, we need to identify continuing education goals and ways of completing them that might

---

1. Many of the stated polyamory relationship principles apply to all healthy relationships: fidelity, steadfastness, and loyalty to the commitments made; trust, honesty, dignity, and respect; mutual support; communication and negotiation; and non-possessiveness. See Kenneth R. Haslam, "The 12 Pillars of Polyamory" (unpublished paper, June 14, 2008), http://www.polyamoryonline.org/articles/12pillars.html.

2. Ralph and Barbara Alterowitz, *The Lovin' Ain't Over for Women with Cancer* (Potomac, MD: CIACT, 2011).

include reading various materials, formal scholarship, or participating in an appropriate study group.

Some of these avenues for continuing learning are also ones that could be utilized to meet the needs of Pastor Wilkins's youth group. Conversations around issues of sex outside of marriage and the pregnancy of under-aged peers are likely to lead Pastor Wilkins to dealing with questions about contraception and abortion. If the discussions are guided by the questions participants have, contraception may surface in the context of preventing pregnancy within or outside of marriage. There are a number of contraceptive aids that might be the focus of inquiry: abstinence; the "rhythm method," now often called Natural Family Planning (NFP); oral contraceptives (pre- and post-sexual intercourse); condoms; spermicidal applications; medical devices inserted into the vagina or uterus; vasectomies; and tubal ligations. Conversations about preventing pregnancy may trigger questions and subsequent conversation about preventing sexually transmitted diseases (STDs).

To inform discussion of the moral and spiritual aspects of a sexual issue, such as abortion and contraception, it is often a good practice to bring in persons with specific expertise—such as medical and legal experts, researchers, and counselors—who have accurate and current information. While disagreement over Roe v. Wade is likely to continue for years to come, many questions about abortion—its legality, proposals to restrict it even in instances of rape and incest, and at what point "life" begins—are in flux. Concern about the rightness of a decision to seek an abortion may raise concerns about the given circumstances, as well as questions of guilt about previous abortions, abortions under consideration, or health or financial and care issues involved.

COMMUNAL DISCERNMENT INFORMED BY SCRIPTURE AND SCIENCE

Sharing information is important, but so is dialogue. How might Pastor Wilkins and her youth leaders open up the opportunity for the youth to explore their questions and concerns? One way to proceed is to design a study by inviting participants to write down their questions or areas of interest. After collecting them anonymously, a series of lessons can be planned. It is important to acknowledge that all are learners, that no question should be ignored, and that participants should be encouraged to use the language they know. Their vocabularies can be expanded in the course of interaction without causing embarrassment to those who use slang or imprecise descriptors. Scripture, current events, case studies, and emerging scientific information are all sources to increase knowledge, fuel conversation, provoke thought, and open dialogue.

Read and pray the scriptures generously. The Scriptures bless the total human being (sexual and spiritual), call us good, and challenge us to use our body lovingly, creatively (versus abusively), and worshipfully. One way to begin is to do a study series that looks at what the Bible has to say about sexuality and sexual issues. For example, I have used Song of Songs in both a young adult class and my seminary course to help students relax about body issues and to see that scripture celebrates the body. Song of Songs clearly celebrates the body, sexual attraction, and desire, as well as the power of the body in human relationships. The writer celebrates it in words like these:

How sweet is your love, my sister, my bride! How much better is your love than wine, and the fragrance of your oils than any spice! Your lips distill nectar, my bride; honey and milk are under your tongue; the scent of your garments is like the scent of Lebanon. (Song of Sol. 4:10-11)

O that his left hand were under my head, and that his right hand embraced me!

(Song of Sol. 8:3)[3]

Portions of Song of Songs can be used in each session as an opening, before exploring more specific portions of scripture.

Read and use scriptures generously to enter into discussion of particular sexual issues. A quick tour through the Bible reveals portions fertile for discussing many different sexual issues. The Book of Genesis is rich. The story of creation (Gen. 1:26-31) reminds us that our physical creation was deemed by God as good and our body, even naked (Gen. 2:25), was not meant to be experienced as shameful. Genesis 19:1-11 offers the opportunity to talk not only about same-sex relationships but also about homo- and heterosexual rape, since homosexual rape is what the men of Sodom try to commit on the messengers from God, and heterosexual rape is what Lot proposes when he offers his daughters instead. The story of Jacob's marriage to Leah and Rachel (beginning in Gen. 29:15) offers the opportunity to talk about polygamy. Since the story of Onan spilling his seed in Genesis 38:1-10 is frequently used as a prohibition against masturbation, it can start a conversation about this sexual practice, even though the action proscribed was not masturbation but Onan's refusal to fulfill an ancient levirate marriage obligation by interrupting coital activity and withdrawing the penis prior to ejaculation (spilling the male seed outside the vagina as a contraceptive action). The story of the efforts of Potiphar's wife

3. Unless otherwise noted, all scriptural quotations are taken from the Revised Standard Version.

to seduce Joseph into a sexual relationship (Gen. 39:6b-23) invites a discussion about extramarital sex and also about the abuse of power that is often involved in inappropriate sexual relationships. (It has the added value of indicating that sexual predators can be male or female.)

The way in which the men of Benjamin obtained wives (Judg. 21:16-24) could open a conversation about sex trafficking and prostitution. Hannah's story in 1 Samuel 1:4-20 contains the issue of infertility. David's relationship with Bathsheba (2 Samuel 11) is an example of infidelity in marriage, as well as abuse of power. The story of Tamar's rape (2 Samuel 13) can open a conversation about rape, including date rape. The passage about the many women King Solomon loved (1 Kgs. 11:1-3) can prompt a discussion of polygamy and polyamory. Mary's pregnancy with Jesus (Matt. 1:18-21) raises questions about premarital pregnancy. A discussion around issues of divorce can begin with a look at what Jesus says about divorce in Matthew 19:3-12. Paul addresses the issues of celibacy and singleness (1 Cor. 7:8, 9, 36-38).

When using Scripture, it is important to recognize, and be forthright about, the cultural context out of which and to which Scripture speaks. Patriarchy—the view that men ought to rule over women—characterized most of the ancient Mediterranean world. Similarly, slavery was widely practiced, and it was routine for the household patriarch to have sexual relationships and bear children with servants. Prostitution was sometimes part of pagan temple worship, and it was the routine practice in some cultures for some well-to-do males to take young adolescent boys as sexual partners in exchange for mentoring. Use contemporary biblical commentaries and other sources to gain the insight needed to be prepared to relate the cultural dynamics underlying the scriptural record.

Awareness and understanding of how biblical cultures are different from the contemporary setting in which we live is especially important. Practices pertaining to marriage and children exemplify these differences. Marriage was not regarded as a love arrangement; marriages were arranged for economic, political, and dynastic reasons, as well as to maintain family lines and connections. Having many children was seen as positive for the culture, a necessity for continuing the marriage and the family line, and a sign of blessing by God. Pregnancy and giving birth to a son were expected of women, giving them status and security. This was probably the motivation for the behavior of Lot's daughters, who seek to become pregnant by their father when they determined that no husbands were available to them (Gen. 19:30-38).

Compare these concepts of marriage with the contemporary marriage practices that impact Pastor Wilkins's youth. It is a fact that young people in the United States today tend to marry at much later ages than even in the 1950s. This delay responds to changing gender roles and to the expectation of many years of formal education, the maturity to make choices, and the financial viability of both partners before entering a marriage relationship. Yet, puberty is occurring earlier than ever, perhaps because of better nutrition or the use of hormones in the foods that we consume. It is also common for couples to live together prior to or instead of marriage. In U.S. culture, the years between puberty and the usual age of marriage have expanded, and there is no longer the assumption that all adults will marry. The average age of marriage in the United States is 25.8 for women and 28.3 for men,[4] but sexual desire has not been delayed. Added to this increased population of single adults is the increase in the number of divorced and widowed persons who remain single, either by choice or circumstances (such as loss of income at remarriage). Pastor Wilkins's youth are actual or potential members of this population of single persons.

How do persons of faith in these situations deal with their active libidos? These issues may arise and should be explored in age-appropriate ministries. Bishop John Spong advocates that faith communities reestablish a form of betrothal that would allow couples to engage in sexual intimacy and/or cohabit within certain imposed strictures.[5] Karen Lebacqz has suggested that an appropriate, mutual vulnerability is the standard for permissible sex outside of marriage.[6] Such responses to our current context can be grist for the discussion mill.

We must also integrate into our Christian faith relevant scientific knowledge, questions, and understandings not known to the biblical writers and their audiences. For example, many translations of the Bible into English use "homosexuality," a word first coined in 1842, for a variety of words in the original Hebrew and Greek of Scripture. How should the words be translated and understood? A close reading raises questions about the differences in how same-sex relationships were experienced in biblical times and now. Is Scripture responding to monogamous, consensual relationships or to abusive and uncommitted same-sex encounters? What role does biblical sexism play in what

4. Casey E. Copen, Kimberly Daniels, Jonathan Vespa, and William D. Mosher, "First Marriages in the United States: Data From the 2006-2010 National Survey of Family Growth," *National Health Statistics Reports* 49 (March 22, 2012), 1, http://www.cdc.gov/nchs/data/nhsr/nhsr049.pdf.

5. John Shelby Spong, *Living in Sin? A Bishop Rethinks Human Sexuality* (San Francisco: Harper & Row, 1988), 177–87.

6. Karen Lebacqz, "Appropriate Vulnerability: A Sexual Ethic for Singles," in *Sexuality and the Sacred: Sources for Theological Reflection*, ed. Marvin M. Ellison and Kelly Brown Douglas, 2nd ed. (Louisville: Westminster John Knox, 2010), 272–77.

is understood? Is homosexuality a choice or inborn? Can our sexual orientation be changed? Should we try to do so? These questions affect how the church responds to LGBT persons, some of whom are undoubtedly teenagers in our youth groups.[7]

CONCLUSION

We need to be honest about the range of positions and beliefs held in the Christian community and in other religious communities with which we have increased contact. They may or may not ordain homosexuals and transgender persons, regard females as equals or as inferiors, condone or prohibit same-sex marriage, or view adultery, divorce, polygamy, and premarital sex differently. The various cultural backgrounds of Christian adherents and converts, as well as secular beliefs and values, require us to understand the stances of various faiths and societies; they filter into the struggles that Christians experience around sexual issues.[8] For example, child marriage and sex trafficking are accepted in some cultures. Those who support such practices have not recognized that God did not create persons to be used or abused by others who have greater power.

Using case studies and news articles is a way to launch into a topic and bring into the conversation the intersection of both religious and cultural beliefs and attitudes. Various states across the United States are asking voters to approve or disallow same-sex unions and/or marriages; this issue will continue to surface politically. In the future, General David Petraeus' infidelity will be raised as we question adultery as a reason for eliminating one from public service, insofar as it may open them to vulnerability to blackmail in the hope of securing classified information.[9] Sex outside of the marriage is also a contested issue. What might be acceptable in the wider culture may be prohibited by our religious values. Couples determine the level of fidelity to which they are committed, whatever the church may say. Monogamy may not be equally valued in a relationship, and attitudes may change in the course of the marriage. Questions about fidelity in marriage affect other persons, such as offspring. This would likely be the case as Pastor Wilkins discusses these issues with her youth. The media-revealed case of Coach Jerry Sandusky's child abuse gives a continuing face to that issue.[10] What might be acceptable in the wider culture may be prohibited by

---

7. Consider, for example, recent news reports of youth and young adult activists. See Michael Schulman "Generation LGBTQIA: lesbian.gay.bisexual.transgender.queer/questioning.intersex.ally/asexual," *New York Times*, January 10, 2013.

8. See, for example, Daniel C. Maguire, "Religions Say...," *USA Today,* August 14, 2006.

9. Thom Shanker, "U.S. Military: culture of abuse and corruption of power? Concern Grows Over Top Military Officers' Ethics," *New York Times*, November 12, 2012.

our religious values. Such cases provide grist for the discussion and discernment mill.

Our aim should be to stimulate thinking rather than indoctrinate. This is particularly necessary if we want to keep the dialogue open and have influence on and conversation with those with whom we are in ministry. We can get persons to articulate a particular belief, but what is needed is for each person to use information to determine a personal belief that guides their behaviors. A continued journey as lifelong learners will help us be fruitful and effective in ministry. Our role as spiritual leaders requires it of us, especially when the issues affect both the spirituality and sexuality of those who are in our care.

Discussion Questions

1. Is there a difference between legal marriage and marriage before God? What does that mean for religious communities?
2. Traditionally, Christians have found polygamy, polyandry (one woman with multiple husbands), and polyamory unacceptable. What Christian convictions and values inform that judgment?
3. The council of a major city is considering expanding laws to require that all adults be held liable if they fail to report child abuse. How might this decision impact confidentiality between youth and lay youth group leaders, such as Ken and Barbara? Between youth and Pastor Wilkins?
4. How should the church community respond to pregnancy outside of marriage among members?

Recommended Readings

Chilstrom, Herbert W. *Sexual Fulfillment for Single and Married, Straight and Gay, Young and Old.* Minneapolis: Fortress Press, 2001.

Countryman, L. William. "New Testament Sexual Ethics and Today's World." In *Sexuality and the Sacred: Sources for Theological Reflection,* ed. James B. Nelson and Sandra P. Longfellow, 28–53. Louisville: Westminster John Knox, 1994.

Gomes, Peter J. "The Bible and Women: The Conflicts of Inclusion" and "The Bible and Homsexuality." In *The Good Book: Reading the Bible with Mind and Heart,* 120–72. New York: William Morrow and Company, Inc., 1996.

10. Tim Rohan, "Sandusky Gets 30 to 60 Years for Sexual Abuse," *New York Times*, October 9, 2012.

Hershberger, Anne Krabill, ed. *Sexuality: God's Gift,* 2nd ed. Scottsdale, PA: Herald, 2010.

Hollinger, Dennis P. *The Meaning of Sex.* Grand Rapids: Baker Academic, 2009.

Miles, Al. *Domestic Violence: What Every Pastor Needs to Know,* 2nd ed. Minneapolis: Fortress Press, 2011.

Thatcher, Adrian. *God, Sex and Gender: An Introduction.* Oxford: Wiley-Blackwell, 2011.

Westheimer, Ruth K., and Sanford Lopater. *Human Sexuality: A Psychosocial Perspective.* Philadelphia: Lippincott Williams & Wilkins, 2005.

20

Sex and the Pastoral Life

Bonnie J. Miller-McLemore

In *The Last Report on the Miracles at Little No Horse*, a novel overflowing with passion, Louise Erdrich tells the nearly unfathomable vocational tale of a woman who has metamorphosed through three life phases—first, a short-lived effort to wed Christ as Sister Cecelia, which ended when her relentlessly ardent piano playing of Chopin drove the convent inhabitants crazy with sorrow and sent her packing; then, as Agnes DeWitt of rural Wisconsin, seeking food and shelter and finding love from a German farmer Berndt Vogel; and finally, undercover as Father Damien, a Catholic missionary priest, dressed as a man but with the desires of a woman, compelled into service on the remote reservation of Little No Horse. Overtly, Erdrich's book explores the question of what qualifies as sainthood, but my interest lies in the flux and flow of passion, its beauty celebrated but also its necessary boundaries respected and tested.

When Agnes walks unexpectedly into Berndt's hard farm life, she trades housekeeping for a bowl of hot oatmeal, only to ignite in Berndt his own passion to unbind the cloth wound tight around her breasts. Right after she appears hungry on his doorstep, cleans her plate, and utters in her mother's German dialect, "*Jetzt muss ich schlafen* [Now I must sleep]," we read: "So he took her to his bed."

As a woman reader who recognizes in my bones vulnerability and self-protection, I immediately thought "to bed" as in "to ravish." But he doesn't mean it that way. "He took her to his bed, the only bed there was, in the corner of the otherwise empty room," and he retires to the "barn he loved . . . [to] lay awake all night," determined by morning to marry her "if she would have him."[1] She refuses. She has already been unfaithful, although whether to her

---

1. Louise Erdrich, The Last Report on the Miracles at Little No Horse (New York: HarperCollins, 2009), 17.

love as a religious of Christ or to the Polish composer, conjured through her keyboard fervor, we cannot say. Either way—once, it seems, is enough.

So begins the ancient tension between desire and constraint that underscores the paradox and lesson that *proper boundaries, respectfully employed, protect and even deepen sexual passion.* Agnes's rationale is merely "her first pawn in a long game . . . the two would play over the course of many months." And he is a more "dogged and ruthless opponent" than she anticipates. In a penultimate move, he agrees to buy a piano, the "sort of thing a husband gives his wife," he says, hoping finally to convince her to wed. Once more she spurns him; she can move to town, she declares, find a room, and support herself by giving lessons. So he yearns, waits, *and* practices. Just as she cannot keep her fingers from pounding out the Adagio of the Pathetique on the arms of the chair, so he cannot "help his own fingers moving" on his rough barn mattress "in faint imitation of the way he would, if he could ever, touch her hips." Only when a side of the house is removed to move the grand piano shipped from Minneapolis into the front room and Agnes sheds every shred of clothes to pour herself into each wrought note, do they both give into love, even if never to marriage. And a deep sexual love it becomes, told in sparingly few but deeply moving details. "Then followed their best times."[2]

Months and miles later, after daringly donning the clothing from a priest found dead in the aftermath of a devastating flood, Agnes becomes Father Damien and travels on to assume the position for which he was intended, and we expect her desires to end. But they do not, even though they are more restricted than ever by duty to her parishioners. Desire reemerges with a "jolt" when she grasps the hand of Father Gregory, an assistant sent by the bishop, the "heat" traveling up her arm "from his heavy palm . . . into her heart." The situation is loaded with contradictions and quandaries: Father Damien willingly despairs "to be discovered" as a woman; Father Gregory fears with an "awful and appalling joy" that his attraction to her (as a "him") marks him among "those whom the Church darkly warned against"; they are both priests promised to celibacy; she is at least temporarily his teacher and superior; yet their bodily attraction is palpable, their pleasure untainted by personal and social distortions, and their clandestine love loyal unto death, unknown to anyone except perhaps a housekeeper rescued by Father Damien from a horrific domestic situation. When they later break bread and confess they "belong" to each other, they feel "spreading from those words a branching fury of impossible difficulty."[3]

2. Ibid., 17, 19, 20, 22.
3. Ibid., 194, 200, 201.

PROMOTING THE BEAUTY OF PROTECTED PASSION

This third and final passion play of *The Last Report*, like the two before it, raises questions about desire's boundaries that this chapter will not address. Fortunately, other chapters in this book provide guidance for navigating the "impossible difficulty" when passion is fanned into flames in the wrong places. In fact, I can only write this chapter because others here and beyond have underscored the importance of maintaining clear sexual boundaries with parishioners and staff. As a prerequisite to this chapter, I assume readers will have labored over the steps essential to the prevention of the abuse of power. I assume readers are committed to nurturing a healthy professional sexual ethic through study, workshops, collegial consultation, professional supervision, and support networks. This allows me to turn to another essential and overlooked theme—the importance of sustaining a passionate sexual life beyond the professional pastoral life.

My purpose here is to affirm passion within its proper place—intimate, committed, just, and mutual relationships outside one's place of employment. I want to celebrate the beauty of sexual passion protected and promoted within such parameters and explore practices that secure its good. In a word, I argue for clear boundaries within ministry *and* good sex outside one's professional pastoral relationships. I start with my own case, not as representative at all (especially given the quintessentially slow awakening and still naïve and illogically modest nature of my own sexuality), but simply as a place to begin, with all its limitation. I will try to draw some general conclusions from my experience in conversation with resources that have informed my work as a teacher and scholar of pastoral theology.

I envision three groups among the readers of this book. There are those who are passionate, at risk because we are sometimes careless and often over-extended, and hence prone to falling into inappropriate relationships due to poor preparation and inattention to professional sexual ethics. This, I fear, includes most of us. There are those less prone to sexual indiscretion but still in need of greater understanding and enjoyment of the sexual reward within enduring intimate relationships. This group includes a lucky few wise and seasoned clergy. Finally, and regrettably, some few readers of this book may have serious emotional, spiritual, and sexual problems. They may be among those who prey on the vulnerable and need criminal or legal intervention and professional healing to prevent abuse. I write this chapter primarily for people in the former two groups who not only need to maintain clear patterns of professional behavior that prevent sexual violation of those in their care, but who also seek to sustain a rich and viable sexual life and, ideally, help their parishioners do the same.

Indeed, when I shared my intentions for this chapter with others, one person who regularly hosts workshops on professional ethics remarked that pastors who attend often want sexual education for themselves. While sexuality pervades popular culture, it still seems foreign in Christian contexts. Throughout Christian history, topics like asceticism, celibacy, and even sexual orientation and appropriate sexual boundaries have received more discussion than the pleasures of sex. Most of us do not feel supported in our sexual passions by *either* our Christian communities *or* popular culture, where sexual freedoms and fantasies are paraded and exploited heedlessly. This is unfortunate since Christianity actually has positive contributions to make on the sacramental value of passionate love.

Get a Life—A Sexual Life

Sometimes, when we perceive someone as overinvested in work, we say that she or he needs to "get a life." This is essentially what Mark, my husband, and I learned three decades ago, early in our shared lives as a couple and as ministers, he in a congregation and I in a seminary. *Get a life—a sexual life outside your professional context.*

There, forever emblazoned in my teaching notes on clergy sexual ethics, is the wake-up call: "Pay more attention to your own primary relationships." Right next to that is another note: "Cancelled anniversary vacation *rescheduled*." It was the mid-1980s, we were newly married and encountering the first wave of disclosure of clergy sexual abuse. I was developing my pastoral care course. He had just returned from a denominational workshop on clergy ethics, awakened. He learned a lot about prevention, but one priority stood out: Our relationship needed to be sustained. Seems simple enough, but no one had advised us to have more sex until then. Of course, it was about much more than that. Still, contrary to the Hollywood portrait, our sexual life would not automatically flourish without tending. It needed time, space, attention, devotion, and, yes, practice. We rescheduled the anniversary trip we had just crossed off our calendars. So "get a sexual life" not only made its way into my teaching, it became memorialized in our lives. I taught students not to take for granted those treasured intimate relationships outside our congregational or professional context. Without "consistent emotional closeness," we risk using inappropriate means for meeting such needs.[4]

This seemed counterintuitive to ministerial assumptions about devotion to one's flock. It certainly was counterintuitive to how many women across generations have been raised to suppress our needs for the sake of others. The words of Luise Eichenbaum and Susie Orbach on the "construction of femininity" are as powerful today as when they wrote them three decades ago. A mother's over-identification with her daughter "makes her annoyed with the child for displaying her needs and for not controlling them as she herself does." Unwittingly, many mothers transmit to daughters the message that there is something wrong with such desires, "something that needs to be kept at bay," thus providing daughters with their "first lesson in emotional deprivation," and, I would add, sexual deprivation.[5] Decades of feminist reconstructions of Christian love, from self-denigrating sacrifice to radical mutuality, have made apparent the delicate and rich balance that must occur between self and other in the give and take of any significant relationship, whether between intimate couples or a minister and her congregation.

This balance cannot be sustained if one doesn't even know one's desires. As Polish psychologist Alice Miller makes apparent in *The Drama of the Gifted Child*, those who go into helping professions are precisely those who have learned well how to take care of others' needs by suppressing their own, thus perpetuating a cycle of further narcissistic wounding.[6] Ministers who meet repressed needs for love and admiration by trying to keep everyone happy face serious challenges in their congregations. In the prototypical struggles of dependency, authority, and power in churches, the "personal authenticity of the minister, priest, or rabbi is the greatest strength," according to Episcopalian pastor John Harris.[7] In a nutshell, one must know one's desires and one must learn to express them openly and appropriately.

---

4. I was especially struck by the overlooked importance of the middle term of "Value" of Lloyd Rediger's acronym PREVENT, which stresses *preparing* for appropriate behavior before challenging circumstances arise; developing a *regular* or consistent pattern of proper behavior; establishing a means of *evaluating* one's accountability with congregational leaders; *valuing* our need for intimacy and close relationships; striving for *excellence* and joy in ministry; sustaining support *networks* with peers; and remaining *terrified* of the traumatic consequences of clergy malfeasance. See G. Lloyd Rediger, *Ministry and Sexuality: Cases, Counseling, Care* (Minneapolis: Fortress Press, 1990) and G. Lloyd Rediger, *Beyond the Scandals: A Guide to Healthy Sexuality for Clergy* (Minneapolis: Fortress Press, 2003), 133–34.

5. Luise Eichenbaum and Susie Orbach, *Understanding Women: A Feminist Psychoanalytic Approach* (New York: Basic Books, 1983).

6. Alice Miller, *The Drama of the Gifted Child*, trans. Ruth Ward (New York: Basic Books, 1981).

7. John C. Harris, *Stress, Power and Ministry: An Approach to the Current Dilemmas of Pastors and Congregations* (New York: Alban Institute, 1997), 3.

Knowing and affirming passion is not just a psychological necessity. It is also a theological mandate. In an article on the church and sexual violence, one sentence from Catholic ethicist Christine Gudorf's assessment really resonates with me: "If the church had done a better job of teaching how marriage is sacramental—and how central sexual pleasure is to the spiritual life and growth that characterizes the vocation of marriage—the sinfulness of sexual violence would be much clearer than it presently is."[8] That is, if we truly celebrated sexual passion in its proper place, sexual violence would stand out as abhorrent by contrast. Gudorf went on to write an entire book on pleasure as an essential component of a Christian sexual ethic. On a mission that extends to recent writings, she has become bolder and clearer: "Sex—good, frequent, mutually pleasurable—is as vitally important to the vocation of marriage as reception of the Eucharist is to membership in the church community. One of the tasks of the church should be to help make marital sex more pleasurable."[9]

This last claim rests on a Catholic understanding of marriage as a means of grace comparable to the Eucharist in dispensing divine life, with sexual intercourse as integral to the bestowal. Admittedly, most Protestants recognize only two sacraments, and marriage is not among them. But this doesn't make Gudorf's blessing of pleasurable sex any less crucial for Protestantism. Marriage remains for Protestants a Christian vocation, and many recognize the sexual passion at its heart as capable of conveying God's love.

Of critical note: I am *not* claiming that sex and sexual pleasure is *reserved for marriage*. This important question belongs to a different text with a larger agenda. I am claiming, however, that *the mandate for sustaining a good sex life beyond the congregation belongs not only to the married; it pertains to all who minister, whether single, vowed celibates, or married.* My agenda here is simply to affirm sexual passion within its proper place: intimate, committed, just, mutual relationships outside one's place of employment. These parameters may not necessitate marriage, even though they do include ideals common to marriage. In her extensive work on just love, Christian ethicist Margaret Farley spells out the norms necessary to morally good, intimate relationships. They must entail no unjust harm, free consent, mutuality, equality, commitment, fruitfulness, and social justice.[10]

---

8. Christine E. Gudorf, "Sexual Violence: It's Sinful to Remain Silent," *SALT: Catholic Journal of Social Justice* (May 1993): 10.

9. Christine E. Gudorf, "Graceful Pleasures: Why Sex is Good for Your Marriage," *Human Sexuality in the Catholic Tradition*, ed. Kieran Scott and Harold D. Horell (New York: Rowman & Littlefield, 2007), 124.

PRACTICES FOR THE LONG HAUL

How does one have a healthy sexual life outside one's ministry? I am not a sex therapist or expert or even someone that is well-informed about sexuality. Worse, I have fit so well the women Eichenbaum and Orbach describe that I struggled in the early years of marriage to give into pleasure and made sex difficult. My impulse to chase and kiss boys as a young girl had been shamed into hiding long ago and had to be reawakened and welcomed back. Nonetheless, I can speak to the challenge and parameters of what makes for a good sexual life through its fits, starts, and flourishing in my own. I list in no particular order practices that have played an important place for me and my husband. When I step back, I see that these are actually suggestions for a loving relationship more generally and not just in the bedroom.

REMEMBER THAT SEXUAL PRACTICE MATURES OVER THE LONG HAUL.

So many Hollywood films make sexual ecstasy look easy. People appear naturally to know just what to do. Although biology serves as a rudimentary guide in many practices that appear inborn (for example, nursing), most such proclivities take practice and learning. With time, sex can get better, not more boring.

WELCOME THE FREEDOM THAT COMES WITH LONG-TERM COMMITMENT.

Why does sex sometimes get better with time? Comfort and trust come with time. Sometime during the first decade of marriage, our sex life shifted. Perhaps our egos were less fragile as we left behind graduate study and early years establishing ourselves in school and congregation. Perhaps it was the renewed commitment we made once we had kids (if we had kids, we had to stick together), the richness that can accompany sex in pursuit of procreation,[11] or just knowing the other's body and pleasures more clearly. Or more basic, Mark got a vasectomy and I no longer had to fool with the unpleasantries of mood-altering hormones, a slippery diaphragm, or an IUD that caused bleeding. Whatever the reason, a more genuine letting-go surprised us when it appeared. Trusting the relationship more deeply allowed us to recognize that

10. See Margaret A. Farley, *Just Love: A Framework for Christian Sexual Ethics* (New York: Continuum, 2006).

11. See Cristina L. H. Traina, "Papal Ideals, Marital Realities: One View from the Ground," in *Sexual Diversity and Catholicism: Toward the Development of Moral Theology*, ed. Patricia Beattie Jung with Joseph Andrew Coray (Collegeville, MN: Liturgical, 2001), 273–274. She writes, "Other than childbirth, I can think of nothing that compares with the physical, psychological, and spiritual exhilaration of intentionally procreative lovemaking" (273).

any particular failure—the kind that stopped sex and left us upset, unsatisfied, frustrated, sickened—was relative, as one of many and surely better times. So, covenanted boundaries of certain kinds can deepen passion.

Practice Forgiveness.

The Christian idea of forgiveness of self and other has as key a role to play in one's sexual life as anywhere. Failure is inevitable and recurring, even if it occurs less frequently as "practice (supposedly) makes perfect." When Gudorf says, "even in loving marriage, sex does not always function ideally,"[12] I laughed and thought, "Not always? How about *never* (even in marriage)?" We have had amazingly wonderful times. But we have had our fair share of frustrations, especially early on. Grace goes a long way.

Love Your Bodies in All Their Idiosyncrasies and Oddities.

This is a hard one for almost all of us. We are at odds with our bodies, no matter how "beautiful" by cultural ideals. Gender and race studies show the horrific distortions of self-perception caused by cultural stereotypes about body weight, color, shape, and so forth. No body part is left untainted. Size wields such a huge and destructive influence here—big breasts and penis, small butt, belly, and nose. Christianity defies this. In the *imago Dei*, no one is ugly. Moreover, the power of sexual love to counter this is partly what makes it sacramental (if not formally a sacrament). It affirms creation and paves the way for God's grace.

Take Risks, Have Fun, Play, and Enjoy Tenderness.

Although two separate categories, I put fun and tenderness together because they both bring to mind intimate practices of our own making, practices I imagine readers might appreciate knowing but those who know us well would rather I didn't share (children, students, colleagues). These practices are personal (for example, how he touches my neck bone, how I kiss his eyes). Imagination and gentleness are what is essential, not any particular actions or techniques. Touch, the most undervalued of senses, has a special place.

Pursue Mutual Pleasuring.

In 1993, Mary Pellauer penned a daring essay on female orgasm that puts women's pleasure and mutual pleasuring at the center of sexual ethics as a moral mandate.[13] Although sex play alternates between giving and receiving, the overall aim is a deep mutuality. I doubt this can exist easily without a wider

---

12. Gudorf, "Graceful Pleasures," 128.

mutuality in the relationship that distributes domestic and public workload as equitably as possible. Here and in bed, mutuality fluctuates over time. Seldom is any division of labor instantly and easily mutual. Rowan Williams, formerly the Archbishop of Canterbury, describes the dynamics: "My arousal and desire must become the cause of someone's desire. . . . We are pleased because we are pleasing."[14]

KNOW YOUR OWN BODY NEEDS AND DESIRES.

The long legacy that labeled masturbation sinful reflects just how far the church went in discouraging sexual self-knowledge, portraying such knowledge as fundamentally selfish and unnatural and viewing pleasure as an unnecessary evil on the way to procreation. The result is an ignorance that actually inhibits joyful procreation rather than sustaining moral holiness. I learned more about what my body is telling me through bearing, birthing, and nursing children. It also helps to remember that we need physical, and not just genital, intimacy (for example, touch and affection).

MAKE TIME AND DEVELOP ROUTINES.

For practicing Jews, sex is a *mitzvah*, a commandment that married couples are obliged to observe. Its purpose is to reinforce the marriage bond on a regular basis. Sex is "a source of tremendous energy . . . that overflows on others," as Gudorf says. Her kids were sometimes inclined to notice "when either my husband or I was tense and irritable" and "suggest that he or I entice the irritable one into a 'little nap,'" their family euphemism for a "retreat to our bedroom."[15] Were all families so open about parental need for love making, it might head off more feuds. Some of our family vacations were less happy precisely because they disrupted routines that had evolved, from late-night weekend sex when our kids were little (and asleep) to early-Saturday-morning sex when our kids were older (and asleep). Routines change with circumstances (for example, children) and abilities (for example, aging).

13. Mary D. Pellauer, "The Moral Significance of Female Orgasm: Toward Sexual Ethics That Celebrates Women's Sexuality," *Journal of Feminist Studies in Religion* 9 (Spring-Fall, 1993): 161–82.

14. Rowan D. Williams, "The Body's Grace," in *Theology and Sexuality: Classic and Contemporary Readings*, ed. Eugene F. Rogers (Oxford: Blackwell, 2002), 312, 313.

15. Gudorf, "Graceful Pleasures," 129.

Rightly Ordered Passion

Passion drives Erdrich's book and, indeed, makes life itself worth living. Unfortunately, the church has trouble with passion. Theologians have worried incessantly about all kinds, not just sexual. Passion is indelibly linked with the body, which is also deeply mistrusted. The worry and distrust are not without sound reasons. Untutored, unmonitored sexual desire, like religious zeal itself, can go grossly awry, injuring everyone in its destructive wake. Early church father Augustine, while frequently blamed for the excessive anti-sexual leaning of the tradition, was at least on to something when he saw the value of rightly ordered desire and placed love of God at the epicenter.

Unfortunately, this insight was accompanied by other convictions that malformed Augustine's legacy—like antipathy toward physical pleasure and its equation with sin, fear about losing control over one's body, and obsessive repression of sexual passion. This antipathy had disastrous results and was further distorted in North America by sixteenth-century Puritanism and nineteenth-century Victorian ideals, leading to Freud's quintessential "return of the repressed" in all manner of inappropriate behavior. This leaves all of us, but especially those called into ministry, at risk of misusing and abusing the passion each of us naturally possesses.

Fortunately, this is not the whole of Christianity or the right reading of the gospel. Christ's embodied passion, the story of Jesus' love for people despite the political pressures of the world around him, stands at the center of our faith. Incarnation itself affirms creation and God's eagerness to assume human form on our behalf, including sexual yearning. Theology is ultimately "love-talk"—talk about love-in-practice—in Marcella Althaus-Reed and Lisa Isherwood's vivid words.[16] Although I cannot easily resolve the ethical dilemmas that run through the three scenarios of Erdrich's book, I can with confidence affirm her blessing of desire. Most of us can and should avoid the "branching fury of impossible difficulty" without missing out on what lies behind it—a love located deep within passionate bodily desire.

16. Lisa Isherwood and Marcella Althaus-Reid, "Introduction: Queering Theology: Thinking Theology and Queer Theory," in *The Sexual Theologian: Essays on Sex, God, and Politics*, ed. Isherwood and Althaus-Reed (New York: T & T Clark, 2004), 2.

Discussion Questions

1. What assumptions do you harbor about sexual passion? What assumptions do you hold about the relationship between Christian faith and sexual pleasure?

2. What did you learn from your own upbringing, and from your parents in particular, about your own sexual desires?

3. What do you think about Alice Miller's view of helping professionals as gifted in meeting others' narcissistic needs while repressing our own? Or what do you think about Eichenbaum and Orbach's portrait of women as learned in depriving ourselves for others' sake? How do these images fit (or not fit) your own experience?

4. Why hasn't the church made a place for open conversation about sexual passions and pleasure? Can you imagine ways to create in church an environment that affirms the potential gracefulness of our sexual desires? How might scripture and tradition be (re)read?

5. What practices have you developed to sustain a healthy intimate sexual relationship outside your place of employment? What impediments have you encountered?

Recommended Readings

Boulton, Elizabeth Myer, and Matthew Myer Boulton. "Sacramental Sex: Divine Love and Human Intimacy." *Christian Century.* March 22, 2011: 28–31.

Farley, Margaret A. *Just Love: A Framework for Christian Sexual Ethics.* New York: Continuum, 2006.

———. *Personal Commitments: Beginning, Keeping, Changing.* San Francisco: Harper & Row, 1986.

Gudorf, Christine E. *Body, Sex, and Pleasure: Reconstructing Christian Sexual Ethics.* Cleveland: Pilgrim, 1994.

Pellauer, Mary D. "The Moral Significance of Female Orgasm: Toward Sexual Ethics That Celebrates Women's Sexuality." In *Sexuality: A Reader,* ed. Karen Lebacqz with David Sinacore-Guinn, 9–32. Cleveland: Pilgrim, 1999.

Schnarch, David. *Passionate Marriage: Keeping Love and Intimacy Alive in Committed Relationships.* New York: W.W. Norton, 2009.

Index of Names

Index of Biblical References